Thinking about Crime

Thinking about **CRIME**

sense and sensibility
in American penal culture

Michael Tonry

OXFORD
UNIVERSITY PRESS

2004

OXFORD
UNIVERSITY PRESS

Oxford New York

Auckland Bangkok Buenos Aires Cape Town Chennai
Dar es Salaam Delhi Hong Kong Istanbul Karachi Kolkata
Kuala Lumpur Madrid Melbourne Mexico City Mumbai Nairobi
São Paulo Shanghai Taipei Tokyo Toronto

Copyright © 2004 by Oxford University Press, Inc.

Published by Oxford University Press, Inc.,
198 Madison Avenue, New York, New York 10016

www.oup.com

Oxford is a registered trademark of Oxford University Press

Library of Congress Cataloging-in-Publication Data
Tonry, Michael H.
Thinking about crime : sense and sensibility in American penal culture
/ by Michael Tonry.
p. cm. — (Studies in crime and public policy)
Includes bibliographical references and index.
ISBN 0-19-514101-6
1. Prisons—Government policy—United States.   2. Crime
prevention—Government policy—United States.   3. Discrimination in
criminal justice administration—United States.   4. Prisons in mass
media—United States.   5. Prisons—United States—Public opinion.
6. Public opinion—United States.   7. United States—Politics and
government—2001–   I. Title.   II. Series.
HV9471.T65 2004
365′.973—dc21   2003004245

1 2 3 4 5 6 7 8 9

Printed in the United States of America
on acid-free paper

Acknowledgments

Isaac Newton, not generally known as a modest man, once, on being praised, accepted it as his due but also observed that in reaching so high he had stood on the shoulders of giants. There are not many Isaac Newtons, and I am certainly not one, but it feels right to acknowledge people without whose existence and works this slight book could not have been written. I have tried to draw on the work of historians and sociologists to understand why modern Americans think as they do about crime and criminals, and how, understanding that, we can do more that is good and less that is harmful. This book could not have been written nor the ideas in it developed had I not learnt from the writings of historians John Boswell, Grant Gilmore, Paul Johnson, David Musto, and Jaroslav Pelikan, and of sociologists Stanley Cohen, Émile Durkheim, Norbert Elias, Kai Erikson, David Garland, Joseph Gusfield, and Edwin Sutherland. With the exception of Garland, none of these are friends. Most of them are dead. A few may count as giants.

This book, whatever its demerits, would be even less had friends not read and reacted to drafts. Among those who tried to save me from error, not always, in their views, successfully, are David Garland, Roxanne Lieb, Charles Loeffler, Amanda Matravers, Norval Morris, Kevin Reitz, Julian Roberts, Michael E. Smith, and Andrew von Hirsch. Sara Harrop, Charles Loeffler, and Vickie Sheridan helped with references, artwork, and avoidance of grosser infelicities of style. Dedi X. Felman, my long-suffering and patient editor at Oxford

University Press, stayed the course, ran interference, and did all the things good editors—in romantic stereotype but seldom in life—do. I am lucky to have such good friends.

Earlier versions of bits of chapter 2 appeared in *Crime and Delinquency*, of chapter 6 in the *UCLA Law Review*, and of chapter 7 in *Punishment and Society*. They are reprinted by permission.

Preface

From capital punishment to three-strikes-and-you're-out to the highest imprisonment rates in the Western world by a factor of five, the United States stands alone in what it does to its citizens to prevent crimes and punish criminals.

There are good reasons to doubt that recent punishment policies have had much to do with recent drops in crime. The strongest is that crime trends for the past 40 years have been broadly similar in every Western country, and in every American state, while punishment policies and practices have varied enormously.

The United States has a punishment system that no one would knowingly have built from the ground up. It is often unjust, it is unduly severe, it is wasteful, and it does enormous damage to the lives of black Americans.

This book explains how contemporary American crime policies came to be as they are, and how they can be reconfigured to be made more effective but less costly, and to do less harm to offenders, their loved and loving ones, and their communities. The story is partly about rising crime rates and public fears, about cynical politics and pusillanimous politicians, and about public opinion and sensationalizing media. The story more importantly is about the ways long-term trends in values and attitudes influence how Americans think about crime and punishment, and how they think about victims and offenders.

Social scientists use the word "sensibilities" to refer to prevailing social values, attitudes, and beliefs. Sensibilities change slowly over time and fundamentally shape what people think and believe. Current crime control policies are to a large part an outgrowth of American sensibilities of the past third century. Nothing wrong with that, one might observe. Policies have expressed the views of the people, and that is what democracy is all about.

There is something wrong with that, though, because we know, looking backward, that the prevailing sensibilities of an era often are deeply regretted later. Mainstream American sensibilities in the past have supported policies—slavery, the near-extermination of indigenous North American peoples, the internment of Japanese-Americans, sterilization of the mentally ill, ostracism of homosexuals—that we now believe to be wrong in some timeless sense. Sensibilities of particular times and places may have supported such attitudes and practices, but few people today believe that justifies them.

And so it is concerning crime and punishment. In some respects this seems obvious. No one any longer calls for drawing and quartering of offenders, for public execution by guillotine, or for the use of torture to extract confessions. In other respects, it may not appear so obvious, even though practices that many Americans endorse—capital punishment, three-strikes laws, prison sentences measured in decades or lifetimes—are as unthinkable in other Western countries as are lynchings and public torture in America.

Assessments of the acceptability of particular policies and practices need to take account of basic human rights and moral considerations. They also need to take account of what historians can tell us about interactions between sensibilities, behavior, and policies in the past.

We know from historical writings on recurring cycles of support for romanticism and classicism in the arts, of tolerance and intolerance of homosexuality and religious pluralism, and of attitudes and policies on drug abuse, that human sensibilities often move in regular cycles and that beliefs and policies move with them.

In trying to understand and assess crime control and punishment, we need to take account of prevailing sensibilities, of timeless human rights ideas, and of what we know about past interactions between sensibilities, cycles of tolerance and intolerance, and public policies. When we do that in relation to drug policy, we learn that "wars on drugs" are typically launched when drug use is beginning to decline, that members of minority groups are typically targeted and scapegoated, and that attitudes and policies typically soften a decade or two later. A similar pattern characterizes "wars on crime."

Had American policy makers in the 1980s and 1990s heeded the readily available historical literature, learned its lessons, and more sensitively interpreted evidence of public concern, the wars on drugs and crime would have taken very different forms. Many fewer Americans would have been sent to prison, and the criminal justice system would have intruded into many fewer black Americans' lives.

What was in effect a form of false consciousness led drug and crime control policy makers to adopt policies that were too harsh, too simple, and too wasteful. Once we understand why American policies evolved as they did we can begin the job of making them better.

That in a nutshell is the main argument. I develop it within these eight chapters. Chapter 1 is a brief summary of the whole. Chapter 2 asks, and then summarizes alternative answers to, the question of why contemporary American crime control patterns developed as they did. Many answers have been offered, including rising crime rates, public opinion, the politics of race, political cynicism, the weakened credibility of government, and post-modernist angst. None of these things is irrelevant, but the best answer focuses on cycles of intolerance and prevailing but fallible sensibilities. Chapters 3 and 4 introduce basic ideas and literatures on cycles of intolerance, sensibilities, and moral panics. Chapter 5 returns to the main story line to show that American crime trends closely resemble those of other countries, that crime control policies are much different, and that prevailing sensibilities explain both why we think our problems are worse and our policies are better (and effective). To illustrate the force of prevailing sensibilities, chapters 6 and 7 examine contemporary policies that would have been unthinkable in earlier times, and mainstream ideas from recent earlier times that have been forgotten. The last chapter returns to the premise that the United States now has a punishment system that no one would knowingly have chosen, and shows how it can be changed to do more good and less harm, especially to members of American minority groups.

Contents

Thinking about Crime

Sense and Sensibility in American Penal Culture

In searching for ways to address rising crime rates in the final third of the twentieth century, American policy makers got lost in a forest of good intentions, public anxieties, and political cynicism. They created a punishment system that no one would knowingly have chosen, but that we do not know how to change. Current policies are too severe, waste lives and money, and often produce unjust results. They have produced an imprisonment rate five times higher than that of any other Western country and seven to twelve times higher than most.

Current policies have disproportionately damaged the lives of black offenders and their families and have undermined black communities. Nearly a third of young black men are in prison or jail, or on probation or parole. More than 13 percent of black men between 25 and 29, more than one in every eight, were in jail or prison in 2001. We lack comparable information about Hispanics, but they are the fastest growing part of the prison population. Unless current policies change, the criminal justice system will soon intrude as deeply into Hispanic Americans' lives and communities as it now does into black Americans' lives and communities.

Ordinary Americans made these things happen. Elected politicians proposed policies and enacted laws, but they would not have done it if they believed American voters would disapprove. Journalists and academics assert that many politicians who proposed tough policies did so cynically, out of personal, political self-interest, and that many realized the policies they proposed would not work and would do harm. "Soft on crime" was a label few politicians dared risk during the 1970s through the 1990s, and many supported policies they believed unwise or unjust rather than risk losing an election. An influential analysis by Katherine Beckett shows that politicians typically led public opinion about crime rather than followed it, in effect raising public fears and anxieties and then proposing harsh, simplistic solutions to ameliorate them. The bottom line, nonetheless, even if those accounts are valid, is that the public could not have been led someplace it was unwilling to go.

At the beginning of a new century, Americans are having second thoughts about the wisdom of current antidrug and anticrime policies, but elected politicians most places are afraid to change them. To do so runs risks of being tarred as soft on crime and, until significant numbers of politicians take that risk and get reelected, most will not take the chance. And until that happens, the unfortunate social facts described in the opening paragraph will continue to be true.

There is lots of evidence that ordinary Americans want to change current policies, and there is lots of evidence that judges and prosecutors at local and state levels are responding. Policy makers in some states are responding, though usually by tinkering at the margins rather than by overhauling current policies. Legislators and executive branch officials in the federal government and in the large, heavily populated states, however, are neither repealing nor fundamentally recasting failed policies. Most remain locked in the politics and attitudes of earlier times and are hunkering down to protect the status quo. The George W. Bush administration's determination, reiterated in 2002, to preserve the federal laws that punish crack cocaine offenses as severely as powder cocaine offenses one hundred times larger is but one illustration. Most crack is sold by young inner-city blacks and most cocaine by older whites. As a result, the 100-to-1 law imposes much longer sentences on blacks. Almost no one defends that outcome on the merits, but political courage to change the law cannot yet be found.

This book explains how contemporary policies came to be as they are, and how they can be reconfigured to be more effective but less costly, and to do less harm to offenders, their loved and loving ones, and their communities. The story is only partly about rising crime rates and public fears, about cynical politics and pusillanimous politicians, and about public opinion and sensationalizing media. The story is also about the ways long-term trends in social values and public attitudes, and short-term effects of moral panics, influence how Americans think about crime and punishment. For two decades, Americans thought they wanted single-minded toughness and they got it. The question is why they thought they wanted it.

"Moral panics" are part of the answer. They typically occur when horrifying or notorious events galvanize public emotion, and produce concern, sympathy, emotion, and overreaction. Examples in recent years include the kidnapping of Polly Klaas in California and the crack-overdose death of Len Bias in Maryland. Results included, respectively, California's three-strikes law and the federal 100-to-1 crack cocaine sentencing law. Sometimes moral panics are about general problems, for example, child abuse or school violence, and the resulting emotions have been harnessed constructively. Often though, moral panics relating to crime lead to poorly considered and overly harsh reactions. In recent decades, moral panics have magnified the effects of longer term changes in values and attitudes.

The ways people think about contentious issues change slowly but predictably. Social scientists use the word "sensibilities" to refer to prevailing social values, attitudes, and beliefs, and show how sensibilities change slowly over time and shape and reshape what people think and believe. Current American crime control policies are to a large part an outgrowth of American sensibilities of the past third of the twentieth century. Nothing wrong with that, one might respond. Policies have expressed the views of the people, and that is what democracy is all about.

There is something wrong with that, though. Looking backwards, we know that American sensibilities of earlier times supported policies—slavery, the near-extermination of indigenous North American peoples, internment of Japanese Americans during World War II, sterilization of the mentally ill, ostracism of homosexuals, denial to women of a right to vote—that we now believe to be wrong in some timeless sense, and not merely in light of current sensibilities. Looking outside the United States in our own and earlier times, similar judgments are widespread about religious intolerance, oppression of women, and exploitation of child labor. Sensibilities of particular times and places may support such attitudes and practices, but few people in our time believe that justifies them.

And so it is concerning crime and punishment. In some respects this seems obvious. No one any longer calls for drawing and quartering of offenders, for public execution by guillotine, or for the use of torture to extract confessions. In other respects, it may not appear so obvious, even though practices that many Americans in our time endorse—capital punishment, three-strikes laws, prison sentences measured in decades or lifetimes—are as unthinkable in other Western countries today as are lynchings and corporal punishment in America.

Concluding that particular policies or practices are consonant with current sensibilities is thus the beginning but cannot be the end of assessments of their legitimacy. That evaluation needs to take account of basic human rights and moral considerations, whatever the public opinion poll results or prevailing sentiments of a particular day or year. It also needs to take account of what historians can tell us about interactions between sensibilities, attitudes, and policies in the past.

We know from historical writings on recurring cycles of support for romanticism and classicism in the arts, of tolerance and intolerance of homosexuality and religious pluralism, and of attitudes and policies on drug abuse, that human sensibilities often move in regular cycles and that beliefs and policies move with them. Persecution of "heretics" in the history of the Christian church, for example, often coincided with periods when the power and authority of the organized church were in doubt. At other times, self-confident church leaders comfortably tolerated dissenters.

In trying to understand and normatively evaluate crime control policies we need to take account of prevailing sensibilities, of "timeless" human rights ideas, and of what we know about past interactions between sensibilities, cycles of tolerance and intolerance, and public policies. When we do that in relation to drug policy, we learn that "wars on drugs" are typically launched when drug use has peaked and is beginning to decline, that antidrug policies and law enforcement practices become harshest during such times, and that zealous drug law enforcement targets and scapegoats members of minority groups. People violating drug laws are treated much more harshly during these cyclical periods of heightened intolerance than they would have been ten years earlier or would be twenty years later.

Why these things happen is not hard to understand. For at least two centuries, significant fractions of American society have held moralistic views about drug dependence and believed that drug use is dangerous, unwise, and immoral. During times when drug use is increasing or has stabilized, other voices argue that moral choices are not the law's business and some argue that drug use is a good or at least culturally tolerated thing. Drug use peaks, and begins to decline, however, because the balance of views has changed. As the decline continues, the balance of social attitudes changes. Fewer people use drugs and feel a need to justify themselves. The moral arguments against drug use become louder and command wider support. People of dissenting views become more reluctant to speak out for fear they themselves will seem foolish, irresponsible, or deviant. More people come to promote, support, or administer harsh policies and fewer are prepared to oppose them. The pattern of harsher laws, more vigorous enforcement, and scapegoating of minority groups occurs.

Eventually, however, the fervor abates, the harsh policies soften, enforcement becomes less single-minded, and the focus on minority groups blurs. Drug use stabilizes or begins mildly to increase. People become more confident opposing majority sentiment and a wider range of views is expressed.

The drug policy cycle just described has recurred in the past thirty years. Drug use peaked in the late 1970s and early 1980s, the harshest laws were enacted and the most vigorous enforcement occurred in the ensuing fifteen years, and signs of gradual easing of both fervor and policy have been evident since the mid-1990s. The signs include the movement to create drug courts for drug-abusing offenders, the enactment of laws in many states calling for diversion of drug-dependent first- and second-time offenders into treatment programs, and the passage of referendums supporting medical use of marijuana.

There is no reason to doubt that something similar is happening in relation to crime. By the most cautious measure, crime rates peaked around 1990 (some would say around 1980) and fell continuously and precipitously during the 1990s. During the several decades when crime rates were rising, there was vigorous debate about trade-offs in crime control policy between civil liberties and public safety. That debate had largely stilled by 1990 and remained still for much of the following decade. Just as people become uncomfortable during peak prohibitionist periods arguing for individuals' rights to use drugs, people become uncomfortable during peak anticrime periods arguing for the need to treat offenders fairly and to recognize the complex causes of much criminality. No one who read American newspapers during the 1990s could have failed to observe that both major parties were consistently tough on crime and loathe to risk any other public perception. Former President Bill Clinton famously observed in 1994, "I can be nicked on a lot, but no one can say I'm soft on crime."

As a result, closely paralleling experience with drugs, crime control policies became unprecedentedly harsh during the early and mid-1990s. That was the time of three-strikes, truth-in-sentencing laws, and zero-tolerance policing, and of a striking increase in the severity of punishments and in the numbers of people in prisons and jails.

And now, the fervor is abating, policies gradually are softening, a wider range of voices is being heard, and the prison population is stabilizing and in some places declining a little.

Had American policy makers in the 1980s read the readily available historical literature, heeded its lessons, and more sensitively interpreted evidence of public concern, the war on drugs would have taken very different forms. And had American policy makers in the 1990s heeded history's lessons, crime control policies would have been very different. Many fewer Americans would have been sent to prison. More public monies would have been available for health care, education, and social welfare. The criminal justice system would have intruded into many fewer black Americans' lives. If only American policy makers had not allowed themselves to be carried away by short-term and predictable transient emotions, America's criminal justice system would look very different.

The organization of American government makes it especially vulnerable to emotional overreaction. American policy makers need to worry even more than policy makers elsewhere that they will be carried away by shifts in sensibilities about crime, drugs, and other unwanted behaviors, or by moral panics, and adopt inhumane and unjust policies that later they will regret.

American institutions provide less insulation from short-term passions and emotions than do governmental institutions in other Western countries. Most prosecuting attorneys are elected and those who are not are selected according to partisan political criteria. A large majority of American state judges are elected. No informed person would deny that appointments of federal judges are fundamentally partisan and political.

Only rarely in Western Europe or the other major English-speaking countries are judges and prosecutors elected. Prosecutors and judges elsewhere are often career civil servants.

Where they are not, they are typically selected through nonpartisan merit procedures. Nowhere else do legislators try to micro-manage sentencing and parole decisions. In the United States, however, policy makers and public officials often pride themselves on responding to changes in public opinion and to heightened anxieties, and are accordingly less likely than those elsewhere to stand firm against winds of emotion when they sweep across the national consciousness.

American policy makers over the past thirty years did not try to keep their heads and retain a sense of perspective. What was in effect a form of false consciousness led to adoption of drug and crime control policies that were too simple, too harsh, and too wasteful. Centuries of experience with the excesses of witch-hunts and the persecution of heretics have taught church officials caution. Those who feel moved to punish heretics know they must search their souls to consider whether that is because controversial beliefs genuinely threaten harm or because they are concerned that the authority of the church is weakening. Likewise, makers of crime control policy should examine their consciences to consider whether they support one policy or another for valid reasons or merely because of fleeting beliefs, opinions, and passions.

Because American policy makers lost their way, hundreds of thousands of people are in prisons because they were in the wrong place at the wrong historical moment. Their bad luck was to have committed crimes, or been convicted and sentenced, during a period when public and official attitudes toward crime were harsh and single-minded.

Many thousands of aging offenders convicted of trifling crimes in the mid- to late 1990s occupy California prisons. Their misfortune is to have been sentenced before the California Supreme Court gave judges the authority to sidestep California's three-strikes law and before prosecutors throughout the state began to restrict its application to genuinely serious cases.

Many thousands of people are serving decades-long sentences in federal prisons for non-violent drug crimes. Their misfortune is to have been sentenced in federal courts before avoidance of sentencing guidelines by federal judges and prosecutors became common practice.

Hundreds of thousands of people, mostly but not only of minority and disadvantaged backgrounds, have spent much of their young adulthood in prison for drug crimes. Their misfortune is that unwisely, but for young people not uncommonly, and typically as a result of peer influences and teenagers' sense of invincibility, they experimented with drug use, got hooked, and got caught—in a time when antidrug policies were unprecedentedly harsh.

Reasonable people disagree over why policies are so harsh, so many people are in prison, and so many of those are black and Hispanic. In the most literal sense, the explanation is that American politicians adopted unduly harsh policies and the public let them do it. That does not explain, however, why the public supported those policies. Conventional explanations range from the inevitable effects of rising crime rates, reflection of the public will, and belief in the crime-preventive effectiveness of tough policies to political cynicism, partisan manipulation of public anxieties, and indifference to the well-being of black Americans.

Current penal policies have trapped American policy makers much as Brer Fox got stuck in Joel Chandler Harris's tar-baby story. Brer Rabbit, not at all interested in becoming Brer Fox's supper, persuaded him that the tar-baby would be juicier and tastier. Brer Fox grabbed hold of the tar-baby's arm, only to find that he could not pull his front paw away. When he tried to push away with the other front paw, that too became stuck. In the end, as Brer Rabbit walked away, smiling quietly, Brer Fox was hopelessly stuck. He had grabbed hold of what he thought he wanted, and he could not break free.

American policy makers, having grabbed hold of current policies, are stuck and do not know how to get loose. It does not matter that we now know that current crime policies cannot be justified on the merits. Although many people long believed that severe crime control policies generally, or particular policies like zero-tolerance policing in New York

City and the three-strikes law in California, substantially reduced crime rates, most informed practitioners and scholars no longer believe that to be true. At the margins such policies probably influenced crime rates, but only as small parts of much more complicated stories. Crime rates fell sharply in all large cities during the 1990s, including the large majority that did not adopt zero-tolerance policing, and in all populous states, including the majority that did not enact three-strikes laws. Particular policies and particular laws in individual cities and states may have influenced crime rate declines in those places, but most of the steep decline was the result of normative and behavioral changes that affected the entire country.

It is more accurate to refer to normative and behavioral changes that affected most Western countries. Crime rates fell in most countries in the 1990s, including Germany, England, Canada, the Scandinavian countries, Scotland, the Netherlands, and the United States. Crime rates have even been falling since the mid-1990s in many of the countries of Eastern Europe, a region that has experienced enormous social and economic disruption.

No one has a good explanation for why crime rates are down in most of the Western world, but such things have happened before. Crime rates fell in most Western countries for a century or more beginning around 1830. Historians differ in their inevitably speculative explanations as to why that happened but not as to whether it happened. Something similar is happening now, and it is affecting Maine, Maryland, Minnesota, and Manitoba on the western side of the Atlantic and Manchester, Mainz, Malmo, and Messina on the eastern.

To some readers it may seem counterintuitive that policies like zero-tolerance policing and three-strikes sentencing had only modest effects on crime. That is because prevailing sensibilities in recent years made Americans want to believe harsh policies would work. Many Americans appear to believe that crimes occur primarily because offenders are bad people or because punishments are insufficiently severe. If that is true, incapacitating the incorrigibly bad people and threatening lengthy prison sentences for the others should reduce crime rates.

In many other Western countries, by contrast, ordinary crime is understood primarily to be the product of personal disadvantage or disability and social disorganization, and it seems counterintuitive that crime can be much affected unless those underlying problems are addressed. Few people deny that offenders have free will and choose to commit crimes. Self-evidently, they have and they do. That recognition, however, can coexist with recognition that childhood abuse, poverty, mental disability, limited opportunities, lack of marketable skills, and socialization into deviant values often lead individuals to make choices they would otherwise not make.

To many disadvantaged inner-city American teenagers, for example, drug dealing, in comparison with other available options, appears to be a sensible and relatively low-risk way to earn money and improve their lives. So they choose to sell drugs. Privileged teenagers much less often see it that way because their circumstances are different, and other avenues to success and happiness are open. So it is not that disadvantaged kids do not make choices, but that the choices available to them are often far less attractive than those open to privileged kids. A just society would take those differences into account in punishing offenders and in setting crime control policies.

Many European policy makers think this way now, and in earlier times so did many American policy makers. Historian David Rothman described the prevalent Progressive Era views during the early twentieth century: "No one raised in a slum could be held strictly accountable for his actions. The wretchedness of the social setting was so great that responsibility could not be assigned in a uniform and predictable fashion. Elemental fairness dictated that the offender be treated as an individual. It was not just a sensible and effective principle, but a just one." Tony Blair's Labour Government in England famously expressed this in the back half of its campaign slogan "Tough on Crime, Tough on the Causes of Crime."

In any case, for countries, states, or societies, changes in crime rates or patterns do not necessarily lead to changes in punishment policies or patterns. Put crisply, at a societal level crime does not cause punishment. Imprisonment rates and the severity of punishment move independently from changes in crime rates, patterns, and trends. Governments decide how much punishment they want, and these decisions are in no simple way related to crime rates. This can be seen by comparing crime and punishment trends in Finland, Germany, and the United States between 1960 and 1990. The trends are close to identical. Violent crime rates in all three countries grew by a factor of 3-to-4 and homicide rates more than doubled. Yet the U.S. imprisonment rate quadrupled in that period, the Finnish rate fell by 60 percent, and the German rate was broadly stable.

Likewise, punishment does not cause crime (or less cryptically, punishment policies do not have major effects on crime rates or trends). This can be seen by comparing crime rates over the past twenty years of comparable and closely related countries that have very different punishment policies. Canada's incarceration rate fluctuated within a narrow band of 100 to 125 per 100,000 between 1980 and 2000 while the U.S. rate more than tripled, growing from 200 per 100,000 in 1980 to 700 per 100,000 in 2002. Yet crime rate patterns in Canada between 1980 and 2000 closely parallel those in the United States with the crucial difference that they were not as high.

And a Scandinavian example: crime rates in Finland and Denmark have moved in parallel since the early 1960s, though Finnish crime rates have been consistently lower. Finland's incarceration rate, twice as high in 1965 (130 per 100,000 compared to 65 per 100,000), fell by half, Denmark's stayed about the same, and both fluctuated in the low 60s per 100,000 in the 1990s. The Finnish incarceration rate in 2000 (56) was marginally lower than Denmark's (61). In both countries the crime rate in 1990 was essentially the same in 2000.

Whether current American crime policies were an inexorable product of recent crime patterns, and whether they can be justified on the merits, or in either case not, they are difficult to alter or repeal. Enacting a three-strikes law, a life-without-possibility-of-parole law, or a law calling for mandatory minimum sentences is incomparably easier than repealing such laws. They were politically popular in the 1980s and 1990s. No candidate or incumbent who supported them imperiled his or her electoral prospects. In contemporary America, politicians' support for laws aimed at prevention of crime, hostility to offenders, or well-being of victims does not require political courage.

Political courage is required, however, to propose or support repeal of tough laws. Even in a time when crime has fallen well down lists of the public's primary concerns, a vote to repeal, narrow, or weaken a three-strikes law can be portrayed as soft on crime. This makes elected officials risk averse. Conservative New York Republican Governor George Pataki in 1995 first proposed reducing penalties for nonviolent offenders under the severe Rockefeller drug laws; in mid-2003, the legislature had still not acted. Conservative Republican U.S. Senator Orrin Hatch, according to a Senate staffer, long believed reducing federal drug sentences was "the right thing to do, but he couldn't do it for political reasons." The United States Sentencing Commission in 1995 proposed repeal of the federal 100-to-1 policy, adopted in 1986, that penalizes crack cocaine offenses as harshly as powder cocaine offenses involving quantities 100 times larger. In 2003, the law remained unchanged.

Leaving things as they are poses no electoral risks. Inertia may result in wasteful public spending or avoidable damage to the lives and interests of offenders, their families, and their communities, but responsibility for these things is diffuse. No one loses elections for failing to lead or support a campaign for repeal of laws that are tough on drugs or crime.

This is unfortunate and ironic, because there is plenty of evidence that broad-based public sentiments support more nuanced, compassionate, and constructive policies than those now in place. Few people argue that violence or theft is morally excusable, or that use of heroin, cocaine, or ecstasy is a good thing. Many more people than a decade ago, however, accept that human lives are messy and complicated, that everyone makes mistakes, that sensible drug and crime policies should recognize that, and that current policies do not.

What is the evidence for the preceding paragraph's claims? Drug policy referenda for starters. Despite unceasing opposition from the federal government, by 2002 voters in eight jurisdictions (Alabama, California, Colorado, Maine, Nevada, Oregon, Washington, and the District of Columbia) had enacted referenda legalizing medical use of marijuana, and Hawaii did so by legislation. In July 2002, the California Supreme Court, in *The People v. Mower*, 122 Cal. Rptr. 2d 326 (2002), held that a person who cultivates or possesses marijuana for medical purposes may not be convicted of unlawful possession of drugs. Earlier, in 2000, California voters enacted Proposition 36, which required large numbers of first- and second-time drug offenders to be diverted from prosecution and imprisonment to drug treatment. District of Columbia voters in November 2002 adopted Ballot Initiative 62, which prescribed a similar preference for treatment over prosecution.

More evidence can be found in results from public opinion surveys showing that crime is no longer widely numbered among the country's most pressing problems. From 1980 to 1990, crime ranked most years in the top three. In March 2002, according to the Gallup Poll, crime ranked fifteenth and drugs twelfth, behind poverty, dissatisfaction with government, and the high cost of living. In a 1994 poll by Peter D. Hart Research Associates, 48 percent of Americans said their preferred crime control strategy would be to address the underlying causes of crime, and 42 percent preferred stricter sentencing. In a 2001 Hart Poll, 65 percent of Americans approved the root causes approach and only 32 percent preferred stricter sentencing.

The general public holds complicated views about punishment that are neither monolithically nor single-mindedly punitive. Ordinary citizens want criminals punished, but also want them treated. They believe punishments in general are too soft, but when they focus on particular cases typically support sentences less severe than judges now impose. They believe that crime is a product of bad character and bad judgment, but also that drug and alcohol dependence, bad home lives, and disadvantage are among crime's major causes.

There is also evidence that many criminal justice officials believe current policies are too severe and too expensive, and long have done. A January 2002 *New York Times* article by Fox Butterfield, for example, reported that some states were changing their laws on sentencing and punishment in various ways to reduce their rigidity and severity. A Ninth Circuit Federal Court of Appeals in *The People v. Andrade*, 270 Fed. 3rd 743 (2001), struck down California's three-strikes law, as applied in that particular case. The court held that a fifty-year sentence for Andrade's theft of $150 in videotapes from K-Mart violated the U.S. Constitution's provision forbidding "cruel and unusual punishments." (The U.S. supreme court, however, in mid-2003 held otherwise.) Several years earlier, in *The People v. Romero*, 53 Cal. Rep. 2d 789 (1996), and in *The People v. Alvarez*, 60 Cal. Rep. 2d 93 (1997), a California Supreme Court composed entirely of judges appointed by conservative Republican governors Ronald Reagan, George Deukmeijian, and Pete Wilson reinterpreted the three-strikes law to empower judges to sidestep it when they believed it appropriate to do so. More recently, there is much evidence that the three-strikes law has fallen into partial desuetude, invoked only for extremely serious cases. *Washington Post* reporter Rene Sanchez wrote that, "prosecutors insist they are careful to use discretion in deciding whether to invoke a third-strike prison sentence." Los Angeles County prosecutor Steve Cooley ran for office and was elected on a platform promising to use three-strikes prosecutions only in very serious cases.

That is a lot of California three-strikes, but together with the California drug referendum it starkly illustrates the problem. Voters, prosecutors, trial judges, and appellate courts have acted in various ways to change California laws to make them more flexible and discriminating. Legislators, however, have not. The three-strikes law remains unchanged on the books. Thousands of people are serving decades-long sentences in California who, had they been sentenced a few years later, would not (if drug offenders) have been sent to prison at all or who (if third-strike property, drug, or minor violent offenders) would not have been sent there for anywhere near so long.

So we appear to be stuck. Voters and many criminal justice officials would support repeal and refashioning of much of the harsh penal legislation of the past quarter century, but elected officials are too risk averse to do it. Crime and punishment has come to resemble the signature issues of single-issue interest groups such as the National Rifle Association or the Right-to-Life movement. Only a few percent of voters in a district may base their electoral choices solely on candidates' positions on gun control or abortion but in places where victory margins are sometimes small, they may make the difference. The safe course is to oppose gun control and oppose abortion, and many electoral candidates do so most of the time, whatever their private views may be.

Crime and punishment has become a comparable issue. No matter how amenable most voters may be to sensible policy changes, the existence of a few percent who will always oppose candidates who appear "soft" on crime or likely to "coddle" offenders can immobilize legislatures.

Crime and punishment may be even more immobilizing than gun control and abortion. There is no "pro-criminal" sentiment to offset "tough on crime" sentiment as there is a gun control movement that opposes the NRA and a pro-choice movement that opposes the right-to-life movement. It was common in the 1990s for politicians to suggest that one must be "for victims" or "for criminals." Given the emotive force of crime as an issue, few public officials are willing to risk the "for criminals" label.

But, unless some elected officials are prepared to propose fundamental policy changes, and work to achieve them, we will not be able to let loose of the tar-baby. America will remain stuck. Too many people who shouldn't go to prison will continue to be sent there and to stay there too long. Too many lives will continue unnecessarily to be blighted.

Chapter 8 sets out three sets of proposals for correcting and ameliorating the worst excesses of the American criminal justice system. The first set is aspirational and calls on American policy makers to learn from both history and contemporary experience that they should not allow themselves to get carried away by the passions of the moment or to adopt policies that will later be regretted.

The second set addresses features of American government that create higher risks in the United States than in other Western countries that policy makers will get carried away. These include most prominently the American practice of electing many judges and prosecutors, and taking partisan political considerations into account when appointing most of the rest. Judges and prosecutors in other Western countries are either career civil servants who have undergone specialized university-level training or are appointed under nonpartisan meritocratic procedures. The American system ties criminal justice policies and decisions in individual cases to election returns and to officials' personal and political self-interest. Rather than buffer policy and decisions about individuals' fates from emotional overreactions, moral panics, and changing sensibilities, American institutional arrangements are almost designed to assure their influence.

The third set of proposals concerns changes to contemporary criminal justice policies. Early release laws should be adopted that allow panels of judges or corrections officials to review the sentences of all offenders serving very long terms to determine whether and when they can safely and justly be released. Three strikes and mandatory minimum laws should be repealed and replaced by sentencing guide-lines that allow judges to draw sensible distinctions among offenders. If that is not viable, all such laws should be amended to authorize judges to disregard them in appropriate cases. A variety of measures should be adopted to prevent enactment of ill-considered legislation, including require-ments that all proposed new laws be accompanied by appro-priations of whatever funds will be required to implement them and by disparity analyses that demonstrate their likely differential effects on minority and women offenders. To be-gin to lessen racial disparities in the courts and prisons, not only proposed new laws but also all existing practices should be subjected to disparity analyses. These would investigate whether and how new and current practices treat minority and women offenders worse than whites and men, and serve as the basis for deciding whether disparity-causing practices can be justified.

We know how to create a humane and effective criminal justice system. Experience with sentencing guidelines shows how to adopt comprehensive sentencing policies that treat offenders fairly and consistently, requiring severe punish-ments for those who deserve them and less severe but appro-priate punishments for others. Accumulating evidence on the effectiveness of drug courts and drug treatment shows that greatly increased investment in drug treatment can prevent crime, save money, and rebuild lives. Accumulating evidence on the effectiveness of a wide range of other treatment pro-grams has undermined the "nothing works" attitudes of the 1980s and 1990s and shows that diversion of public funds from prisons to treatment programs would pay financial and crime-prevention dividends. If American criminal justice sys-tems would eliminate the worst policies of the last thirty years, we could re-create systems that were no longer out-of-step with our own history or with the practices of other Western countries.

2

Why So Many Americans Are in Prison

American imprisonment rates, more than 700 per 100,000 residents behind bars at the end of December 2002, have reached unprecedented levels compared with other times in U.S. history or with current times in other Western countries. In other Western countries between 50 and 150 residents per 100,000 are in prison or jail on an average day. In Sweden, one in every 2,000 people is locked up; that is the lowest rate. In Portugal, the highest, it is one in 650. By contrast, in the United States, one of every 120 people is in prison or jail; that is five to twelve times the rates in other Western countries (A. Kuhn 1998; Bureau of Justice Statistics 2003). When those under 16 and over 70 are disregarded, one in eighty Americans each day awakens inside a prison or jail. Nearly one of every seven black American men in their late twenties is among them.

American punishment policies are unusually severe in other respects. Only in the United States are constitutional and other safeguards of criminal defendants systematically being reduced; throughout Europe, under the influence of the European Human Rights Convention and Court, defendants' procedural protections have been expanding for the last twenty years (Kurki 2001). In the United States, legislatures and courts are cutting back on prisoners' rights and privileges; in Europe, they are steadily expanding under the influence of the European Convention for the Prevention of Torture and Inhuman or Degrading Treatment or Punishment (Morgan 2001). Among advanced Western countries, only the United States retains and uses the death penalty, and with increasing frequency. Only the United States has adopted broad three-strikes and extensive mandatory minimum sentencing laws.

Only in the United States is "prison gerontologist" an imaginable civil service career ladder. Only the United States uses life-without-possibility-of-parole sentences; elsewhere even murderers sentenced to life terms are eligible for parole or executive-branch pardon, and are typically released after eight to twelve years. In much of Europe, fourteen years is the longest prison sentence that may lawfully be imposed. Only in the United States are prison sentences longer than one or two years common; in most countries, fewer than 5 percent of sentences are for a year or longer. In the United States in 1994, the average sentence among people sent to state prisons for felonies was seventy-one months, and that was before the effects of three-strikes and truth-in-sentencing laws were being felt. Among those in prison in recent years, more than half were serving terms exceeding ten years (Bureau of Justice Statistics 1998, table 1.3). In 1997 the mean average sentence an inmate in a state prison would serve before release was ninety-one months (Bureau of Justice Statistics 2000, table 4.8).

All of this is a drastic change from earlier times. In the 1930s, for example, the United States had incarceration rates comparable to or lower than those of many European countries, including England, France, Switzerland, and Finland (Tonry and Hatlestad 1997, chap. 3). Through the early 1970s, American rates were not much higher than those elsewhere.

More recently, in the 1960s, the United States was in the international mainstream of criminal justice policies. In many respects, it was leading the way toward creation of criminal justice practices that were humane and effective, setting standards that other countries tried to emulate. The death penalty was withering away, the incarceration rate was dropping and comparable to those in other Western countries (Blumstein and Cohen 1973; Zimring and Hawkins 1991), the courts were establishing, expanding, and refining defendants' procedural protections, a prisoners' rights movement was taking shape, and crime control was not generally viewed as a partisan or ideological issue.

So what happened? Why did American crime control and punishment policies become so much harsher than in earlier American times or in other places now?

Eight different plausible stories can be told. The first is empirical. American crime rates are higher or have increased more than other countries', and punishment patterns and policies simply reflect that reality. Crime rates increased and carried punishments with them.

The second is psephological. No matter what the crime trends and rates, the public demanded tougher penalties, and elected officials bowed to that demand.

The third is cynically political. Conservative Republican politicians realized they could use crime, and also welfare, immigration, and affirmative action, as "wedge" issues designed to separate white working-class voters from the Democratic Party. The text of this story is about crime; the subtext is about race. Current policies are the result.

The fourth story is structurally political. Developments of the past quarter century have fragmented the electorate into a mélange of single-issue political groups. People have lost confidence in government's ability to achieve positive goals. Politicians have had to seek broad-based support around emotional but essentially negative issues, including opposition to crime, welfare, and immigration, that offend no politically powerful groups.

The fifth, the arrival of the "risk society," and the sixth, postmodernist angst, are related. I separate them somewhat artificially to isolate their central claims. The risk society story is that the insecurities and social isolation of our times have made us preoccupied with uncertainty, danger, and risk. Modern crime control and penal policies accordingly are concerned above all to identify, quantify, and reduce risk or the perception of risk. Insecurity is so profound and so pervasive that traditional concerns about fairness, justice, and equality have become unaffordable luxuries.

The sixth, the postmodernist angst story, is that a wide range of economic, social, and cultural changes have made people anxious, risk averse, and insecure, and desperate for comforting explanations and easy cures of what ails them. No simple and reassuring explanations exist, so politicians have provided scapegoats. Criminals are among the most vulnerable and viscerally plausible scapegoats and politicians have tried to placate voters' discomforts and win votes by being tough on criminals.

The seventh is historical and is based on comparison of social, political, and legal developments over the past three centuries in the United States, Germany, and France. It attempts to explain why American punishment policies and attitudes are so different from those in the two most powerful European countries. Its key themes are deep cultural differences in attitudes toward the degradation of prisoners and toward the application of egalitarian values to offenders. Eighteenth-century France and Germany were inegalitarian societies with well-developed social hierarchies, while eighteenth-century America already aspired to be an egalitarian society without established hierarchy.

Those differences, it is said, explain punishment practices and attitudes then and now. In France and Germany, high-status criminals in the eighteenth century were often treated with respect, housed decently and comfortably, and, if punished, punished in ways that seemed dignified. Common, low-status criminals were treated roughly and without respect. As part of the shift toward more egalitarian values, as part of the rejection of the social hierarchies of the past, France and Germany have "leveled up," have attempted to accord all offenders the dignity and respect previously granted only the elite.

Eighteenth-century America, by contrast, was a place that rejected notions of aristocratic or social hierarchy, and elite offenders often were dealt with in the same ways as were others. Fast-forwarded to the twentieth century, egalitarian ideas about punishment persist, but in the absence of cultural commitment to leveling up. Instead, something like leveling down has occurred. Commitment to ideas that prisoners should be treated with respect and dignity translates into mild punishment practices. The absence of that commitment opens up possibilities of harshness, debasement, and lack of compassion.

The final story is historical: complex, regularly recurring, but poorly understood interactions among crime trends, public attitudes, and policy making shape our sensibilities and through them our thought, policy debates, and policies. A succession of upsetting incidents has produced a series of moral panics that, among other things, has led to artificially heightened anxieties and fierce overreactions. Current policies are a predictable and understandable, but regrettable, result. This is much the most plausible and complete story and I tell it in considerable detail in chapter 5.

Other stories have been offered besides these eight, but they are so idiosyncratic or obviously inadequate that they can be dismissed out of hand. One, associated with German sociologist Zygmunt Bauman (1991) and Norwegian criminologist Nils Christie (2000) is that current policies are the inevitable outgrowth of "modernity." The modern state goes about its business in a depersonalized neutral way. The "punitive shift," according to criminologist Simon Hallsworth (2000, p. 148), "is born then out of the progressive development of ever more rational forms of organization and their application in the criminal justice system."

This ignores the commonplace realities that nothing like American penal policies exist in any other Western country—suggesting that the modernity thesis applies nowhere else, which would be odd. It also does not acknowledge that arguments in favor of current American policies almost always include ideas about accountability, personal responsibility, and moral culpability. Conservative American proponents of recent policies such as James Q. Wilson, John DiIulio, and William Bennett would be surprised to learn that their proposals were not predicated on normative premises.

Another dismissable story is that contemporary policies and practices, far from reflecting the onset of modernity, reflect the erosion of modernity and "speak directly to punitive passions and are profoundly inspired by them" (2000, p. 156). Somewhat similarly, American sociologist Jonathan Simon argues that a long-term civilizing process has somehow been reversed, at least temporarily, and that "cruelty-seeking" has become a basic theme in "contemporary penality" (2001). Like the modernity story, this one suffers from the difficulty that the phenomenon it explains primarily characterizes the United States, though it purportedly applies more generally. As chapters 3 and 5 show, people characterized by majority culture as seriously deviant always suffer from negative stereotypes and seldom benefit from others' empathy. That is not new, and it cannot explain why American policies were adopted when they were, and not earlier, or why similar policies were not adopted elsewhere. Rhetoric about cruelty and punitive passions does not a plausible story make.

The first of the eight main stories, about the effects of rising crime rates on imprisonment rates, is flatly wrong. There is no simple or direct relation between crime rates and punishment policies or imprisonment rates, though rising crime rates are important. Taken together, the first six stories, whatever their surface plausibility, suffer the same fundamental defect as the modernity and cruelty stories. They, or substantially comparable developments, characterize all wealthy Western countries but only the United States has adopted crime control policies and practices of unprecedented severity.

Most of the more familiar explanations for why contemporary U.S. crime control policies emerged as they did have some merit, but none by itself is convincing. No single factor could cause so massive a change in policy (Garland 1990, 2001a). A sophisticated and nuanced explanation would take all into account.

Sociologist David Garland has recently attempted to explain why English and American crime policies have evolved as they have, and he offers a rich, complex explanation, which I discuss below. His explanation confronts a major difficulty, however. American imprisonment rates grew by 400 percent between 1970 and 2002. English rates grew by 80 percent and remained lower in 2002 (around 125 per 100,000) than American rates were in 1970 (140 per 100,000). The English imprisonment rate in 2002 was not significantly higher than the highest rates of other periods. The American rate is nearly four times higher than at any time in American history before the last thirty years' run-up. Similar social, economic, and cultural forces may have affected sensibilities, politics, and policies in both countries, but the consequences were fundamentally different.

Historian James Whitman's effort to explain differences between France and Germany, and the United States, is full of wisdom and insight, but it suffers from a temporal limitation that parallels the geographical limits of Garland's argument. Garland's analysis does not hold up across space; Whitman's fails across time. If comparisons of French and German practices with American ones today can be explained by reference to cultural attitudes toward egalitarianism and degradation, why did things look so differently for the first two-thirds of the twentieth century? Before 1970, American punishment practices were among the mildest in Western countries and the United States was at the forefront of efforts to rehabilitate offenders and advance offenders' and prisoners' rights. France and Germany lagged far behind.

Many explanations have been given for why American policies and practices developed as they did. Some are plainly wrong. Most are at best fragments of the whole explanation. Many people, however, subscribe to various of them and it seems to me useful to canvass them and show why they are inadequate before offering a better explanation.

Crime Rates and Trends

The first explanation for why so many Americans are in prison, that U.S. crime rates are higher or faster rising than other countries', has virtually no validity. Crime rates in the United States in the 1990s were, for the most part, not higher than those in other Western countries. We know this from the International Crime Victimization Survey, conducted by national governments in most major Western countries since 1989 (e.g., Mayhew and van Dijk 1997; Kesteren, Mayhew, and Nieuwbeerta 2000). For property crimes, the United States is in the middle of the pack. Chances of being burglarized, having your pocket picked or your car stolen are considerably higher in England and several European countries. For violent crimes, American rates are among the highest, along with Australia, Canada, Spain, and France, but not the highest. Chances of being robbed, assaulted, or victim of a stranger rape are higher in several other Western countries. Where the United States stands out is in gun violence. Our rates of robberies and assaults involving guns, and of gun homicides, are substantially higher than elsewhere (Zimring and Hawkins 1997). That is important. However, less than a fourth of those sentenced to prison are convicted of violent crimes of any type, so that is not why U.S. prison patterns and penal policies are so different.

If absolutely higher crime rates do not explain the severity of American punishment policies, perhaps crime trends do. Perhaps there is a necessary connection between crime rates and imprisonment rates. When crime rates rise, imprisonment rates follow, and that is why the number of people locked up increased by nearly seven times in the past thirty years, from around 300,000 in 1972 to 2,000,000 at the end of 2002. There is a surface logic to this claim: more crime yields more arrests yields more convictions yields more prison sentences yields higher prison populations and imprisonment rates. Whatever the logic, however, comparisons of crime and punishment trends in the United States with those in other countries show that there is no inexorable relation between crime and punishment rates.

Figures 2.1–2.3 show trends in imprisonment, homicide, and violent crime rates in the United States, Germany, and Finland from the 1960s to the early 1990s. They stop then because crime rates in the United States began a steady decline in 1990–91 and my aim is to compare national experiences while crime was rising. There are some differences in what the data represent in the three countries. The imprisonment rates, based on the numbers of convicted offenders in prison per 100,000 population, are comparable. The homicide rates are calculated somewhat differently; the Finns, for example, include both attempted and completed homicides whereas the United States counts only completed homicides. The violent crime rates include robbery, rape, and serious assaults, and there are differences in the legal definitions of these crimes in each country. For my purposes, the technical differences in how crimes are defined are unimportant, however, since my interest is not in comparing the rates of crime in the three countries but in comparing crime rate trends. The figures show trends in what each country counts as homicide and serious violent crime, and my interest is in the trends and how they compare with imprisonment trends.

In the United States from 1960 to 1993, as figure 2.1 shows, homicide, violent crime, and imprisonment rates rose together through 1980. Imprisonment rates, however, also rose in 1981–86 when crime rates fell, and rose continuously thereafter including after crime rates peaked in 1991. Between 1960 and 1991, and ignoring intermediate peaks and valleys, violent crime rates rose by a factor of four and homicide rates nearly doubled. On the face of it, this pattern supports the hypothesis that rising crime rates lead to rising prison populations. The German and Finnish experiences show the hypothesis to be false.

That there is no necessary connection between crime and imprisonment rates is shown in figures 2.2 and 2.3, which show comparable data for Germany and Finland during the same period. Violent crime rates overall and for homicide increased in both countries about as much as in the United States, but imprisonment rate patterns are completely different.

Figure 2.2 shows the German data. Violence rates increased by three or four times and homicide rates more than doubled.

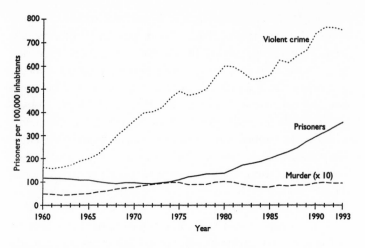

Figure 2.1 Imprisonment, violent crime, and murder rates in the United States, 1960–1993 (per 100,000 population)
Note: Crime rates are somewhat differently calculated in the United States than in Finland and Germany; U.S. incarceration rates do not include jail inmates.
Sources: Bureau of Justice Statistics, *Prisoners*, various years (Washington, D.C.: U.S. Department of Justice, Bureau of Justice Statistics); Federal Bureau of Investigation, *Crime in the United States*, various years (Washington, D.C.: U.S. Government Printing Office).

The imprisonment rate, however, fell through the mid-1970s and remained essentially stable thereafter, fluctuating within a narrow band.

Figure 2.3 shows the Finnish data. The crime trend pattern is the same as in the United States and Germany: homicide rates more than doubled and violent crime rates grew by a factor of three or four. The Finnish imprisonment rate, however, 160 per 100,000 at the start, equal to or higher than the American rate at the time, fell continuously to 60–70 per 100,000.

I could have used data from other countries to make the same point (A. Kuhn 2001). Crime rate trends in France in the same period were about the same as those in the United States, Germany, and Finland. Imprisonment rates zigzagged,

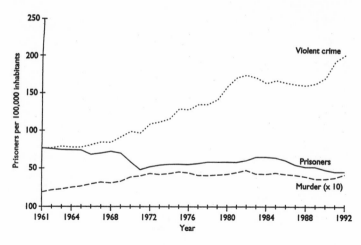

Figure 2.2 Imprisonment, violent crime, and murder rates in Germany, 1961–1992 (per 100,000 population)
Note: Violent crime and murder rates are somewhat differently calculated in Germany than in the United States; the German imprisonment rate excludes pretrial detainees.
Source: German Ministry of Justice (unpublished data provided to author).

with periods of steep increase alternating with steep declines. In France, large-scale pardons and commutations generally accompany national celebrations like the inauguration of a new president or the two-hundredth anniversary of the storming of the Bastille. There were also a series of policy decisions to reduce use of imprisonment by means of newly authorized community penalties (Kensey and Tournier 2001).

It is well known why German imprisonment rates held steady and Finnish rates fell. German governments in the late 1960s and early 1970s decided that prison sentences under six months serve no valid purpose. By separating offenders from jobs, families, and loved ones, and stigmatizing them with the label "ex-convict," short prison sentences damaged prisoners' prospects of later living a law-abiding life. At the same time, a prison sentence of a few months is too short for treatment programs to have much effect. As a result, the

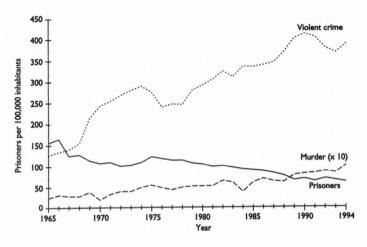

Figure 2.3 Imprisonment, violent crime, and murder rates in Finland, 1965–1994 (per 100,000 population)
Note: Violent crime and murder rates are somewhat differently calculated in Finland than in the United States; the Finnish imprisonment rate includes pretrial detainees.
Source: Finnish Ministry of Justice (unpublished data provided to author).

German parliament enacted laws discouraging use of short prison sentences and authorizing expanded use of community penalties. In particular, a system of day fines was established, enabling judges to impose burdensome punishments that were simultaneously scaled to the seriousness of the crime and calibrated to the offender's wealth and income. (One "day-fine unit" is usually one day's net after-tax income, with upward adjustments to take account of wealth.) The government also established a program under which prosecutors could dismiss charges against suspects who accepted responsibility and agreed to pay the fine or perform the community service that would have been ordered had they been convicted. No subsequent German government, including Helmut Kohl's conservative Christian Democrats, felt a need to change those policies. The day-fine system and the prosecutorial diversion schemes have several times been broadened to apply to more cases (Weigend 2001).

Government officials in Finland in the 1960s observed that Finnish crime rates were approximately the same as those in Denmark, Norway, and Sweden but that the Finnish incarceration rate was two-to-three times higher. That must mean, they concluded, that too many people were in prison. Patrik Törnudd (1993, p. 4), a participant in the discussions at the time but writing a quarter century later explained: Finnish officials, policy analysts, and academics "shared an almost unanimous conviction that Finland's internationally high prisoner rate was a disgrace and that it would be possible to significantly reduce the amount and length of prison sentences without serious repercussions on the crime situation." They decided to reduce the use of imprisonment, and Finnish governments ever since have held to that decision. Over a quarter century, year-by-year, the incarceration rate fell until, by the 1990s, Finnish crime *and* imprisonment rates were comparable to those of other Scandinavian countries (Lappi-Seppälä 2001).

There are two important points to be made about the contrast between the United States and the German, Finnish, and French experiences. First, violent crime rates increased rapidly in all four countries over several decades but only in the United States did imprisonment rates increase continuously or substantially. Second, the German, Finnish, and French patterns resulted from policy decisions that increased incarceration was neither an appropriate nor an effective response to rising crime rates. American politicians decided otherwise. American imprisonment rates did not rise because crime rose. They rose because American politicians *wanted* them to rise.

A benign account of the formulation of recent American punishment policies is that policy makers believed that something had to be done to stop the increases in crime rates and adopted deterrence and incapacitation as their strategies. The only problem with this is that the most drastic policies were adopted long after crime rates began to fall. As figure 2.1

showed, crime rates for most crimes peaked around 1980, fell through the mid-1980s, rose for a while for reasons largely associated with the crack cocaine epidemic, and have since fallen sharply. The first three-strikes laws, however, were enacted in Washington state and California only in 1993–94 and the federal "truth-in-sentencing" law authorizing $8 billion for state prison construction was passed in 1994. The meanings of these data comparing U.S. crime and imprisonment patterns to those of other countries are complex but, whatever else they may show, they do not show any simple interaction between crime trends and imprisonment patterns.

Public Opinion

The second explanation for why American punishment policies are so harsh is that public opinion wished it so. Survey results sometimes in the 1980s and 1990s showed that "crime" and "drugs" were "America's most pressing problem," that large majorities thought sentencing is too lenient, and that the people wanted tougher punishments. On this account, elected officials merely respected the public will and adopted harsher policies. Imprisonment rose as a result. If that is wrong, blame the public.

There are two serious and well-known deficiencies in this story. The first relates to what "the public" wants. The answer is complicated, but it is not very different from what practitioners want—penalties no more severe than are now imposed and substantial efforts to rehabilitate offenders. The second relates to whether politicians follow or lead public opinion. The answer is that they lead it, but claim to follow it.

A mountain of public opinion scholarship and research shows that the belief that the public is monolithically and unqualifiedly harsh is fundamentally mistaken (Roberts et al. 2002). Most people necessarily base their opinions about punishment on what they know about crime from the mass media. As a result, many people regard heinous crimes and bizarre sentences as the norms, many believe sentences are much softer than they are, and many believe crime rates are rising when they are falling. As a result, majorities nearly always report that judges' sentences are too lenient. Yet, and this is true not only in the United States but also in Australia, Canada, and England, when people are asked to propose appropriate sentences for individual cases, they generally propose sentences shorter than are actually imposed (Roberts et al. 2002).

A different body of research powerfully demonstrates why results of opinion polls sometimes should not be taken at face value. Dan Yankelovich (1991), long-time head of a large public opinion survey firm, urged that readers of polls never lose track of the difference between public *opinion* and public *judgment*.

Public opinion is what people say off the top of the head as a first reaction. It may be uninformed or misinformed, ignorant or insightful. For some purposes evidence of this sort is useful. On simple subjects where only preferences matter (Will you vote for Bush or Gore?), it may be all we need to know, though even there we know that preferences change quickly and often can not be taken at face value (for example, throughout the 1990s, more people told interviewers they would vote for black candidates than did). On complex matters (How should the United States balance environmental concerns with energy needs? Should criminal penalties be increased or decreased?), ordinary public opinion surveys tell us what is on people's minds, or what they know or think they know, but not what their informed opinion would be.

Public judgment is what people say when they know enough to have an informed opinion. A great deal of opinion research on many subjects has been premised on this distinction. Here is how it typically works. At the outset a group of people are asked to answer a series of questions about a subject. The results are a measure of their opinion. They then participate over a few hours or a few days in seminars and discussions about the subject. The people running the project try hard to be sure the information presented is balanced and evenhanded, and participants discuss the subject at length. Participants are then asked for their views. The results are an indication of public judgment.

The results of the before and after surveys can be compared and it can be seen what difference knowledge makes to what people think. This has been done on numerous subjects, including the environment, nuclear power, the death penalty, and criminal punishment. Public judgment is nearly always substantially different from public opinion. Having more and better information often changes what we think. There is nothing surprising about this. That is everyone's experience in day-to-day life—it is why we try to avoid making rash decisions about things that are important to us—but it is easy to forget when thinking about surveys of public opinion.

Research of this type on punishment often begins by giving people vignettes that describe the characteristics of a crime and a criminal. They are then asked what sentence they would impose, provided information on sentencing practices and options, and asked again—a few hours later or the next day—what sentences they would impose. This has been done in at least a dozen American states and, though the details vary, in outline the results are always the same. Many hypothetical offenders who at the outset would have been sentenced to prison are instead sentenced to various community punishments.

Another major and recurring finding is that when public judgment is wanted, when ordinary citizens have the information to reach informed conclusions, they have the same complex and ambivalent attitudes toward criminals that judges and lawyers have. They believe crimes are the products of bad moral choices, disadvantaged backgrounds, and substance abuse. They want offenders to be punished and to be rehabilitated. They are much more often willing to pay more taxes for treatment programs than for prison building. They insist on prison sentences only for the most violent crimes (Tonry and Hatlestad 1997, chap. 5; Roberts et al. 2002).

Public opinion surveys show that crime is no longer widely numbered among the country's most pressing problems.

Crime ranked in the top three from 1980 to 1990, but by March 2002 had fallen to fifteenth. In 1994 less than half of Americans preferred policies that address the underlying causes of crime over stricter sentencing. By 2001 nearly two-thirds of Americans favored approaches that address the root causes of crime (Peter D. Hart Research Associates, Inc. 2002).

A final point about public opinion on punishment is also important. Prevalent sensibilities in recent decades have predisposed Americans to heightened intolerance of crime and criminals. Nonetheless, public opinion findings showing that Americans regard crime or drugs as the nation's most pressing problem typically follow, not precede, media and political concentration on crime. Politicians who attempt to win favor by demonstrating their toughness nearly always say that they are honoring citizens' wishes. The evidence shows, however, that emphasis by politicians and the media on crime issues is what causes public anxiety to increase. This is best shown in a book by Katherine Beckett (1997), who analyzed interactions among media attention to crime and drug issues, politicians' relative emphasis on those issues, and the results of opinion surveys. She did this in relation to crime policy in the 1970s and drug policy in the 1980s. Content analyses of newspaper and television coverage were compared with public opinion survey results and showed a recurring pattern. Politicians focused on crime policy, or the media increased their crime coverage, or both, and then, after those things happened, opinion surveys showed heightened public concern about crime or drugs, and heightened support for tough policies.

So public support for harsh policies has coincided with their adoption. However, it is not public opinion per se that leads to harsher policies, but politicians' proposals and posturing and sensational media crime coverage that lead to changes in public opinion. Americans were prepared to support the crime control policies of the 1980s and 1990s. Evidence on public judgment, however, shows that they would also have supported policies that aimed to enhance offenders' chances of achieving law-abiding lives. Responsibility for recent policies lies not with the public but with the public officials who failed to provide balanced and humane leadership.

This leads to the third explanation for why American punishment policies are so harsh—that conservative politicians for partisan advantage banked the fires of public fear of crime and then offered harsh policies to dampen those fires. I refer to conservative politicians even though by the 1990s moderate and some liberal Democrats were equally outspoken in their anti-crime toughness. No one seems seriously to question that Bill Clinton's decision never to let the Republicans get to his right on crime was a tactical response designed to check Republicans' partisan use of the crime issue. It worked for Clinton, but not for the tens of thousands of people whose lives were changed for the worse by the consequences of his strategy.

Partisan Politics

Crime and punishment have been high on American political agendas since the late 1960s. Before Republican Barry Goldwater raised "crime in the streets" as a partisan issue in his unsuccessful 1964 presidential campaign, public safety was generally seen as one among many important but unglamorous core functions of government, like public health, public transit, and public education. Public officials were expected to do their work conscientiously and well, and systematic knowledge was widely seen as relevant to the formulation of policies and the improvement of institutions and practices. Reasonable people differed over the best approaches for addressing particular problems. As American Law Institute deliberations in the 1950s of provisions of the proposed Model Penal Code demonstrate, however, the debates were seldom partisan or ideological (this is discussed in detail in chapter 7). Criminal justice policy was a subject for practitioners and technocrats, and sentencing was the specialized case-by-case business of judges and corrections officials.

In recent decades, however, crime control has been at the center of partisan politics, and policies have been shaped more by symbols and rhetoric than by substance and knowledge. Political scientists and journalists tell the story of how that happened. Until the 1960s, the Democratic Party had dominated electoral politics in most of the South since the end of Reconstruction. Policy differences and personal rivalries were fought over within a state's Democratic Party, rather than between parties. The civil rights movement, however, created a fissure between racial and social policy liberals and racial and social policy conservatives, initially in the South but eventually nationally.

Republican strategists seized the opportunity in the 1970s and 1980s to appeal to "Nixon [later Reagan] Democrats" by defining sharp differences between the parties on three "wedge issues": crime control, welfare, and affirmative action. Those issues were meant to separate Democrats from their traditional white working-class supporters by speaking to legitimate anxieties in ways that, beneath the surface, also appealed to racial enmity and stereotype. On the surface, these three issues are about protecting citizens from crime, public funds from cheating, and workers from unfair treatment. Below the surface, they were largely about race, and in political imagery were given black faces. Illustrations include George Bush's 1988 use of black Willie Horton to personify the dangers of soft crime policies; Ronald Reagan's 1980 use of black Linda Taylor, Chicago's "welfare queen," to embody welfare fraud; and Jessie Helms's television ads in his 1990 Senate campaign against black Charlotte mayor Harvey Gantt illustrating the dangers of affirmative action with images of an unemployed white worker's wringing hands.

On crime control, conservatives blamed rising crime rates on lenient judges and soft punishments, and demanded "toughness." On welfare, conservatives blamed rising welfare rolls on "welfare cheats" and laziness, and demanded budget cuts. On affirmative action, conservatives blamed white un- and underemployment on "quotas," and urged elimination of affirmative action (Edsall and Edsall 1991; Applebome 1996; Gest 2001).

Crime's role as a wedge issue had important consequences. Issues that are debated on television and examined in fifteen- and thirty-second commercials necessarily are presented in simplistic and emotional terms. The appeal palpably is to public opinion, not public judgment. Matters about which judges and prosecutors agonize in individual cases are addressed in slogans and symbols, which often lead later to adoption of ham-fisted and poorly considered policies.

Few corrections officials, judges, or informed scholars, for example, support broadly defined three-strikes laws, mandatory minimum sentence laws, or sexual psychopath laws in the forms in which they are typically adopted. This is not because they do not want criminals to be punished, or are unsympathetic to victims' suffering, or are indifferent to public safety needs, but for practical reasons. Such laws seldom achieve their nominal purposes—there is no credible evidence that they are significant deterrents to crime—but generally generate serious unintended consequences. They are too rigid and often result in unjustly harsh penalties. They result in circumvention by judges and lawyers who believe their application inappropriate and unjust in many cases. They are often redundant because people who commit serious crimes almost always receive severe penalties anyway (Tonry 1996, chap. 4).

Many more practitioners and scholars would support such laws if they were narrowly drawn and carefully crafted to encompass only genuinely serious crimes and genuinely threatening offenders. However, in a "sound-bite politics" era, few politicians were prepared to act as voices of moderation and parsimony, and as a result new sentencing laws often lacked those qualities.

As important, when crime control became one of the central issues in American politics, it ceased being a specialized policy subject and became instead a symbol or metaphor for, broadly, concepts like "personal responsibility" and vindication of victims' interests, and, more narrowly, ideas about criminals' immorality and irresponsibility. Analysts of contemporary crime control policy often say that its principal aims are "expressive" rather than functional (J. Kennedy 2000; Garland 2001a). A broadly defined sexual psychopath law, three-strikes law, or mandatory minimum sentence law may be ineffective or cruel or unduly costly, but none of that may matter. If the law's proponents, and voters, view it as an expression of revulsion with crime and outrage toward criminals, whether it will work or achieve just results in individual cases is often politically irrelevant. When issues are defined in polar terms of morality and immorality or responsibility and irresponsibility, few elected officials want to be found at the wrong pole.

Few informed people will disagree with the broad outlines of this account. Many liberals might say that the conservative emphasis on toughness was cynical and intellectually dishonest. Many conservatives might respond that they believe that tougher penalties reduce crime rates and, through public opinion polls and electoral support for "tough-on-crime" candidates, citizens have shown they support such policies; what better basis for policy making can there be?

Of the explanations offered so far for the severity of current punishment policies, this is the most plausible. Current American imprisonment policies, and the avoidable damage they do to prisoners, their families, and their communities, and the fiscal and opportunity costs they impose on governments (Hagan and Dinovitzer 1999), may merely be by-products of an effective political strategy for winning elections. However, that the Right won, whether cynically or honestly motivated, does not explain why such political appeals were successfully made and such policies adopted in the United States, and not in other countries, and now, and not at other times.

Political Reconfiguration

So what is needed is an explanation for why crime and punishment served so nicely as a wedge issue, and why so many elected officials were prepared in recent decades to behave in ways that opponents and many observers perceived as demagogic. Social scientists have offered analyses of political and governmental trends of recent decades that attempt to explain why crime has received so much more and more sustained attention from governments and politicians than have other equally important public policy issues.

Sociologist David Garland has argued that American and English politicians and governments came to focus so much on crime almost by default, and that vigorous anticrime efforts should be seen as expressions of the weakness, not the strength, of the state (Garland 2001a). Since the 1960s, Garland argued, external forces have made it difficult for the state demonstrably to solve its citizens' problems. The state's credibility has suffered as a result. Governments cannot insulate their citizens from the disruptive effects of economic recessions, globalization, and multiculturalism.

But crime is different: "The essential and abiding attractiveness of the 'sovereign' response to crime . . . is that it can be represented as an immediate, authoritative intervention. . . . Like the decision to wage war, the decision to inflict harsh punishment or extend police powers exemplifies the sovereign mode of state action" (Garland 2001a, pp. 134–45). Garland explains that evidence—of what works, of foreseeable effects—is irrelevant because the goal is not crime reduction per se, but the credibility of the state. Whether policy initiatives have any effect on crime rates or not is beside the point. What matters is that policy-makers be seen to be doing *something*, and that policies express anger and outrage with crime, and the people who commit it, and its consequences for victims (Garland, 2001a, p. 110).

Sociologists Theodore Caplow and Jonathan Simon (1999) offer two interconnected reasons (among others) why U.S. crime policy developed as it did. One, paralleling Garland's ideas about the weakness of the state, is the anomaly that enormous expansion over the last thirty years in the role of government, particularly the federal government, coincided with sharp and continuous decline in public confidence in government. The second is the weakening of broad-based political coalitions and the growth and influence of single-issue political movements.

The scope of federal government activity has expanded greatly. Before the 1960s, for example, many subjects now seen as important federal responsibilities received little federal attention. These include health care, education, street crime, consumer protection, occupational safety, employment practices, child care, environmental protection, the arts, and discrimination on grounds of age, race, sex, and disability. Few people any longer argue that any of these subjects is not the Congress's business. The enormous expansion of the federal government's agenda transformed American politics.

The result, Caplow and Simon (1999) argue, was a spiral of failure. Declining student performance was attributed to lack of discipline and intellectual rigor in schools. Illegitimacy and chronic poverty were blamed on perverse incentives provided by the main federal income support program, Aid to Families with Dependent Children. Rising crime was blamed on lenient judges and parole boards.

As evidence of government failure, Caplow and Simon cite the massive escalation of costs of federal government programs between 1970 and 1995 without corresponding benefits. Federal expenditures for health care outpaced inflation by five to one, for education by three and a half to one, for Aid to Families with Dependent Children (AFDC) by three to one, and for criminal justice by six to one. None of these systems was widely credited as being conspicuously successful, but they are interconnected and their defects are mutually reinforcing. The extraordinary costs of the health care system prevented any serious effort to alleviate poverty. The deficiencies of the antipoverty programs undermined the public schools. The failures of the schools poured into the criminal justice system.

All of this led, they say, to a remarkable collapse of confidence in government. In response to the survey question,

"How much of the time do you trust the government in Washington to do the right thing," 75 percent of a representative national sample in 1964 answered "just about always" or "most of the time." When the same question was put to a similar sample in 1995, only 25 percent gave those answers (Caplow and Simon 1999).

For Caplow and Simon, as for Garland, penal policies and politics are primarily about other things. Government can express outrage and appear to respond to the public by taking drastic and dramatic action against crime and criminals. Enactment of harsh policies serves as an end, not a means.

The inherently expressive character of much crime control policy distinguishes it from other policy subjects. Government and government leaders get credit in most realms for policies that achieve results, and lose credibility when policies fail. Announcement of new educational or health care policies by itself is insufficient. What matters is whether they satisfy their aims, or demonstrably move in that direction. In recent years, the expressive content of crime control policies has been enough.

Caplow and Simon's second observation is that American politics after the 1960s moved away from broad-based parties with traditional class and regional constituencies toward "single issue" movements. The proportions of the electorate with strong loyalties to the Republican or Democratic parties steadily fell and the proportion of voters with no attachment to either party grew. Elections increasingly are won, or lost, not because voters support the values or platforms of a party, but because of the ways they react to media imagery and particular issues. In an era in which few people believe strongly in government's ability to do good, it is difficult to base political campaigns on broad positive agendas. Some popular subjects—national defense, antiterrorism programs, and environmental protection are examples—attract such wide support that they seldom distinguish parties or candidates.

What is left are candidates' images and personalities, issues of overriding importance to single-issue groups, and things to be against. About images and personalities I have nothing special to say; candidates try to present themselves favorably and modern electronic media make those efforts ever more effective.

The single-issue groups, however, have transformed politics. Elections are won and lost over such issues as abortion, affirmative action, gun control, school prayer, gay rights, and capital punishment. These controversies, Caplow and Simon (1999) note, do not lend themselves to the compromise and horse-trading that long characterized American politics.

Single-issue organizations and campaigns invite people to join the side of good against evil. To antiabortion activists, abortion is cold-blooded murder. To their adversaries, the issue is women's ownership of their own bodies. To advocates of strict gun control, the private possession of firearms is foolish and dangerous; to their adversaries it is the keystone of liberty. To proponents of gay rights, the issues are equality and human rights; to opponents, traditional values and the sanctity of the family. School prayer for proponents is about belief in God and respect for private faith; for opponents, about cultural hegemony, intolerance, and subtle coercion.

Candidates and parties are loath to take sides in any of these conflicts. The well-organized pressure groups that represent such interests have few means of achieving their goals outside of federal courts, Congress, and the state legislatures. They want to prevent other people from doing things, or to require other people to do things, and only courts and lawmakers have the power to do that. Supporters of these groups will reliably vote against candidates on the wrong side of the issue. Only a small minority of voters may care deeply about the issue, but in a close election they can make the difference.

Faced with voters who split on so many issues and are profoundly skeptical about the ability of government to improve their lives, parties and politicians have been required to emphasize policy initiatives that command broad support. In our time, these initiatives are generally negative. Opposition to communism and the Soviet Union long played this role. Early in the twenty-first century, opposition to terrorism and other countries' fundamentalist regimes may be used in this way, but it will seldom differentiate parties or candidates. What is left are domestic initiatives—such as crime, welfare, and immigration—that can be debated in moral terms, respond to broad-based anxieties and empathies, and affront no powerful constituency.

Like some of the other explanations for American punishment policies, this is plausible and probably valid. Confidence in government is low and single-issue groups are powerful. These developments to some extent distinguish American politics and government from those of other Western countries. Faith in government is higher in other countries as is acceptance of the view that government has positive obligations to improve citizens' lives. Disagreements about values and morals exist in every country, but galvanizing single-issue movements like the National Rifle Association or the National Abortion Rights Action League are not common. Anti-immigrant movements are the closest equivalent, but that is more akin to U.S. anti-immigrant or crime movements than to American single-issue movements. Nor in most other countries are issues such as school prayer, capital punishment, and affirmative action the subjects of great controversy.

The question remains, though, why alone among Western countries has the United States adopted penal policies of unprecedented severity?

Risk Society

One explanation builds on literatures in sociology and anthropology on "risk" and "the risk society." These literatures have only recently been applied to crime and crime control policy. The anthropological literature, most famously associated with Mary Douglas (1985, 1992), concerns the social construction of risks and such questions as why in a particular place and time something is seen as unacceptably risky and how to understand and evaluate actors' differing perceptions of risk.

The sociological literature is most famously associated with Anthony Giddens (1990, 1991, 1998) and Ulrich Beck (1992, 1996). Part of the backdrop for each is concern for the environmental risks created by modern industry and technology, and how those risks are assessed at individual and social levels. Giddens, after noting the secularism and uncertainty of our time, described contemporary society as a "risk culture" (1991, p. 3), in which all of life is subject to "contingencies." "Living in a 'risk society' means," he wrote, "living with a calculative attitude to the open possibilities of action, positive and negative, with which, as individuals and globally, we are confronted in a continuous way in our contemporary social existence" (1991, p. 28). For Giddens, this does not mean that people living in contemporary societies are more exposed to risk than people living in other times, or are more anxious about risk, but are more self-aware.

Beck bridges Douglas's interest in the social construction of risk and Giddens's interest in how the greater fluidity of contemporary life influences our lives. As social structures have weakened, and work, family, and gender roles become less fixed, individuals have more control over their lives, more choices to make, and less certainty about the future. He refers to this evolving aspect of contemporary life as "individualization" and it is fraught with risk (Beck and Beck-Gersheim 1995). As with Giddens, there is neither necessarily more nor worse risk now but greater awareness of it.

Deborah Lupton (1999), in a recent survey of writing on risk, synthesizes the main themes:

> [T]he contemporary obsession with risk has its roots in the changes inherent in the transformation of societies from pre-modern to modern and then to late modern (or postmodern, as some theorists prefer to describe the contemporary era). Late or postmodernity generally refers to broader socioeconomic and political changes that have-

taken place in Western societies since World War II, producing the sense for many people that we are 'living in new times.' . . . For the individual, it is argued, these changes are associated with an intensifying sense of uncertainty, complexity, ambivalence, and disorder, a growing distrust of social institutions and traditional authorities, and an increasing awareness of the threats inherent in everyday life. (Lupton 1999, pp. 10–12)

So far, so good. Stripped of jargon, there is nothing here that any regular newspaper reader will find surprising or unfamiliar. What is the relevance of the risk literature for understanding crime control or punishment policies? Not much.

Lupton offers three observations about the implications of risk analysis for crime. First, situational crime prevention strategies focus on prevention of crime rather than on rehabilitation of offenders (1999, p. 94). This is true, but neither momentous nor new. Situational crime prevention is a complement to law enforcement techniques and not inconsistent with rehabilitation efforts. The idea is that much crime is opportunistic and spur-of-the-moment, and it can be reduced by changing situations to make opportunities less attractive. Examples include increased street lighting, use of CCTV, redesign of public spaces, and substitution of paper or electronic tickets for cash payments. Such initiatives make crimes more difficult, more likely to be observed, and less likely to succeed. People have, however, always tried to lessen their chances of victimization by locking doors, buying dogs, hiring guards, carrying weapons, and avoiding dark alleys at night. Modern prevention techniques are larger in scale and more sophisticated in technology but not different in kind. Situational crime prevention in any case is but a tiny part of contemporary crime prevention efforts.

Second, emphasis on risk or dangerousness treats offenders not as individuals but as members of "risk groups" (1999, pp. 94–95). This also is true, and nothing new. Incapacitation has always been the flip side of rehabilitation. The converse of the belief that an offender has been rehabilitated and is capable of living a crimefree life, and hence should be released from prison, is that he has not, is not, and should not.

Until recent decades, such decisions were usually based on individualized assessments of rehabilitation and predictions of risk, but they were intuitive and subjective, and less reliable than are such decisions when based on validated risk prediction instruments (Clear and Cadora 2001). Beginning in the 1920s, sociologists and others began developing base expectancy tables to predict offenders', prisoners', and parolees' likelihood of future offending (e.g., Burgess 1928; Ohlin 1951; Gottfredson, Wilkins, and Hoffman 1978). These are actuarial calculations aimed at identifying groups, on the bases of particular characteristics, whose members have greater or lesser probabilities of reoffending. Contemporary risks and needs assessments, prediction instruments, and targeted incapacitation policies are applications of that long-established technology. Surveillance and punishment policies based on actuarial calculations do raise questions concerning whether, when, and within what limits such information may justly be used in individual cases. There is nothing intrinsically new about any of this. The relevant conceptual, jurisprudential, and empirical literatures all date back at least a half century.

Third, "the figure of the criminal is frequently positioned as risky and needing exclusion from others" (Lupton 1999, p. 144). Among the implications of this are that people assess some places—"the inner city, the shopping mall, housing estates [public housing]"—where criminals are likely to be as dangerous, and avoid those places, and that members of some groups, such as "injecting drug users," are stereotyped as potential criminals. All true, and often regrettable, but the discovery neither needed nor awaited the appearance of the risk society literature.

Lupton, however, is a specialist in "cultural studies," not a crime specialist. The criminologists do no better a job of demonstrating how risk society analysis aids understanding of crime policy changes (Hope and Sparks 2000; Stenson and

Sullivan 2001). The best work on the subject, most of it qualitative, examines the interacting ways objective risk, anxiety, and fear of crime affect people's daily lives in different settings and circumstances (e.g., Jefferson and Hollway 2000). The worst of it is jargon-ridden and obscure (e.g., Stanko 2000), or ideological and polemical (e.g., Stenson 2000).

Social scientists not working in the risk society framework also worry about increased use of prediction instruments throughout the criminal justice system. Sir Anthony Bottoms (1995) includes this as part of a new "managerialism," and Malcolm Feeley and Jonathan Simon (1992) portray it as "actuarial justice." Both works emphasize increased use of risk prediction, but neither claims that risk is a new consideration in criminal justice decision making.

Most of the risk society literature discusses punishment policies in England and the United States, as if the phenomena to be explained are the same in both countries. Though most who write on this subject are based in England, it does not seem to have occurred to them that American penal policies are incomparably harsher than the English and imprisonment rates are five times higher. A theory that applies equally to both cannot explain those differences and is invalidated by them.

By this point, the explanation for contemporary American crime control and punishment policies has gotten pretty complicated. Crime rate levels and changes by themselves do not have much explanatory power. Rising crime rates and mass media developments provide a plausible basis for heightened public concern, but ordinary people's views are more complex, ambivalent, and temperate than is widely recognized. Frightening stereotypes and valid fears provide an intelligible reason why voters respond to "tough-on-crime" rhetoric and appeals, but do not explain why politicians in our time chose to campaign on those issues rather than others. The account of structural changes in American politics is part of the explanation—there is little support in the early twenty-first century for ambitious broad-based policy initiatives by government, and it is always easier to mobilize support against something than for something. Social, economic, and cultural changes in American life in the past thirty years have made life more uncertain and, in the Giddens/Beck sense, risky.

Like the dots in a pointillist painting, all of these claims provide points of understanding, but they lack a pattern that provides an intelligible picture. Three more complex stories try to do that. One is David Garland's story, discussed in the next section, of the force of postmodernist angst. The second is James Whitman's explanation for why American punishment policies and practices differ so greatly from those in France and Germany. The last, best, and most complete story is that the pattern can best be understood in relation to the intertwining of cyclical changes in sensibilities with recent moral panics and political opportunism.

Postmodernist Angst

This story overlaps the risk society story, but is more complex, comprehensive, and sophisticated. The final third of the twentieth century was a period of disruption, uncertainty, and change. Few people were unaffected by recessions, globalism, or economic restructuring; nor by social changes associated with the women's, civil rights, and gay rights movements; nor by increased immigration, ethnic diversity, and cultural pluralism. Routines and expectations had to change. Peoples' lives became less constrained and predetermined but greater autonomy and wider possibilities brought greater uncertainty. Values and certainties were undermined and questioned. And, for much of the last thirty years, crime rates increased and fear of crime penetrated into more people's lives, and more deeply. Most crimes, especially the street and violent crimes that are most feared, are committed by people at the social and economic margins, and disproportionately by members of racial and ethnic minorities. Because most of the forces and developments that destabilize our lives are distant and impersonal, but criminals are near at hand and identifiable, broad-based anxieties are displaced onto blamable criminals. Politicians know that government action cannot fundamentally affect crime rates and patterns but want to be seen to be doing something, and accordingly promote and enact policies meant primarily to express disdain for offenders and hurt them.

"Underlying the debate about crime and punishment," Garland wrote, "was a fundamental shift in interests" (2001*a*, p. 76). Sir Anthony Bottoms of Cambridge University in 1995 famously characterized the sensibilities to which expressive policies are a putative response as "populist punitiveness." He, like Garland, attributes populist punitiveness to increased crime rates and the uncertainties associated with what he, like Garland, calls "late modernity." Populist punitiveness exists, Bottoms says, and it explains why governments adopt harsh policies and why harsh policies are well received. Garland's story, however, goes further and explains both why governments adopted particular policies and why they won public favor.

Garland's story, rich, subtle, and multifaceted, is told in what he calls a "history of the present." He sketches the origins of modern criminal justice institutions, traces the 1970s loss of faith in individualized and relatively nonpoliticized practices, describes social and cultural changes, surveys changes in criminology, crime prevention, and crime control policies, and then explains why policies changed as they did. It is an ambitious work, and much the most distinguished of its kind. What follows is not a review of the entire work and cannot do it justice, but is an effort to distill central themes.

Garland's story has four main components. The first is the salience of "high crime rates as a social fact" (2001*a*, p. 106). The second is the use of expressive punishments as a demonstration of state sovereignty. The third is the risk society story of instability, change, risk, insecurity, anxiety, and displacement. The fourth is the "criminology of the other." I summarize these components briefly, quoting Garland extensively, rather than paraphrase wordily and imprecisely.

First, crime has become a "normal social fact," more widely distributed, and avoidance of crime a ubiquitous feature of everyday life:

> [B]y the 1970s society's vulnerability to high rates of crime came to be viewed for what it was—a normal social fact. At the end of the 1990s, despite much publicized decreases, American and British rates of crime and violence remain at an historically high level. . . . Whatever successes police and politicians may claim, crime avoidance remains a prominent organizing principle of every day life. (2001a, p. 194)

Garland describes how political campaigns and the mass media amplified awareness of crime. Independently of that, he argues that victimization is more widespread than in earlier times. No longer primarily localized in low-income, disadvantaged, and minority neighborhoods, victimization has become in a sense more fairly distributed and threatens affluent and middle-class people.

Second, crime's status as a new social fact exposed the "myth that the sovereign state is capable of delivering 'law and order' and controlling crime" (2001a, p. 109). This created a predicament for policy makers. They can accept and adapt to the limits of sovereign power, or they can pretend not to know it and retreat into an *expressive* mode.

"[T]he essential and abiding attractiveness of the 'sovereign' response to crime (and above all of retaliatory laws that create stronger penal sanctions or police powers)," Garland writes, "is that it can be represented as an immediate, authoritative intervention. Such action gives the impression that *something is being done*—here, now, swiftly and decisively" (2001a, pp. 134–35; emphasis in original).

Third, the new social fact of crime, particularly as it impinges on the middle class, importantly exacerbates the "sense of ontological insecurity" of late modern society:

> [T]his new element of precariousness and insecurity is built into the fabric of everyday life. . . . Little surprise too that people increasingly demand to know about the risks to which they are exposed by the criminal justice system and are increasingly impatient when the system fails to control "dangerous" individuals. . . . Crime has become one of the threats that the contemporary middle-class household must take seriously—another problem to manage, another possibility that must be anticipated and controlled. (2001a, p. 155)

The vulnerability of the middle class is doubly important. It provides receptivity to politicians' populist appeals. Perhaps as importantly, middle-class prosecutors, judges, probation officers, and prison officials shared the widespread sense of precariousness and danger. Previously, these peoples' social distance from "the poor people's problem" of crime, and their low levels of victimization, made compassion easy to express and others' vulgar punitiveness easy to disdain. Their own sense of personal insecurity, however, made many "more supportive of punitive responses to crime" (2001a, p. 150) and less committed to the more humane and constructive policies that in earlier times they supported. A group that might have been expected to resist expressive policies became less inclined to do so.

Fourth, is Garland's "*criminology of the other*, of the threatening outcast, the fearsome stranger, the excluded and the embittered [which] . . . functions to demonize the criminal, to act out popular fears, and to promote support for state punishment" (2001a, p. 137; emphasis in original). The outcasts in the social and political climates of the 1980s and 1990s inevitably were the welfare poor, urban blacks, and marginalized working-class boys.

So, putting all this together, why are harsh expressive policies adopted? "Because," Garland writes, "the groups most affected lack political power and are widely regarded as dangerous and undeserving; because the groups least affected could be reassured that something is being done and lawlessness is not tolerated; and because few politicians are willing to oppose a policy when there is so little political advantage to be gained by doing so" (2001a, p. 132).

This snapshot of Garland's argument omits much that is creative and insightful but does, I believe, capture its flavor. The important question is whether it adds anything importantly new to the five stories already told. I think not. The salience of the new fact of crime is part of every story, as are the insecurities of "late modernity." Garland's sovereignty argument bears strong resemblance to Jonathan Simon's governing-through-crime thesis. The centrality of expressive punishments, and their frequent disengagement from substantive crime prevention, is common ground. And along the way, Garland develops, albeit less extensively, the political cynicism and ideological subplots of the other stories.

The postmodernist angst story by itself is not enough. There have been other equally unsettled periods in American history that produced widespread dislocation and insecurity but did not produce the kind of sensibilities that led to contemporary crime control and punishment policies. It is easy and not unnatural for people living of a time to think that time uniquely challenged or troubled, but that is a reflection merely of chronocentrism, the temporal equivalent of ethnocentrism. Both where and when we stand, observe, and generalize shape what we see and think. Anyone who thinks the three decades 1970–2000 were uniquely unsettling has forgotten the three decades 1920–1950. That period experienced the rise of Nazism, fascism, and Soviet communism, as well as the Roaring '20s, the Great Depression, World War II, the Iron Curtain, and the onset of the Cold War. Nothing very dramatic happened to crime control and penal policy during those thirty years and the American system of individualized and indeterminate punishment that had taken shape by 1930 looked much the same in 1950.

More eloquently and comprehensively than anyone else, Garland puts all the stories into one mosaic, but the whole is not greater than the sum of its parts. What is still needed is an explanation for why the United States adopted crime control and punishment policies of unprecedented severity, but neither England nor any other Western country that experienced comparable crime, social, economic, and cultural changes and trends did so.

Garland's story has real power, but ultimately does not offer a convincing explanation, and he himself seems not entirely convinced. Having explained how crime trends, social and cultural changes, recognition of the limits of state power, and the "criminology of the other" all shaped the development of current policies, in the end he reduces those developments to background conditions; they are not singly or jointly causes. He insists that he does not mean "to imply that political decisions and policies are determined, or made inevitable, by events and circumstances occurring elsewhere" (2001a, p. 139), and that contemporary crime control policies were "not inevitable" (2001a, pp. 76 and 201). He also insists that "public attitudes about crime and control are deeply ambivalent" (2001a, p. 203) and that "[t]he populist current in contemporary crime policy is, to some extent, a political posture or tactic, adopted for short-term political advantage. As such it can quickly be reversed" (2001a, p. 172).

Garland's account of the relationship between postmodernist angst, crime control policies, and punishment practices, notwithstanding its many merits, does not explain why U.S. policies are as they are.

Earlier I quoted a passage from Garland about the changing sensibilities and interests that underlay the construction of contemporary crime control and punishment policies. But where do the sensibilities and interests come from? The seventh and eighth stories answer that question.

Democracy and Degradation

The challenge historian James Whitman set for himself was to understand why "over the last quarter century, America has shown a systematic drive toward increased harshness by most measures, while continental Europe has not" (Whitman 2003, p. 38). One explanation is that, "for the most part, though, American-style politics has failed to exert an American-style influence in German or French criminal justice," and, as a result, "bureaucrats have succeeded in keeping control of the punishment process, without becoming subject to decisive pressure from a stirred-up public" (2003, p. 15).

That last observation, if warranted, and lots of evidence suggests it is, powerfully refutes most of the preceding stories about increasing punitiveness in America. France and Germany have experienced rising crime rates, economic destabilization, more punitive public opinion, ethnic tensions, and postmodernist angst no less than the United States, and yet "as of the year 2000, mildness is still, at heart, the watchword of punishment practices in each country" (p. 70).

Whitman's *description* of contemporary differences between continental Europe and America is not an *explanation*. For that he goes back two centuries and identifies two differences between Europe and America that reverberate in our time. The first is the American distrust of government and government officials that developed in the fifty-year build-up to the American Revolution and has characterized Americans ever since. This he contrasts to the strong European states of the eighteenth century and the continuation of support for strong states today. Germany and France have state apparatuses that, compared with American government, are relatively powerful and relatively autonomous.

The second difference relates to the alternate ways European and Anglo-American cultures ameliorated the consequences of eighteenth-century status differentiation. Social hierarchy and status differences were, of course, marked in Europe, Britain, and the American colonies, and extended to the ways people who committed crimes were dealt with. Status mattered, and it can be illustrated by the forms of execution and imprisonment. Hangings are unattractive: the victim slowly asphyxiates, the bowels let loose, and the body wracks with spasms. Beheadings are nearly instantaneous and the headless body, if supported, stays in place. In Britain and Europe, low-status people were hanged; high-status people were beheaded. And so with prisons: low-status people were kept in crowded, squalid places, while high-status people were allowed comfortable facilities to which visitors and personal servants had access.

Whitman describes starkly different ways that Europe and Anglo-America responded to the status hierarchy in punishment: Europe leveled up, aspiring to treat all offenders with respect and civility, at least in principle like high-status prisoners; England and American leveled down, treating all prisoners in principle like low-status prisoners. In this framework, Whitman argues that much American punishment is degrading, as low-status punishment has always been degrading, while French and German punishment is premised on treating prisoners with respect and sympathy. Similarly, American egalitarianism leads to beliefs in uniform and mandatory punishments, while the European response to historic anti-egalitarianism leads to beliefs in individualization and mercy. This is why, Whitman argues, the French regularly and the Germans occasionally announce broad-based amnesties and commutations, without enraged public outcry, and it is why the trend in recent decades has been toward greater mildness in punishments.

Whitman's two theories, about strong and weak states, and punishment systems that level up or level down, fit nicely with contemporary differences in punishment systems. France and Germany grant autonomous officials substantial authority to individualize mild punishments. America, and to a lesser extent, England, attempt through legislation to limit the discretion of officials to deviate from comparatively uniform systems of harsh punishments.

Whitman's analysis is creative and original and genuinely enriches efforts to understand differences between legal systems. What it does not do, alas, is explain American policies of the past quarter century. The difficulty is that three properties of French and German punishment practice that his theory explains—moderation in punishment, individualization, and mercy—until twenty-five years ago were more characteristic of the United States than of Europe. Individualization of punishment was the reigning premise of American sentencing and punishment systems for a hundred years beginning in the 1870s.

Parole is the starkest example. First established in America as a means to let prisoners out when they had become rehabilitated, parole systems were established in most Western countries, including by 1930 in every American state (Rothman 1980). American parole boards had broad discretion, at narrowest to release any prisoner who had served a third of his or her sentence. The extreme cases were California and Washington State, where every sentence was "one year to the statutory maximum" and the parole board decided all release dates. The English parole board was not established until the late 1960s. Parole systems in most European countries had only narrow scope: prisoners typically became eligible for release only after serving half the sentence and had to be released when they had served two-thirds (Bottomley 1990).

So Whitman's argument, elegant though it is, fits 1975–2002, but not 1875–1975. A different explanation is required that can explain not only why American punishment practices and policies are as harsh as they are, but why they have changed so dramatically in a quarter century. The final story provides that explanation.

Cycles and Sensibilities

Each of the preceding seven stories helps explain the origins of American crime control and penal policies. However, four of them—rising crime rates, toughening public opinion, the emergence of the risk society, and postmodernist angst—characterize all Western countries and accordingly cannot explain why U.S. policies are so much harsher than those elsewhere. The democracy and degradation story offers an imaginative theory to explain why American punishment differs so greatly from French and German. Unfortunately, however plausible it would be if only the past quarter century needed explaining, its plausibility disappears in the face of the preceding hundred years when the United States spearheaded the movement toward humane and respectful handling of offenders.

The two remaining stories—about cynical politics and structural changes in governance—are a bit more distinctively American, but not entirely. The particular racial subtext of American politics is ours alone, but nearly every Western country has recently experienced nativist, xenophobic, and anti-immigrant political movements that could have manifested themselves as law-and-order movements. Jonathan Simon's account of the disproportionate influence of single-issue interest groups describes a distinctively American phenomenon, but the larger arguments that he and Garland offer about governance apply to, at least, all the English-speaking countries. But none of Australia, England, or Canada has so far done more than flirt with American-style crime policies and punishment practices, so those stories also do not explain why here and not there.

The distinctive and overarching story of cycles, sensibilities, and moral panics has already been sketched. Sensibilities associated with the developments described in the other stories coincided unhappily with a downswing in recurring patterns of tolerance and intolerance of deviance to produce widespread public susceptibility to calls for adoption of unprecedentedly repressive policies. The emotional force of ubiquitous mass media coverage of such events as the crimes of Willie Horton, the murders of Megan Kanka and Polly Klaas, and the crack overdose death of Len Bias produced moral panics that provided occasion for such calls. And

American governmental institutions and political culture provided many fewer buffers to the force of that emotionalism than do the governmental institutions and political cultures of other countries. This large and complicated story is told in chapter 5. Before that, chapters 3 and 4 provide fuller accounts of cycles, sensibilities, and moral panics.

3

Cycles and Sensibilities

Capital punishment, indiscriminate private possession of handguns, and mass imprisonment of black men in early twenty-first century America will someday be widely deplored and deeply regretted. Nearly all Americans regret and deplore the past subordination of black people in the American South, and yet it was approved and accepted by most southern whites for at least a century after the Civil War. The moral, religious, and social policy arguments against slavery did not change but people's beliefs and values did, and now human slavery and deliberate racial or ethnic subjugation are, almost literally, unthinkable. In most Western countries today, adoption of American policies on capital punishment, handguns, and mass imprisonment is almost as unthinkable as adoption of slavery would be. Prevailing sensibilities elsewhere attach greater importance to ideas about human rights and the value of human lives and life chances than do prevailing American sensibilities.

So why are American crime control policies as they are? Usually policies toward crime and punishment are portrayed as the outcome of disagreements between liberals and conservatives, or between advocates of due process and advocates of public safety, or between people who care about criminals and people who care about victims. The views caricatured in the first member of each of those pairs, it is said, predominated in the 1960s and the views caricatured in the second in the 1990s. And that is all we need to know to understand why 140 per 100,000 Americans were in jail or prison in 1970 and over 700 per 100,000 in 2003. That is true in one important albeit grotesquely oversimplified sense, but it is deeply shortsighted. Policies do, of course, reflect beliefs and values, but those come from somewhere, and somewhen. If Americans were more self-aware of why we believe what we believe, our policies about crime would be very different and we would not be fated to suffer our descendants' disapproval.

For some subjects, beliefs and values oscillate in predictable cycles. Americans have lately been caught up in a period in which excessive hostility and emotional overreaction toward criminals and drug users could have been predicted (and was) and current penal policies are the result.

Truths and Trivia

What we see, think, and believe depends as much on when we stand as where. This is true of trivial things—people who were once enamored of bouffant hairdos, polyester pantsuits, or platform shoes have a hard time imagining that was ever true and a harder time picturing themselves dressed that way now. Fashions change, tastes evolve, and few of us are immune to influence in such matters. What once we liked, we now dislike, and vice versa.

We are almost as susceptible to influence, however, about things that are important. Periods of romanticism and classicism in the arts have alternated throughout history, as have periods of tolerance and intolerance of homosexuality and religious pluralism, and peoples' opinions and beliefs have oscillated with them. And the same thing is true in recent centuries in relation to punishment, with moralistic ideas about deserved punishments and moral responsibility alternating with instrumental ideas about problem-solving and human fallibility.

Beliefs and attitudes about punishment, religious pluralism, and sexual tolerance are different in kind from preferences for polyester pantsuits. Wearing unfashionable clothes or hairstyles can be done naively or defiantly. It can be gauche or anachronistic, elicit disapproval or ridicule, and result in embarrassment or humiliation, but the sanctions for being different are entirely social.

Being seriously on the wrong side of contemporary views about religious beliefs can be lethal. Apostates have been being killed for as long as organized religion has existed (Erikson 1966; Johnson 1976). From shortly after the death of Jesus, through the Protestant Reformation and at least through the hangings of Quakers by Massachusetts Bay Calvinists, Christians have been killing Christians because of their heretical views. In numerous periods from the first century A.D. to the eighteenth, interspersed among more tolerant eras, Christian heretics were martyred because of their heterodox beliefs. As the confidence and strength of the early Christian church waxed and waned, beliefs that were punished by death in one century were tolerated and sometimes celebrated in the next. The radical simplicity and antimaterialism of St. Francis of Assisi in the thirteenth century might well have been intolerable heresy in the twelfth or the fourteenth. According to historian John Boswell, the "Franciscans came perilously close to being declared heretical before their final acceptance by the church" (Boswell 1980, p. 275).

Histories of homosexuality tell similar stories of periods of tolerance that alternated with periods when the consequences ranged from ostracism to death (Boswell 1980; Greenberg 1988). Boswell describes classical antiquity and the Early Middle Ages as periods when homosexual relations were widely accepted and celebrated, albeit separated by the sixth through ninth centuries when homosexuality was strongly disapproved.

Then the pendulum swung: "During the 200 years from 1150 to 1350, homosexual behavior appears to have changed, in the eyes of the public, from the personal preference of a prosperous minority, satirized in popular verse, to a dangerous, antisocial, and severely sinful aberration" (Boswell 1980, p. 295). Homosexuality passed from being an uncontroversial matter of preference or idiosyncrasy in most of Europe to being a criminal act that most contemporary legal compilations made punishable by death. Sensibilities changed and, more importantly, laws changed with them. The change was lethal, as Boswell demonstrates:

> Kings themselves were no longer safe. In the twelfth century the king of France could elevate to the episcopate a man thought to have been his bed partner, and the king of England [Richard II] could fall head over heels in love with another monarch [Philip II of France] without losing support from either the people or the church. But by the fourteenth century all this had changed, and its opening decades witnessed first the downfall of the Templars [who had been accused of sodomy, among other things] at the hands of Philip IV and then the execution (at the hands of his daughter Isabella) of the last openly homosexual monarch of the Middle Ages, Edward II of England. (Boswell 1980, p. 298)

The animosity toward homosexuals is made "pellucidly clear," wrote Boswell, by the nature of the executions of Edward and his lover Hugh le Despenser: "Hugh's genitals were cut off and burned publicly before he was decapitated, and Edward was murdered by the insertion into his anus of a red-hot poker" (Boswell 1980, p. 300).

Comparative tolerance is typical now in Western countries, though far from complete. Memories of Oscar Wilde's final, sad years and of intolerance in some parts of the contemporary world remind us that things are often otherwise.

Being on the wrong side of contemporary views about punishment can also be fatal, or life-diminishing, but in a different way and to different people. Being homosexual or subscribing to particular religious beliefs is part of who people are or want to be. In tolerant times, those are Good Things, and in intolerant times, perilously they are not.

The central question concerning crime and punishment is not whether crime is a good thing—not whether people should be entitled to be criminals in the same way they are free in tolerant times to be homosexual—but how the state should punish criminals. The prevailing ethos can have drastic consequences for people convicted of crimes, and include differences between life and death or between prison sentences measured in years or in decades. In earlier centuries, Michel Foucault (1977) and many others relate, breathtakingly cruel punishments were sometimes practiced. Foucault famously began *Discipline and Punish* with a description of the 1757 execution of Damien, condemned to have the flesh torn from his breasts, thighs, arms, and calves by red hot pincers, his hand burnt with sulfur, and the wounds dressed with a blend of molten lead, boiling oil, burning resin, wax, and sulfur. He was then to have his body drawn and quartered by four horses.

That time has passed, but prevailing attitudes toward punishment continue to change with the times. Thousands of executions occurred in the United States in the early twentieth century, but steadily declined in the 1940s, 1950s, and 1960s. In more recent times, an American offender's chances of execution are vastly higher early in the twenty-first century than they were in the 1960s. During the 1970s and 1980s, the average lengths of prison sentences for serious crimes more than tripled, and then increased some more in the 1990s.

Even a few years can make an enormous difference in punishments imposed and suffered for particular crimes. Young men convicted of draft evasion late in the Vietnam War often received the maximum lawful prison sentence of five years. Within a few years, a short prison term or probation became typical and shortly after that an amnesty was enacted. The same behaviors, occurring at about the same time, incurred vastly different consequences depending on when the sentence was imposed or the case dealt with.

There are many other examples of punishments varying greatly depending solely on when they were imposed. Before the U.S. Supreme Court declared capital punishment for rape unconstitutional under the Eighth Amendment in *Coker v. Georgia*, 433 U.S. 584 (1977), many actual or alleged rapists, especially black men accused of raping white women, were executed.

As tolerance of drug use and Drug War fervor fluctuate, authorized and imposed sentences for drug crimes vary radically. The U.S. Congress enacted mandatory minimum sentences for drug crimes in the 1950s and 1960s, then in 1970 at the urging of, among others, Republican Congressman George H. Bush, repealed nearly all of them, because they were seen to be too rigid and too harsh. In the 1980s and early 1990s, at the urging of, among others, Republican Vice President and later President George H. Bush, the U.S. Congress enacted new mandatory minimum sentences of unprecedented severity for drug crimes. People involved in 500-gram heroine transactions could receive very different punishments depending on whether the transaction occurred in the 1970s, the 1980s, or the 1990s. Closer to many more people's homes, because of the commonality of use or experimentation with marijuana, penalties for small-scale trafficking in marijuana have fluctuated nearly as widely as for cocaine trafficking. Marijuana offenses punishable by multi-year prison sentences in the 1960s in many places were largely ignored in the 1970s. In 2001 handling of marijuana cases is wildly inconsistent, ranging from de facto decriminalization and widespread open use in some parts of the country to inconsistent but sometimes harsh handling elsewhere.

Punishment practices and policies change for reasons, but the quality of the reasons may be good or bad. It is important to be sure that the reasons why punishment policies are to be made harsher are sound, and that they result from something other than raw emotion or short-term upset. Recent toughening of penalties and policies concerning domestic violence or child abuse, for example, can probably pass that test. Both behaviors fundamentally damage victims' lives and neither appears before to have received sustained attention from the criminal justice system. So might penalty increases be justified for particular crimes, corporate and white-collar crimes, for example, for which reliable evidence gives reason to believe that ethically defensible increases would measurably prevent future victimization. When, however, the reason is short-term overreaction or political expediency or animus to minority groups, the test is failed.

Stark shifts in social practices, including punishment, occur because many or most people in a time and place share perceptions and beliefs that justify them, unmindful or indifferent that their perceptions and beliefs may be time-bound, and that they themselves in a few years or decades may see them to have been wrong. In the abstract, we understand that things change. That's life. In the particular, individuals' lives are diminished, shortened, and taken not only because of who they are or what they believed or did but also because of when they are, or believe, or do.

Aristophanes' "The Frogs" tells of two boys playing near a stream who find a frog and, for fun, kill it. They killed the frog in jest, Aristophanes reports, but the frog died in earnest. People whose lives are diminished, ruined, or taken because of the penal ethos of the era in which they live are like Aristophanes' frog. Impersonal forces of history or the penal policies of a moment may explain what happened to them, but their suffering and loss are real.

It would be easy but wrong to think that cruel punishments are primarily of antiquarian interest, that we are more civilized now, that we do not allow our collective judgment to be overwhelmed by passing emotion, or that we do not do things to offenders that we or our descendants will later regret. There is no reason to suppose that people now in positions of power are any less susceptible to the ethos of our times than our ancestors were to theirs. The United States in the final decade of the twentieth century was in the throes of a cyclical period of extreme intolerance of drug users and people who commit crimes. Many Americans early in the twenty-first century have a hard time recognizing the cruelty of current drug and crime policies, because they have become used to them, but most people in earlier periods of intolerance were equally unaware of injustices that later generations condemned.

Sensibilities

Sensibilities are time- and place-bound ways of thinking that include ideas and express values that are widely shared and little questioned. Sometimes sensibilities change slowly and sometimes they change rapidly, but when a particular sensibility is widespread it influences what people think, say, and believe.

Sensibility is a central idea in this book, so I devote several pages to explaining what I mean by it. Two influential conceptions of sensibility have recently received attention in writings on crime and punishment. For English penologist Nigel Walker, sensibilities are characteristics of individuals that make them more or less susceptible to different kinds of pain (and pleasure). For sociologists Norbert Elias and David Garland, sensibilities are characteristics of societies and are the products of long-term economic, social, and psychological developments that shape the values and beliefs of members of a society.

By sensibility, I mean the ethos or zeitgeist of a moment that influences but does not determine what most people think and believe about a particular subject. It differs from Walker's conception because it refers to something social and collective rather than idiosyncratic and individual, and it differs from Elias's and Garland's because it is more contingent, and more susceptible to conscious reflection and reconsideration.

Nigel Walker (1991) uses the term to describe the unique characteristics of individuals that cause them to experience punishments differently. He points out that a serious effort to impose comparable punishments on like-situated offenders would take account of offenders' diverse sensibilities and adjust punishments accordingly. Different offenders, Walker argues, for example, will experience imprisonment in different ways. For an active Los Angeles gang member, a three-year sentence may be a rite of passage. For a single man in his twenties, not otherwise involved in crime, it may be unpleasant and disruptive. For a young single-parent mother, it may be soul-destroying. For an employed middle-aged head of household, it may be the destruction of a family and ruination of a life. For a sickly 75-year-old, it may be a death sentence. For an effeminate teenage boy, or a claustrophobe, it may be sheer terror. Three years in prison for one person often will not result in the same kind or amount of suffering as it does for another. To pretend otherwise is to ignore basic differences between human beings, to fail to take differences between individuals seriously. Walker makes these points not prescriptively, but argumentatively, to demonstrate that punishment theories or policies that call for equal punishments for broad categories of crimes or criminals are psychologically and ethically misconceived. In Walker's sense, sensibilities differ between individuals and, for individuals, over time. For Elias and Garland, sensibilities differ between societies and, within societies, over time.

Modern attention to the nature, course, and power of sensibilities at societal levels derives from the work of the late German sociologist Norbert Elias (1978 [orig. 1939], 1982 [orig. 1939]). For Elias and for David Garland, a Scottish sociologist now at New York University, who is partly responsible for revived interest in Elias's work, sensibilities are characteristics of societies. They are the prevailing ethoses of time-bound societies and shape the beliefs and values of individuals. Elias used the idea of sensibilities to explain changes in societies' norms and practices, and Garland uses it to explain contemporary changes in penal policy. Societies differ in their cultural, historical, material, religious, and social circumstances, and these differences shape the prevailing sensibilities.

Elias, in *The Civilizing Process* (1939), connects changes in sensibility and individual psychology with wider changes in social, economic, and geopolitical organization. These changes, as Garland summarizes:

> eventually have an effect on the psychic organization of the individuals involved and, in particular, on the structure of their drives and emotions. . . . To the extent that

this process of socialization is successful, the emotions and behavior of the individual become more evenly ordered, less spontaneous, and less given to wild oscillation between extremes. Individuals are thus trained and psychologically equipped to sustain social conventions and to display a particular pattern of sensibility. (1991, pp. 144–45)

For Elias, some changes in sensibilities have been more or less linear and together make up what he calls the "civilizing process." Operating through changing sensibilities, the civilizing process has been underway since the late Middle Ages. It made the sight of brutality, suffering, pain, and violence unpleasant and unappealing. These things became increasingly unacceptable or, at least, were moved out of sight. In our time, they have been stylized into the seemingly-real-but-understood-to-be-unreal cartoons of modern mass entertainment and thereby detached from day-to-day life (Bettelheim 1977).

Elias described "typical civilization curves." One example is the history of meat preparation and eating: "The curve running from the carving of a large part of the animal or even the whole animal at table, through the advance in the threshold of repugnance at the sight of dead animals, to the removal of carving to the specialized enclaves behind the scenes, is a typical civilization curve" (Elias 1978, p. 121). Sixty years after Elias wrote, most people buy meat in tidy plastic-wrapped packages even further removed from the visceral realities of killing and dismembering. Increasing numbers of people in Western countries, more in Europe than in North America, have become vegetarians, and their numbers will grow, further extending Elias's meat-eating civilization curve.

Capital and corporal punishments have followed a similar pattern. Albert Camus, in *Reflections on the Guillotine* (1960), chronicled the gradual evolution of capital punishment in France from drawing-and-quartering in a public square preceded by painful embellishments like disembowelment, successively to strangling, hanging, guillotining in public, and guillotining behind prison doors. Camus explained the sequence in terms of the increasing revulsion people felt about killing human beings. Only by moving the corporal reality and mess behind doors and out of sight could the killing continue. Later, after Camus wrote, French sensibilities no longer tolerated even secretive executions and capital punishment stopped.

The implicit march toward increased decencies in Elias's civilization process may or may not be overly optimistic. That sensibilities in Elias's sense exist, change over time, and influence individuals is, however, incontrovertible. Our beliefs, preferences, tastes, and values are shaped by the culture and society in which we live. These differ and change. Those differences are much of what makes us who we are. Just as it is easy to forget that we speak prose, it is easy to overlook basic matters about which most people in a time and place unthinkingly agree.

The relevance of Elias's work for thinking about punishment and penal policy is demonstrated in David Garland's 1990 book *Punishment and Modern Society*. Garland showed that efforts to understand penal policy that incorporate only normative analyses and arguments about practical effects are incomplete. They must also take account of the social functions punishment serves.

In his later book, *The Culture of Control: Crime and Social Order in Contemporary Society* (2001a), Garland attributes recent trends in punishment policies and practices to changing sensibilities associated with the emergence of economic and social changes that he and others encapsulate in the term "late modernity." Garland tries to show how secular changes have shaped sensibilities. Changes in crime rates and patterns are not irrelevant to penal policy changes, but larger social forces do the heavy lifting.

Garland's relevance here is that he offers a sophisticated account of the role of sensibilities in the making and implementation of penal policy. Sensibilities as Elias described them are shaped by the kinds of social changes Garland describes, and in turn shape how we think and what we believe.

Note the verb: shape. Close synonyms might include influence, conduce, and predispose, but not determine, cause, or foreordain. Sensibilities exist, and they change, but only rarely do they determine. They are more malleable than is implied by Elias's and Garland's functionalist notions of deeply bedded and evolving social norms that shape human psychologies.

Elias and Garland do not allow for regular alterations in sensibilities, but some at least do alternate, particularly in relation to behaviors widely regarded in a place and time as deviant. Nor do they treat sensibilities as the proper object of self-conscious assessment. If men and women are thinking animals, we can search for and appraise the sensibilities that shape our thought, and reject, or work to constrain, those we disapprove or recognize to be destructive.

Evolutions in sensibilities can be seen in the United States in relation to capital punishment, not exactly in parallel to Camus' story about France, but with similarities (and with the crucial difference that the United States resumed use of capital punishment with enthusiasm). As in France, executions were moved from public squares to prisons, and methods of dispatch shifted from the cruel and messy to the hygienic and painless—from hanging, shooting, and electrocution to death by lethal injection. Many punishments—maiming, branding, whipping, torturing, beheading, and burning at the stake—are, for most people, as unthinkable in the United States as they are in other Western countries.

American constitutional law doctrine about the death penalty has, until recently, followed a course that resembles a weak and crabbed version of Elias's civilizing process hypothesis and demonstrates changing penal sensibilities. The U.S. Supreme Court resorts to consideration of "evolving standards of decency" to decide whether particular punishments are unconstitutional under the U.S. Constitution's Eighth Amendment prohibition of "cruel and unusual punishment." Several Supreme Court Justices, most prominently Thurgood Marshall and William Brennan, argued that evolving standards of decency by the early 1970s were no longer compatible with the death penalty and urged that it be declared unconstitutional. Supreme Court Justices Harry Blackmun and Lewis Powell expressed the same view after their retirements.

For a time in the 1960s and early 1970s, it appeared possible that a majority of the Supreme Court might agree. That did not happen, but the Court did decide in *Coker* that evolving standards forbade capital punishment for rape and by implication for all lesser crimes of sex, violence, and property. In the June 2002 case of Daryl Atkins, a Virginia man with an IQ of fifty-nine, the Supreme Court decided that a "national consensus" now exists that mentally retarded offenders are categorically less culpable than the average offender and for that reason cannot constitutionally be executed. The Court usually looks for mundane empirical evidence on which to base a conclusion about evolving standards, usually by counting up the number of U.S. states that do or do not permit a practice. What saved Atkins, unlike the many retarded persons who have been executed since the court decided *Penry v. Lynaugh*, 492 U.S. 302 (1989), upholding the practice of executing mentally retarded offenders, is that states have been changing their laws. When *Penry* was decided, two states forbade such executions and fourteen states' laws did not authorize capital punishment at all. By the time *Atkins v. Virginia*, 122 S. Ct. 2242 (2002), was decided, eighteen states forbade such executions and twelve states plus the District of Columbia did not authorize any capital punishment. Thus, thirty states, a majority, do not execute retarded offenders. Standards of decency, in the Court's view, have changed enough that offenders such as Atkins should be allowed to live. A counting exercise such as that is an odd way to decide what is ultimately a moral or human rights issue, but the sequence of cases does illustrate an evolutionary process.

Developments regarding capital punishment illustrate a basic difference between the United States and other Western countries. Something like Elias's civilizing process appears to have operated in every country, and capital punishment is now almost everywhere forbidden. For the past thirty years, however, the United States has moved in a different direction. Why? Because American constitutional and governmental arrangements provide less insulation from the effects of cycles of intolerance. Xenophobia, animus towards immigrants and ethnic minorities, and harsher attitudes toward crime and disorder have characterized many countries in recent years. In some, including the United States, opinion surveys show majority support for the death penalty and harsher crime policies. In other countries, however, crime policy is not a central feature of partisan politics and electioneering and judges and prosecutors are either civil servant or appointed in nonpartisan ways. Officials setting policy can generally devote most of their attention to substantive matters and comparatively little to the results of public opinion surveys.

By contrast, crime has been a partisan political issue in the United States for nearly forty years, and most prosecutors and judges are elected or appointed in openly political processes. Crime control features, often polemically, in executive and legislative elections, and policies are often heavily influenced by measures of public opinion, however well or poorly informed that opinion may be. American governmental arrangements, when public opinion turns harsh and mean-spirited, rather than ameliorate the effects of public emotion, often exacerbate them.

The important point here, though, is that something like sensibilities exists, whatever we call them, and they influence what we say and do and think. But there are three important qualifications.

First, almost never is their influence monolithic. No matter what ways the sensibility winds are blowing, there are almost always people who adopt contrarian stances: who opposed slavery in eighteenth-century Virginia, promoted female enfranchisement in the nineteenth century, opposed Japanese internment during World War II, and favored decriminalization of drugs in the 1980s.

Second, some normative disagreements are so deeply rooted that they are not especially susceptible to changes, at least short-term changes, in sensibilities. Examples in our time concern abortion, capital punishment, and gun control. The proportions of the population subscribing to one or the other side of these controversies ebb and flow, but large numbers of people hold to their views no matter which is ascendant.

Third, most importantly, some ideas are timeless. Most basic Western ideas about law, ethics, and morality are examined in Aristotle's *Nicomachean Ethics* and Plato's *Republic* and *Laws*. Concepts such as virtue, justice, fairness, freedom, and equality go in and out of fashion, and conceptions change, but they are seldom completely forgotten. Sometimes they are forgotten or overlooked by many people and are omitted from the orthodoxy of the day. Sometimes they are or imply inconvenient truths that are dangerous to express, and many people are afraid to express them. Sometimes cognitive dissonance, the human tendency to rationalize and accept what we cannot change, operates and many people come to believe what is convenient or safe.

It became fashionable in the 1980s and 1990s in the literatures of postmodernism and multiculturalism to denigrate such notions as "timeless ideas." There is something, of course, to be said for the multicultural argument. Non-Western societies have different histories and cultural traditions than those shared by Western countries and ideas like "freedom" and "individual rights" may have different genealogies and cultural meanings. Within Western countries, though, the notion of timeless ideas is coherent and meaningful. Ideas such as liberty, tolerance, and justice are widely shared. They do not exist in nature as does a rock or a tree, but they are durable social constructions in Western culture and are at the hearts of documents such as the French Declaration of the Rights of Man, the U.S. Bill of Rights, the United Nations Declaration of Human Rights, and the European Convention of Human Rights. People who want to argue that all cultural meanings are contingent and hence time- and place-bound may be right in a trivial, reductionist sense, but as a practical matter they are wrong. So I use the term "timeless idea" understanding that it is inaccurate in a geological sense, but believing it a useful shorthand in our time, place, and culture for core cultural ideas that are widely shared and have been for centuries.

Some people always hold onto the timeless ethical ideas. Erasmus understood that Protestant persecution of apostates, sometimes unto death, was wrong after the Reformation, and no less wrong than were Roman Catholic persecutions of Jews and heretics during the Inquisition, even if the prevailing sensibilities of the time made that a dangerous view to express (Johnson 1976). George Washington and Thomas Jefferson knew that slavery was wrong, as did many white American southerners before and after the Civil War, even if Washington freed his slaves only at his death and Jefferson never did (Ellis 2002). There were people who opposed Jim Crow laws, the Red Scares of the 1920s, and McCarthyism, and sometimes spoke out about it, even at danger to their own lives and interests.

There are also mundane tastes and preferences that vary with time and place and are the opposite of timeless. Some people did not like Rudy Vallee, the Beatles, or *The Fellowship of the Ring*. It is difficult to devise timeless analyses of the merits or demerits of Nehru jackets, stiletto heels, gangsta rap, 100 percent cotton, or the color mauve. Their appeal for some people depends on personal idiosyncrasy, and for others on what most or a sizable number of people in the larger society or a smaller subgroup think at a particular time. Because we are social animals, we are influenced by social influences and prevailing opinions.

The trick, as a people, is to achieve clarity on which subjects, tastes, and preferences are timeless and which are ephemeral. The former matter, and we need always to keep them in sight, even though that is not easy. As to the latter, we can comfortably let a thousand flowers bloom, and revel in their gaudy impermanence and exotic scents, knowing that others equally alluring will soon blossom in their places.

Cycles

Historians have shown how tastes and perceptions change over time, and how the beliefs and values of people change with them. Jaroslav Pelikan, in *Jesus through the Centuries* (1985), showed how each era reinvents or reinterprets the historical Jesus: in some eras he is the Messiah, sometimes a social and political reformer, sometimes the founder of the church, sometimes a charismatic leader, sometimes a spiritual ascetic. The historic Jesus was who he was, but people in different times saw what they wanted or needed to see. Over shorter periods, historians have documented similar metamorphoses in the characterization of such prominent figures in American history as Washington, Jefferson, and Lincoln.

Pelikan, unlike Elias, does not describe a perceptible if sometimes interrupted march of progress, but a series of conceptions of Jesus that reflected the needs, beliefs, and sensibilities of successive times. Nor does Pelikan describe cyclical patterns of sensibility. Sensibilities do, however, fluctuate and cycles of taste and belief recur. In one representative realm, literature and the arts, Grant Gilmore described typical fluctuations in aesthetic preference, taste, and belief:

> We have become used to the idea that, in literature and the arts, there are alternating rhythms of classicism and romanticism. During classical periods, which are, typically, of short duration, everything is neat, tidy and logical; theorists and critics reign supreme; formal rules of structure and composition are stated to the general acclaim. During classical periods, which are, among other things, extremely dull, it seems that nothing interesting is ever going to happen again. But the classical aesthetic, once it has been formulated, regularly breaks down in a protracted romantic agony. The romantics spurn the exquisitely stated rules of the preceding period; they experiment, they churn around in an ecstasy of self-expression. At the height of a romantic period, everything is confused, sprawling, formless and chaotic—as well as, frequently,

extremely interesting. Then, the romantic energy having spent itself, there is a new classical reformulation—and so the rhythms continue. (Gilmore 1974, p. 102)

Historian David Musto has described similar cycles in American attitudes toward alcohol and drug use (1973, 1987*a*, 1987*b*). At least three times since the beginning of the nineteenth century, the United States moved from periods of widespread, tolerated recreational use of alcohol and drugs to puritanical periods of uncompromising prohibition. The first period of extreme intolerance began in the 1820s and culminated in prohibition of alcohol in eight states by the 1850s (Gusfield 1963). The temperance movement of the late nineteenth century led to national Prohibition; more generalized intolerance of drug use and users produced the first major federal narcotics laws, the Harrison Act of 1914 and the Marijuana Tax Act of 1937. The first signs of the contemporary period of extreme intolerance appeared around 1970, when the Nixon administration declared its war on drugs. Those attitudes toward drug use took firm hold in the early 1980s and the United States remains in their grip.

According to Musto, peoples' normative beliefs about drug use vary with successive phases of cycles of tolerance and intolerance of drug use. Live-and-let-live attitudes prevail in periods of relative tolerance, like the 1870s–1880s and the 1950s–1960s. In the late nineteenth and early twentieth centuries, for example, cocaine and opium (and derivatives) were widely used in patent medicines, most addicts were conventional, law-abiding people, predominantly women, and cocaine was widely seen as a harmless recreational drug. Conan Doyle's Sherlock Holmes was a regular user of cocaine but that made neither the author nor the character notorious.

In the 1960s, marijuana was widely and openly used; it and many hallucinogens were seen by many as recreational drugs less harmful than alcohol. Numerous local jurisdictions, including prominently Ann Arbor, Michigan, and Berkeley, California, effectively decriminalized use, possession, and small-scale trafficking of marijuana. Alfred Blumstein (1993) showed how the realization that white middle-class kids were getting criminal records and sometimes going to prisons for minor drug offenses led to a drastic reduction in drug arrests of young whites in the early 1970s. President Carter in 1977 called for federal decriminalization of private marijuana possession. A few years earlier Peter Bourne (not then, but later Carter's primary drug policy advisor; now he would be called the "drug czar") wrote that cocaine "is probably the most benign of illicit drugs currently in widespread use. At least as strong a case could be made for legalizing it as for legalizing marijuana" (Musto 1987*a*, p. 265).

Conversely, during periods of extreme intolerance, recreational drug issues tend to be seen in black and white, and adoption of policies of unrelenting vigor is not uncommon. Liberal Republican Governor Nelson Rockefeller of New York, for example, in 1972 proposed and won adoption of the Rockefeller Drug Laws that established long mandatory minimum sentences for drug offenses, forbade plea-negotiating prosecutors from waiving prison sentences, and paid for additional courts and judges to implement the new laws. Every American state during the 1970s and 1980s adopted mandatory minimum sentence laws for drug crimes. The U.S. Congress in 1986 enacted the harshest drug sentencing laws in U.S. history, including the 100-to-1 law that punishes crack cocaine trafficking, then as now primarily committed by blacks, as harshly as powder cocaine offenses, then as now primarily committed by whites, 100 times larger. In 1988, legislation was enacted providing for appointment of a federal drug czar to lead the war on drugs. By 1989 the per capita drug arrest rate had risen by a factor of six in ten years, and by 2000, the number of people held in federal and state prisons and jails for drug offenses had climbed to 324,489, up 1,370 percent from 1980 (when there were 23,900). In 1994 Congress authorized the death penalty for various drug-related crimes. At various times during the 1980s and 1990s, Americans responding to opinion polls named drug abuse as or among America's most pressing problems.

Musto has several times written of the seeming anomaly that prohibitionistic sentiments become strongest and drug policies harshest after drug use has begun to decline (e.g., 1987*a, b*). At various periods, drug use comes into vogue, use increases, and dangers of abusive use become more evident. Eventually, as Daniel Kagan has summarized Musto's argument:

> The trend reverses; drug use starts to decline faster and faster. Public opinion turns against drugs and their acceptability begins to evaporate. Gradually, drug use becomes associated, truthfully or not, with the lower ranks of society, and often with racial and ethnic groups that are feared or despised by the middle class. Drugs become seen as deviant and dangerous and become a potent symbol of evil. Trailing behind this decline come large-scale legislative and law enforcement efforts . . . aimed at curtailing drug sales and use through energetic prohibition and enforcement and ever-harsher punishments against sellers and users. During this period, public opprobrium intensifies into outright fear, hatred of drug dealers and users, and a burning anger and intolerance toward anyone and anything associated with drug use. (Kagan 1989, p. 7)

During periods of relative tolerance, people feel comfortable invoking traditional American notions of individualism and personal autonomy to justify making their own choices about drug use. Drug use is widely seen as only mildly deviant or not deviant at all. People feel comfortable arguing on the merits for the benefits and pleasures of drug use, for individuals' rights to make their own choices, and against state intrusion into those choices.

In periods of extreme intolerance, drug use is widely seen as deviant. Few people feel comfortable risking moral disapproval or stigmatization by arguing in favor of drug use or tolerance of drug users. Musto notes that, "in the decline phase of drug use . . . we tend to have an overkill, that is to say people become so righteous and so zealous that we can have excesses in the name of fighting drugs. There is very little opposition to draconian policies because no one wants to stand up for using drugs" (1987*b*, p. 43).

The important thing about the Gilmore and Musto accounts, for my purposes, is that they tie sensibilities and beliefs to recurring segments of cyclical patterns. Gilmore observes that, during classical periods, rules of composition and structure are stated "to the general acclaim." Formalism, in other words, is not foisted upon a society or an era, but embodies aesthetic qualities that people value, or believe they value, which is almost the same thing. Romantic aesthetic values likewise become predominant in a period not because they are compelled but because they are celebrated. Musto writes that people "become so righteous and so zealous" during the decline phase of drug use that they adopt views and support policies that most people in other times would see as draconic. People behave like this not because they are coerced or cajoled into it but because that is how they feel.

It is a truism that our upbringings, past experiences, material circumstances, and immediate environments shape the way we see and understand the world. People tend not to be conservative until they have things to conserve, and so the frequent pattern that youthful radicals become middle-aged moderates and elderly conservatives. Or, the somewhat different Chinese developmental stereotype that people are Confucianist while young, Realist in maturity, and Taoist when old. And history is full of stories of whole societies overwhelmed by fear, insecurity, or anger to do or tolerate horrible things that later appear unthinkable.

It is one thing, however, to acknowledge that our characteristics, interests, and experiences influence our wants and beliefs, and quite another to urge, with some of the sillier postmodernists, that what we see depends solely on where we stand. Since one standpoint is as good as any other, it is said, we can not see anything (or we can see many things, but no perception is any more "privileged" or any less "contingent" than any other). That may be a plausible position to adopt in relation to aesthetic assessments of bellbottoms, bouffant hairdos, or gangsta rap but not in relation to fundamental normative issues over which human beings have puzzled for millennia.

Even during periods of intolerance, some people recognize cruelty and excess. Thoughtful people have always recognized the polar possibilities in the value-laden domains of religion, sexuality, and criminal punishment, the alternatives that lie between them, the practical and principled arguments that can be made for one position or another, and the inexorability of the processes by which one set of beliefs displaces another. Unfortunately, all that tends to get forgotten by most people in the heat of a historical moment.

Human beings have been round the bend and back enough times that we should be able, by learning from history, to escape being condemned to repeat at least its worst excesses. Witches and heretics have burned sufficiently often, to later regret, that there is no need to burn them again in order to be able again to regret it. That lesson should have been learnt for good by now and, at least in most Western countries, probably has been. Similar lessons can and will be learned about tolerance of human sexual diversity, experimentation with and use of intoxicants, and punishment of wrongdoers.

4

Moral Panics and "Windows of Opportunity"

Historians teach that crime rates and patterns change slowly, in accord with regular long-term trends, that sensibilities generally change with them, and that some sensibilities fluctuate in accord with cycles of tolerance and intolerance. Sociologists have shown that public attitudes and opinions about crime sometimes change rapidly and decisively. The interaction between long-term cycles and rapid changes in attitudes goes a long way toward explaining American crime control and punishment policies of the past thirty years.

During the past half century, historical sociologists and sociologists of deviance have conceptualized a phenomenon called a "moral panic" that helps us understand times when public passions take over and produce decisions, policies, and behaviors that might not otherwise have happened. Moral panic theory offers insights into the development of contemporary crime and drug policies, and the politics that surround them.

The term was coined and the concept popularized by British sociologist Stanley Cohen (1972). He was trying to explain how an unruly weekend in an English seaside resort in 1964 developed into a national crime crisis that, in turn, led to overwrought newspaper headlines, widespread anxieties, police abuse of authority, poorly considered legislation, and exemplary punishments. Stuart Hall, another British sociologist, used the concept to explain what he saw as overreaction to an outbreak of London street muggings in the 1970s. Here is Hall's description of a moral panic:

[W]hen the official reaction to a person, group of persons, or series of events is out of all proportion to the actual threat offered, when "experts" perceive the threat in all but identical terms, and appear to talk "with one voice" of rates, diagnoses, prognoses, and solutions, when the media representations universally stress "sudden and dramatic" increases (in numbers involved or events) and "novelty," above and beyond that which a sober, realistic appraisal could sustain. (Hall et al. 1978, p. 16)

For Cohen and Hall, a moral panic was something negative, irrational, and regrettable; shocking or frightening incidents occurred, raw emotions took over, fears magnified, panic set in, inhibitions weakened, and public officials overreacted. Whether, however, the result of a moral panic is negative and to be regretted depends on its nature and result, and who makes the assessment. The term is usually used by activists and the media and the use is generally negative.

Some venerable earlier sociological works can also be reread as accounts of moral panics expressed in other language. Out of chronological sequence, I discuss three seminal writings: Cohen's "Clacton riots," Kai Erikson's classic 1966 explanation of the Salem witch trials, and Edwin Sutherland's landmark 1950 account of the origins of twentieth-century sexual psychopath laws.

Those works illustrate three features of moral panics that are germane to my cycles-and-sensibilities theme, and how it can help us understand changes in punishment and drug policies. Cohen shows how notorious events can, for a short time, cause people and governments to lose their heads and overreact. Erikson shows that moral panics often occur at times of broader uncertainty and insecurity; the Salem witch trials had much more to do with Salem than with witches. Sutherland demonstrates that moral panics about some subjects, in his case sexual predators, tend to recur at more or less regular intervals.

Mods and Rockers

Easter weekend 1964 in Clacton, a small, slightly scruffy, seaside resort on England's east coast was cold and wet, the coldest in eighty years. People were disgruntled, shopkeepers because business was slow on the usually busy weekend, young people because they were uncomfortable and there was little to do. A few small groups scuffled and threw rocks at each other and two groups of working-class youth, called Mods and Rockers, began separating out. There were fights, loud music, and some vandalism, and motorcycles roared up and down. Eventually there were ninety-seven arrests, twenty-four criminal charges (two or three for violent crimes), and £513 in property damage (then around $1,500; in modern equivalent $10,000–15,000). Smaller scale "riots," involving less violence, less damage, and fewer arrests, broke out in other seaside resorts on three-day weekends later in 1964 and early in 1965.

The following Monday, all the English national newspapers ran histrionic stories, usually on page one: "Day of Terror by Scooter Groups" (*Daily Telegraph*), "Youngsters Beat Up Town—97 Leather Jacket Arrests" (*Daily Express*), "Wild Ones Invade Seaside—97 Arrests" (*Daily Mirror*). Within weeks the Malicious Damage Act 1964, a toughened law on vandalism, was introduced, enacted, and implemented.

Cohen reconstructed in detail what happened in the riots and, afterwards, in police, pretrial, and court proceedings. Among the things documented were public hysteria, media hyperbole, police harassment and intimidation of young people, abuse by judges of pretrial detention, and vindictive punishments. Anyone interested to know whether I have exaggerated Cohen's account and conclusions will have to read his book but most will conclude that I have not.

Whatever the exact nature of the Clacton episode, reactions clearly were exaggerated. This is shown by the following statement made in parliamentary debate by Henry Brooke, the Home Secretary (the English equivalent of the U.S. Attorney General):

> Some of the reports of what happened at Clacton over the weekend were greatly exaggerated. . . . At Clacton more than 1,000 young people came by one means or another, apparently with little money on them, intending to sleep wherever they could find some form of shelter. The weather was bad over the Easter weekend and there was little or nothing to do. They became bored, tempers flared and a certain amount of fighting broke out. There was nothing like a riot or gang warfare. Clacton was not sacked. (S. Cohen 1972, p. 136)

Brooke proceeded, reports Cohen, to note that acts of assault, theft, or malicious damage were isolated and committed by small groups of individuals. The incidents nonetheless, as they developed in the media and in popular and political imagery, reified the Mods and Rockers into threatening youth gangs and created a sense of crisis in English seaside resorts for years to follow.

Things like the Clacton riots have happened throughout history. Something or someone emerges who dramatically threatens established values and interests, the media and state agencies overreact and exaggerate the nature and scale of the threat, public opinion becomes polarized and demands decisive government responses, public officials adopt extreme policies, and no one has very much patience for suggestions that the problem is less serious or more complicated than it looks.

Quakers and Salem Witches

Kai Erikson's *Wayward Puritans* (1966) describes three challenges that affected Massachusetts Bay Colony in the seventeenth century. Two look like moral panics. The first, the persecutions in 1656–65 of Quakers, whose radically decentralized religious beliefs were seen as an attack on Puritan

Christianity, resulted in cut-off ears, executions, and private violence. The persecutions ended only after Charles II ordered that they stop.

The second was the event we now know as the Salem witch trials. It began early in 1692 in the Salem home of Reverend Samuel Parris, where a number of girls aged 9 to 20 met regularly with a slave woman from Barbados named Tituba. Some of the girls began to act secretively and strangely. The two youngest "began to exhibit a most unusual malady. They would scream unaccountably, fall into grotesque convulsions, and sometimes scamper along on their hands and knees making noises like the barking of a dog" (Erikson 1966, p. 142).

Salem's only doctor could find no medical explanation. He concluded that the Devil had come to Salem and the girls were bewitched. Ministers advised that the Devil must be met head on and that the girls would have to identify the witches who were harassing them. The girls identified three women, including Tituba. At the trial, the girls rolled around, as Erikson describes:

> [in] apparent agony whenever some personal fancy (or the invisible agents of the devil) provoked them to it. It was a remarkable show. Strange creatures flew about the room pecking at the girls or taunting them from the rafters, and it was immediately obvious to everyone that the women on trial were responsible for all the disorder and suffering. When Sarah Good and Sarah Osborne were called to the stand and asked why they sent these spectres to torment the girls, they were too appalled to say much in their own defense. But when Tituba took the stand she had a ready answer. . . . Tituba gave her audiences one of the most exuberant confessions ever recorded in a New England courtroom. She spoke of the creatures who inhabit the invisible world, the dark rituals that bind them together in the service of Satan; and before she had ended her astonishing recital she had convinced everyone in Salem Village that the problem was far worse than they dared

imagine. For Tituba not only implicated Sarah Good and Sarah Osborne in her own confession but announced that many people in the colony were engaged in the devil's conspiracy against the Bay. (Erikson 1966, pp. 143–44)

The three defendants were convicted. Two were executed. The third died in prison.

A year later, Salem's witchcraft hysteria ended. In December 1692 Massachusetts Bay Colony Governor Phips reprieved the final eight persons sentenced to death, discharged every prisoner, and issued a general pardon to all persons under suspicion. By then, however, nineteen people had been executed, one man had been crushed to death under rocks for refusing to testify at his trial, two died in prison, 150 people were in custody, and 280 more had been accused.

Kai Erikson did not describe the Quaker persecutions or the Salem trials as "moral panics." The term was not yet in use. Instead, he viewed these events in a Durkheimian framework, as "crime waves," which, together with responses to them, helped identify and protect the boundaries of normatively acceptable behavior. Why those behaviors, and why such extreme responses? The answers for Erikson are that the Colony was a Puritan theocracy that had outlived its historical moment, and the boundaries were genuinely ambiguous and in doubt. The bloody repression was an act of cultural self-defense: "Historically, this kind of behavior is often associated with people who are no longer sure of their own place in the world, people who need to protect their old customs and ways all the more narrowly because they seem to have a difficult time remembering quite who they are" (1966, p. 114).

In chapter 2, I discussed claims that contemporary American drug and punishment policies are a product of existential angst (Garland 2001a) and emergence of a "risk society" (Giddens 1990). I rejected those arguments because the social and economic changes of the final third of the twentieth century, and the heightened senses of insecurity and anxiety they fostered, occurred in all Western countries, but no other country adopted anything like American crime control poli-

cies. They may have been necessary, but they were not sufficient conditions. As Erikson's account of Salem makes clear,
however, deep insecurities do provide fertile soil for moral
panics.

Sexual Psychopaths and Predators

There have been at least three periods of heightened concerns
about sexual predation of children in this century, beginning
in approximately 1910, 1940, and 1990. The best known book,
*Moral Panic: Changing Concepts of the Child Molester in Mod-
ern America* (1998), by Philip Jenkins, tells of three periods
that seem each to have been moral panics precipitated by
isolated but horrifying incidents of child sexual abuse. The
incidents galvanized media attention, public fears, political
reactions, repressive legislation, and enhanced enforcement.
The latest, in our time, is manifested in the rounds of passage
in the 1990s of sex-offender registration and notification laws
and sexual psychopath laws providing for civil commitment
of sexually "dangerous" people (Lieb, Quinsey, and Berliner
1998).

Nearly a half century earlier, long before moral panic theory took shape, Edwin Sutherland, then the most prominent
American criminologist, explained why the sexual psychopath laws of the 1940s were passed. The background conditions included press concentration on sex crimes, which
"produces a widespread uneasiness which, given a few local
incidents, readily bursts into hysteria" (1950, p. 144). The
process:

> The diffusion of sexual psychopath laws, consequently,
> has occurred under the following conditions: a state of
> fear developed, to some extent, by a general, nationwide
> popular literature and made explicit by a few spectacular
> sex crimes; a series of scattered and conflicting reactions
> by many individuals and groups within the community;
> the appointment of a committee which organizes existing

information regarding sex crimes . . . and presents a sexual psychopath law to the legislature. (1950, pp. 146–67)

The same things happen today, only more, and faster. Although Sutherland wrote of national news coverage, he was trying to explain why individual U.S. states adopted sexual psychopath laws. Horrifying incidents happened in individual states, which, in climates already made sensitive to such things by national news coverage, overreacted, created committees, and passed laws that Sutherland deeply disapproved. They were based, he said, on a series of propositions about identification and treatment of sexual offenders that are "all false or questionable, [but] they have nevertheless been very effective in the diffusion of the laws" (1950, p. 147).

In our time, however, any incident anywhere, given a drumbeat of national publicity, can influence policies in every state. Polly Klaas was killed in California, but the concerns her story raised influenced passage of California's three-strikes law and similar new laws, though generally more narrowly drafted, in many other states. Megan Kanka was killed in New Jersey, but within a few years, prodded by congressional threats of loss of federal funding, all fifty states passed Megan's laws requiring registration of sex offenders and allowing notification of their presence in the community (Lieb, Quinsey, and Berliner 1998). This is partly because national media, especially television, permeate nearly every pore of American life in vivid, repetitive, often hysterical colors. It is also partly because conservative American politicians have for nearly two decades been playing the crime card and exacerbating public fears and then proposing or enacting repressive legislation in order to allay them (Edsall and Edsall 1991). Law reform need no longer await the outcome of deliberations of Sutherland's expert commissions.

The term "moral panic" can be used in ways that range from loose polemic, in which it operates as hyperbole to describe whatever contentious issue is on the writer's mind, to careful depiction of a complex of social, psychological, and policy responses to troubling events. Usually the term connotes something rash and impulsive, and is usually used as a device for explaining things the writer does not like, but the concept, properly understood, is more neutral than that.

Reasonable people, for example, differ about the desirability of the sex-offender registration procedures required by "Megan's Laws." Opponents or skeptics see them, or at least some of their features, as the undesirable fruits of a moral panic—overbroad, stigmatizing, and inviting vigilantism. Proponents, however, see that tragic death as having, at last, focused attention on the need for more effective protection of children from sex offenders and provided some momentum to the effort to achieve it.

In crude and oversimplified terms, the enactment of Megan's Laws might be seen as a victory for law-and-order conservatives and a loss for due process liberals. Of course, it is more complicated than that and views on a subject as difficult as this one seldom closely parallel standard political lines.

Moral panics focus attention on a troubling event or problem and generate emotions that can be harnessed. Sometimes something happens as a result that otherwise would not have happened. Sometimes the result is unequivocally bad as, for example, when a crime by an immigrant provokes mob attacks against immigrants. Sometimes horrible events provide windows of opportunity for desirable policy changes. Desirability is in the eye of the beholder.

Here is an example. The gunshot deaths of Martin Luther King and Robert Kennedy precipitated passage of the federal Gun Control Act of 1968, the first meaningful federal gun control law of modern times. To gun control advocates, those tragic deaths provided the occasion and momentum to win enactment of important and necessary legislation that might otherwise have been unattainable. From that perspective, the emotion and upset generated by the two assassinations produced something good.

To gun control opponents, however, the 1968 Act was the unwanted effect of a moral panic about gun deaths and the consequent reaction produced bad policy. To them, the 1968 legislation was ill-conceived and in derogation of fundamental American values (and they worked for decades, eventually successfully, to weaken it). Thus, if Megan's Laws might be seen by some liberals as the unwanted fruits of a moral panic, some conservatives saw the 1968 gun control legislation in exactly the same way.

So we need to distinguish the dynamics of moral panics from their outcomes. Sometimes a perceived crisis can trigger changes that warrant applause and sometimes that warrant condemnation. Deciding which is which inevitably is contentious and implicates questions of values and ideology.

Thinking about this may be helped by switching from the sociologists' conception of moral panics to political scientists' parallel but less polemic concept of "windows of opportunity." A sizable literature on how social science research influences policy making developed in the 1970s and 1980s. The aim was to understand why credible research findings seemed seldom to influence policy making in direct or straightforward ways (e.g., Lindblom and Cohen 1979; Weiss 1983, 1986; Tonry and Green 2003). The precipitant was frustrations felt by many social scientists that research findings were ignored even though they seemed clearly to demonstrate ways to improve public policies. In our era, similar frustration is often expressed by researchers concerning policy makers' failure to change punishment policies aimed at deterring crime in the face of evidence casting fundamental doubts on the deterrent effects of harsh or increased penalties (e.g., Hood 2002).

The literature showed that research findings influenced policy making much more often than despairing researchers recognized, but often partially, indirectly, and after the passage of considerable periods of time. Various theoretical and conceptual frameworks were developed that could be used to examine the influence of ideology, politicians' self-interest, and bureaucratic inertia. The simple and seemingly obvious but not unimportant points were made that whether policy makers take account of research findings depends in part on whether they are paying attention and whether the time is right. When the time is right, a "window of opportunity" opens through (or during) which people are especially open to persuasion. The trick is to identify which windows are open and when and to devise effective communication strategies to bring the right information to the right people.

Liberal reformers and others who believe that policy making should be rational and evidence-based may see an upsetting event as opening a window of opportunity for the making of better policies. The King and Kennedy assassinations may, in this light, have opened a window through which evidence could pass about the use of handguns in violent crime, handgun accidents, and handgun suicides, with the salutary result that legislation was enacted that created tighter controls on gun distribution. Likewise, more recently, identification through DNA and other evidence of innocent people who have been wrongly convicted of murder or rape and sentenced to life imprisonment or death may provide a window of opportunity for meaningful reform or repeal of capital punishment laws.

That is fine as far as it goes, but so phrased it overlooks that people other than researchers and due process liberals have strong policy preferences and that windows of opportunity can open for them as well. Some people, for example, hold strong views about moral responsibility and the rightness of severely punishing or executing people who commit serious crimes and may be frustrated that their views are not more fully reflected in policy. The death of Polly Klaas, and the reaction it provoked, could be seen as opening a window for more persuasive communication of moral views about deserved and severe punishments.

Whatever the terminologies, notions like moral panic and window of opportunity represent two-edged swords that can cut to left or right, toward sympathetic understanding or condign punishment, toward due process or crime control. Which way the sword cuts depends on the environment in which it swings. The political environment of the United States during the last three decades of the twentieth century was dominated by moral and political conservatives. They won many of the contentious conflicts over crime control and drug policy, sometimes by capitalizing on emotions generated by events and upsets that liberals saw as moral panics.

That the right so often successfully took advantage of distressing events to promote their policy agenda may be why "moral panic" as used by academics generally has negative connotations. There are other reasons. Evidence and rational analysis should be central features of policy making. Decisions made in the heat of an overwrought moment often ignore both, and everyone, whatever their politics, should regret that.

We should not lose sight of an important difference between moral panics that precipitate passage of gun control legislation or repeal of death penalty laws and ones that precipitate passage of three-strikes laws or repeal laws that protect defendant's procedural protections. The latter take away people's liberty and lives, sometimes mistakenly. The former merely restrict peoples' access to guns or frustrate their wishes to see others killed.

The anger, emotion, and urgency that moral panics generate can be harnessed to various ends. Sometimes, as with gun legislation, the momentum of a moral panic can overcome the resistance of special interests and achieve a public good. More often, they produce the kinds of results that Cohen, Hall, Erikson, and Sutherland decried. The great danger is that they lead to actions and policies based on stereotype, anger, and emotion, rather than on careful assessment of problems, cool reflection, and rationality.

During recent decades of decline in rates of crime and drug abuse, American sensibilities, as David Musto predicted, have been harsh and punitive, have been predisposed to target members of minority groups as enemies, and have been intolerant of the views of dissenters from the current conventional wisdom. Penal sensibilities associated with a period of declining crime rates amplified the effects of a series of moral panics and made things worse.

5

Crime Trends and the Effects of Crime Control Policies

Prevailing sensibilities in the contemporary United States have produced, or at least allowed, drug and crime control policies of severity unprecedented in recent American history and unmatched in other Western countries today. There was a de facto moratorium on capital punishment in the United States in 1970 and belief was widespread that the Supreme Court would soon declare the death penalty unconstitutional. For eight years, from 1968 to 1977, no one was executed. In 2001, capital punishment was authorized in thirty-eight states and the federal system, sixty-six people were put to death, and at year's end 3,625 were on death row (Death Penalty Information Center 2002). In June 2001 the execution of Timothy McVeigh, shown "live" on closed circuit television to more than 230 people, was the first execution by the federal government since 1963. By contrast, in 2001, no Western European country, or Australia, Canada, England, or New Zealand, allowed capital punishment. Courts in South Africa and Hungary had declared their countries' capital punishment laws unconstitutional. The dozens of Eastern and Southern European countries joining the Council of Europe agreed to forego capital punishment as a condition of membership.

Concerning imprisonment, the U.S. prison and jail incarceration rate of more than 700 per 100,000 population in 2002 was five times the rate of 144 per 100,000 in 1970 and is nearly five times higher than that of any other Western country. In 1970 Congress repealed most federal laws requiring mandatory minimums. In the states, mandatory minimum sentences were modest in scope and severity, usually at most calling for one- or two-year minimum sentences. There were no meaningful three-strikes or sexual psychopath laws. Few prisoners were sentenced to terms of life-without-possibility-of parole or to non-parolable terms measured in decades. All of those sentences, including lengthy mandatory minimums, are commonplace in America in 2001 and rare or nonexistent elsewhere.

Why are contemporary American sensibilities as they are and why do they allow harsher punishments than characterize other times and places? The best available evidence shows that gross crime trends are determined by fundamental social and structural forces that affect most Western countries, and that they follow much the same broad patterns irrespective of national differences in crime control policies and punishment practices. If that is true, and the relevant historical and empirical literatures demonstrate that it is, it is unrealistic to suppose that short-term changes in penal policy or practice can affect rates, patterns, and trends in any particular country other than at the margins. Other countries experienced crime rises in the 1970s and 1980s, followed by declines in the 1990s, the same patterns the United States experienced, but did not adopt penal policies of unprecedented severity. Why did the United States?

Historians and sociologists of deviance offer guidance. Historians show that crime rate patterns in Western countries are broadly similar and that attitudes, public debate, and policy vary in predictable ways over extended periods in relation to rises and falls in cycles of deviant behavior. Sociologists show how, usually unpredictably, short-term moral panics occur during which problems are exaggerated, public attitudes become polarized, traditional values of moderation and balance are cast aside, moral entrepreneurs become influential, and extreme policies are adopted. The misfortune for our time is that long-term deviance cycles during which intolerance and excessive severity are to be expected have coincided with a series of moral panics, and the long-term cycles and the short-term panics have each exacerbated the other's effects.

The historical and sociological literatures explain and document social processes that shape how people perceive threats in the world around them. Both fit within what might loosely be called a Durkheimian framework, after the French sociologist Émile Durkheim. Durkheim argued that one of the criminal law's functions is to identify and reinforce basic social ideas about right and wrong, that "crime brings together upright consciences and concentrates them." The criminal law is seen as performing a dramaturgical function, with punishment directed primarily at the community and not at the offender, and working not directly through deterrence and incapacitation but indirectly through affirmation and reiteration of basic norms.

Crime and punishment are seen as parts of every human society, mechanisms that help set and then illuminate the boundaries of acceptable behavior. The primary aims of the criminal law and punishment are to state, restate, and reinforce prevailing norms: "[Punishment] does not serve, or else serves only quite secondarily, in correcting the culpable, or in intimidating possible followers. From this point of view, its efficacy is justly doubtful and, in any case, mediocre. Its true function is to maintain social cohesion intact" (Durkheim 1933 [orig. 1893], p. 108).

Durkheim's dramaturgical functions of law are among the ways that socialization occurs and through which sensibilities are shaped. Criminal law and punishment, however, are not the primary means of socialization into right values. That function belongs to primary social organizations such as the family, the church, the workplace, the community, and to kinship and friendship networks.

Cycles of tolerance and intolerance and moral panics operate at an even deeper contextual level, however, than do legal institutions, and have greater influence on men's minds and actions. If legal institutions and their operations serve as a backdrop to the socializing and norm-declaring roles of primary institutions and networks, cycles and moral panics operate as a backdrop to them. However, because of the ways they influence sensibilities, and through sensibilities how people perceive and interpret the world, cycles and panics play the more powerful roles.

Four principal claims are made in this chapter. First, human life is characterized in many spheres by cycles, by regular oscillations between recurring states or conditions. Second, in the United States and in other Western countries for which data are available, crime rates change slowly, over extended periods, and for reasons that have no apparent relationship to changes in crime control policies or criminal justice institutions. Third, in relation to drug policy there is a regular interaction between drug use cycles and punitive antidrug policies, with the harshest policies being adopted when drug use is declining rather than, as at first impression probably to most people seems more likely, when drug use is rising. Fourth, though to my knowledge there is no historical literature on interactions among crime rate cycles, sensibilities, and crime control policies, there is little reason to doubt that the patterns characterizing drug use cycles apply to crime and crime control policies.

Oscillations

Human behaviors, values, and beliefs oscillate over time, moving back and forth between what are widely seen as fundamentally different positions. The business cycle's periods of alternating expansion and contraction are a cliché, but the world economic downturn of 2001–2003 confirms its underlying reality. For the past two centuries in Western countries, regular shifts have taken place in the breadth of popular support for conservative and liberal political parties, and governments have shifted with them. Histories of Christianity document regular fluctuations over 2,000 years between periods of doctrinal orthodoxy and fierce, often deadly, resistance to apostasy, and periods of heterodoxy and tolerance. Histories of homosexuality document a similar aeonslong fluctuation between periods of comfortable tolerance and lethal intolerance.

Grant Gilmore describes the regular alternation between classical periods' celebration of formal rules of structure and composition in the arts and the confused, sprawling, formless, and chaotic agonies of the romantic periods that follow. Gilmore is important not only because he illustrates recurring alternation between opposed perspectives, but because he describes the psychological power of orthodoxy. Prevailing sensibilities affect how people think. During classical peaks, tradition, form, regularity, and structure are admired because most people believe formalism is an aesthetically important ideal, and at romantic peaks most people believe that experimentation, spontaneity, and exuberance are important values. What this shows is that people's beliefs are at least influenced and often determined by the values of the era in which they live and, accordingly, that many individuals would have believed different things had they lived in different times.

People's beliefs about norms, values, and ideals are importantly different from their beliefs about other things, for example, technology. Beliefs about optimal characteristics of internal combustion engines are not fundamentally cyclical but evolutionary. At any developmental stage, some engines are preferred because they are cleaner, more efficient, more reliable, or more durable but, by those criteria, earlier engines are almost inevitably inferior to those later developed. For such things, something like perfectionism is an intelligible frame of reference. Ideas about romanticism, homosexuality, religious pluralism, and punishment are not like that.

Long-Term Crime Trends

Crime rates rise and fall over extended periods for reasons that appear to have little to do with the actions or policies of governments. Historians who have studied such matters agree on a number of propositions about the history of crime rates.

First, violent crime rates in the British Isles and continental Europe fell steadily from the twelfth century, the earliest time for which quantitative data are available, until the 1950s or 1960s (Eisner 2001, 2003). Figures 5.1, 5.2, 5.3, and 5.4, from Swiss historian Manuel Eisner's work, show long-term trends in homicide rates in England, Scandinavia, Holland and Belgium, and Germany and Switzerland. The figures use a log linear scale to show the data. This allows each band shown to represent an order of magnitude difference from those above or below, but within each band the intervals are comparable. The dots on the figures represent quantitative data from individual studies of official records for particular places for particular times. Any individual study can be second-guessed in terms of the reliability of the data source, the representativeness of the incidents that were recorded, and the adequacy of population estimates used to calculate homicide rates. So long, however, as they fall within the "right" band of the figure, being off even by a large margin does not upset the basic patterns.

Looked at as a whole, the data tell remarkably consistent stories in all four regions. In each, homicide rates were between 30 and 100 per 100,000 population in the earliest pe-

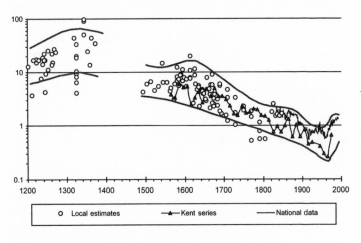

Figure 5.1 England—local estimates and national series
Source: Eisner 2003. History of Homicide Database.

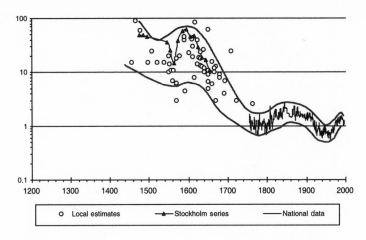

Figure 5.2 Scandinavia—local estimates and national series for Sweden
Source: Eisner 2003. History of Homicide Database.

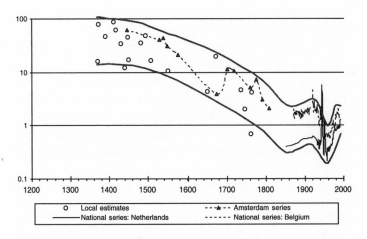

Figure 5.3 Netherlands and Belgium—local estimates and national series
Source: Eisner 2003. History of Homicide Database.

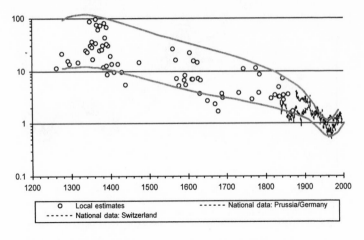

Figure 5.4 Germany and Switzerland—local estimates and national series

Source: Eisner 2003. History of Homicide Database.

riod and then, in a series of sharp falls alternating with lengthy plateaus fell below 10 per 100,000 in the eighteenth or nineteenth century to 1 or 2 per 100,000 in the twentieth century. Eisner offers a variety of explanations that range from broad theory, including Elias's civilizing process and increasing state roles in order maintenance, and individualism, to technology (steadily improved medical care has reduced the likelihood of death from many types of assault). The fundamental and uncontroversial point, however, is that homicide rates in Western Europe decreased continuously for at least five centuries.

Second, if only more recent periods for which more, and more reliable, data are available are considered, violence rates declined in Western countries from the early to mid-nineteenth century until the 1950s or 1960s and rose thereafter but to levels well below either the medieval or nineteenth century starting points (Gurr 1981, 1989; Lane 1992, 1999). American historians refer to this pattern as a "U-shaped" or "reverse J-shaped" curve.

Roger Lane, America's leading historian of crime and policing, has written: "In the United States, as everywhere in the developed world, rates of homicide and other violent crimes, if graphed, would form a kind of long, ragged, reverse J-curve. That is, while short-term events might create zigs and zags, the basic curve dropped from the mid-nineteenth century to the mid twentieth" (Lane 1999, p. 205).

Crime rates then rose for several decades in the United States and in all other Western countries. More recently, however, crime rates have again begun to decline in many Western countries (including Australia, Canada, Denmark, England and Wales, Finland, Germany, the Netherlands, and the United States) as measured by official police data on recorded crimes, data from surveys in which people are asked about crimes by which they have been victimized, or, in most countries, both. It is too early to know whether significant increases in violent crime rates in most Western countries since the 1960s signaled a change in the eight- or two-century-long trends or whether they were merely short-term perturbations like previous up-ticks associated with wars and periods of sustained unrest. Short-term perturbation is the best guess. The falling crime rate in the 1990s in most Western countries, and within federal countries, in most states, irrespective of wide variations in crime policies, imprisonment rates, and punitive sensibilities, suggests the latter.

Figure 5.5 depicts the U/reverse J-shaped American violent-crime-rate pattern for most of the past two centuries. It also shows major criminal justice policy changes from 1840 to 1960. During the period of continuous long-term decline in violent crime rates, most of the major institutions of modern criminal justice systems were established: the penitentiary (1820s through 1840s), the first probation programs (1850s and 1860s onwards), the rehabilitation-premised reformatory for young offenders (1870s), parole (1880s onwards), and the juvenile court (1899 onwards). By 1930 nearly all of these institutions existed in every American jurisdiction (Rothman 1980). The ubiquitous indeterminate sentencing systems that characterized every jurisdiction, and survived everywhere

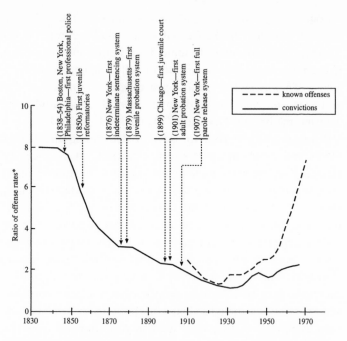

Figure 5.5 American violent-crime-rate pattern with policy changes
Sources: Gurr 1981, 1989.

little changed until 1975, had taken shape. In 1850 something that resembled a combination of modern "truth in sentencing" and "determinate sentencing" existed throughout the United States; by 1930 it existed nowhere.

One might not unreasonably suppose that the invention of the modern criminal justice system is, or was widely seen to be, the reason why crime rates declined so much and for so long. Despite the shift from determinate to indeterminate sentencing, however, and the invention of so many new and unprecedented institutions, changes in criminal justice policies, practices, and processes are seldom mentioned as likely or leading causes of the century-long decline in crime rates (Rothman 1980; Friedman 1993; S. Walker 1998). Roger Lane reported that other leading police historians "believe police impact on non-'order' offenses was minimal and . . . [were]

almost contemptuous about the efficacy of patrol, Walker [1977] pointing out that the thin blue line was too thin to make much difference, Fogelson [1977] insisting that the duty was more often shirked than shouldered" (Lane 1980, p. 38). Lane's "own more fully considered position would be that the cops 'worked' only as part of the demand—created fundamentally by a changing economic order—for a more disciplined society and workforce. Acting alone, or out of phase with this deeper economic need, as in an age of labor surplus, their impact was (and still is) minimal" (Lane 1980, p. 38).

Samuel Walker, one of America's leading criminal justice historians, observes of the nineteenth-century police, "It is unlikely that the police did much to prevent crime and disorder . . . there were too few officers spread too thin, spending too much of their time avoiding work" (1998, p. 66), and of prisons that "the impact of the prisons and the other new institutions on crime is a matter for much speculation. Crime and disorder declined throughout the nineteenth century, but it is unlikely that the prison was responsible for that, any more than were the police" (1998, p. 109).

Instead, the primary explanation provided by Ted Robert Gurr (1981, 1989) and Roger Lane (1982 and 1999) is a combination of a centuries-long decreasing tolerance for violence in Western countries and the effects of the bureaucratization of modern life. The first of these is consistent with Elias's "civilizing process," and the second with Foucault's ideas. Since the early nineteenth century, individuals have been socialized into conformity by public schools, factories, the military, and other institutions. This is not unlike the Foucauldian thesis in *Discipline and Punish* (1977) that prisons, mental institutions, and the army exemplify a wider range of "disciplinary institutions" that mold people into the roles demanded by the modern state and economy.

Political scientist James Q. Wilson (1993; Wilson and Herrnstein 1985) argued that a major part of the explanation lay in the waves of religious revivalism of the nineteenth century. These, he proposed, strengthened moral and ethical standards of right behavior and personal responsibility, which then became central features of the socialization of children in families, schools, churches, and communities. That in turn explains the decline in crime rates. Conversely, in the latter half of the twentieth century, traditional norm-creating processes broke down and the decline in "the moral sense" is a major explanation for the rising crime rates of the 1960s through the 1980s.

Wilson's explanation of the effects of nineteenth-century social changes is not very different from Durkheim's views or the Northern European notion of "positive general prevention" (Törnudd 1997; Lappi-Seppälä 2001). Most people abstain from committing serious crimes because of internalized ideas about right and wrong, which are the product of socialization by primary institutions such as the family, church, and school, and not because they will be punished if they are caught. In Wilson's view, social changes of the last fifty years broke down these socialization processes, but religious reawakening in the nineteenth century strengthened them.

None of Gurr, Lane, and Wilson, it bears repeating, however, primarily attributes nineteenth-century crime trends to the invention and implementation of the institutions of individualized and indeterminate sentencing. This stands in stark contrast to the last twenty years in the United States when public figures and many academics have attributed crime rate declines to criminal justice policy changes such as increased use of imprisonment, three-strikes laws, and zero-tolerance policing. I take this up later on in this chapter.

To anticipate: contemporary sensibilities being as they are, many Americans are predisposed to believe that harsh anti-crime policies are morally right and likely to work. As crime rates fell, it was natural to believe anticrime policies were the reason why, especially for political figures like California Governor Pete Wilson and New York City Mayor Rudolph Giuliani for whom harsh anticrime policies were part of their political identities. Having their policies "work" was in their political self-interest, and it takes no subtle psychology to recognize that people tend to believe what is in their self-interest to believe. People like Wilson and Giuliani, assuming they really believed their policies worked, were almost certainly mistaken. Crime rates fell in every Western country in the 1990s, whatever the governing crime control philosophy and practices, and in every American city and state, whether or not they adopted three-strikes laws or zero-tolerance policing.

Drug Use and Drug Policy

There is a regular interaction between declines in drug use, enactment of harsh public policies, and demonization of minority groups. The pattern has recurred in the past twenty years in the United States, with drug use peaking in 1979–80 for most drugs (and 1982–84 for cocaine), the harshest anti-drug laws being passed in the late 1980s, and black inner-city residents being portrayed as the enemy in the drug wars (Tonry 1995, chaps. 1, 3). The same pattern holds for crime in general: crime rates have fallen since 1990–91 (some would say since the early 1980s), the harshest laws were passed in the early 1990s, and blacks and Hispanics have been the principal targets of the crime wars.

Since my interest here is in how secular trends affect people's thinking, the bases for the preceding assertions are only sketched. The basic outline of the argument comes from historian David Musto's (1973, 1987a) work on the history of American drug policy, embellished a bit by evidence from historian Joseph Gusfield's (1963) work on the history of alcohol policy.

During the past two centuries, the United States has experienced three peaks of prohibitionistic moralism: the 1850s when by 1856 eight states had enacted alcohol prohibition; 1915–35, the era of national Prohibition; and 1980 to the present.

Nineteenth-Century Alcohol Prohibition

Antebellum prohibitionism culminated at least forty years of temperance activism, but was truncated by the Civil War, which distracted activists and policy makers. Three things, however, stand out in Gusfield's account of the history of alcohol policy. First, the prohibition and temperance movements of the nineteenth century were partly a product of status conflicts between cultural groups—initially settled, generally abstemious, American Protestants of British descent against newly arrived, often Catholic, often bibulous European immigrants. Prohibition was a device through which a "cultural group act[ed] to preserve, defend, or enhance the dominance and prestige of its own style of living within the total society" (1963, p. 3).

Second, particular minority groups, in the eyes of the dominant settled Protestants, came to personify the dangers and the lifestyle represented by alcohol:

> The symbol of abstinence as a symbol of respectability was enhanced when large numbers of Irish and German immigrants entered the United States and made up the unskilled labor forces of the growing urban centers during the 1840s and 1850s. In the culture of the Irish and the Germans, use of whiskey or beer was customary and often a staple part of the diet. Both groups were at the bottom of the class and status structure in American society. In the evolution of class symbols, the groups at the lowest rungs of the ladder affect the behavior of those above by a process of depletion in which those traits originally shared by both groups become progressively deprized among the more prestigeful. The incoming group thus widens the status gap between it and the natives. If the lowly Irish and Germans were the drinkers and the drunkards of the community, it was more necessary than ever that the aspirant to middle-class membership not risk the possibility that he might be classed with the immigrants. (Gusfield 1963, p. 51)

Easily recognized lower status groups like the preponderantly Catholic Irish and German immigrants personified the dangers and moral laxity of alcohol consumption. Conversely, alcohol use and abuse personified the irresponsibility and lesser worthiness of the newer immigrants.

Third, when drinkers refused either to accept calls to abstention or to acknowledge the wrongfulness of their behavior, they became enemies:

> When one group acts in a manner contradicting the other's belief in the legitimacy and domination of its own norms, the situation becomes that of a conflict between enemies. . . . The assumption that the norms-violator recognizes the legitimacy or domination [of prevalent norms] . . . is contradicted when the norms-violator is perceived as an enemy . . . someone who is hostile and must be approached as an enemy; who must be forced to accept the dominance of the reformer . . . [is] a hostile enemy who must be coerced through legislation. (Gusfield 1963, pp. 67–70)

All three of these themes—drug policy as an arena of cultural conflict, identification of low-status minority groups with immorality, and conversion of people who reject dominant values into enemies—recur in both the alcohol and drug wars of the twentieth centuries.

Twentieth-Century "Drug" Prohibition

David Musto has several times written of the seeming anomaly that prohibitionistic sentiments become strongest and drug policies harshest after drug use has begun to decline. Use of psychotropic and other mood-altering substances is always a contested subject. Peaks in the prevalence of use followed by drops are often accompanied by a hardening of anti-drug sentiments in the population, a reduction in perceived ambiguities about the issues drug use raises, and a shift toward more vigorous, moralistic, and punitive policies and practices. Here I develop only his further point about a tendency at such times of declining drug use for socially marginal minority groups to be stereotyped as immoral and irresponsible drug abusers.

In a revised version of his book published at a time when the modern drug wars were well underway, Musto wrote:

"One cannot help but be concerned that the fear of drugs will again transfer into a simple fear of the drug user and will be accompanied by draconian sentences and specious links between certain drugs and distrusted groups within society, as was the case with cocaine and Southern blacks early in the Twentieth Century" (1987*a*, p. 27).

Throughout U.S. history during periods of high intolerance of drug use, minority group stereotypes have been associated with deviant drug use. In the mid-nineteenth century, per Gusfield, immigrant Irish and Germans were targeted. In the late nineteenth and early twentieth centuries, even though middle-class women were the modal category of opiate users, Chinese opium smokers and opium dens were among the images invoked by opponents of drug use and are part of the backdrop to the Harrison Act of 1914, the first major federal antinarcotics legislation. At about the same time and in the 1920s, it was blacks and cocaine. In the 1930s, imagery of Mexicans and marijuana was prominent in the anti-marijuana movements that culminated in the Marijuana Tax Act of 1937 and in many state laws criminalizing marijuana use. In the antidrug atmosphere of the 1980s, crack cocaine, the emblematic drug of the latest drug war, became associated in public imagery with disadvantaged black residents of the inner cities (Musto 1987*a*, *b*; Tonry 1995, chap. 3; Mauer 1999).

Musto observes that excesses in overzealous law enforcement, stigmatization of minority groups, and stereotyping of drug users occur when drug use is declining, because "people become so righteous and so zealous." They become zealous because drug use comes to be seen in terms of a contrast between moral right and immoral wrong. They become righteous because right is on their side.

Cycles of Intolerance of Criminals?

The two preceding sections offered two propositions. Crime rates change slowly, in response to long-term underlying social and normative changes. At least in relation to drug use policies, penal sensibilities vary depending on whether drug use is increasing or decreasing, with the harshest sensibilities developing shortly after usage peaks and has begun to fall. Taken together, those propositions support a hypothesis that penal sensibilities concerning crime parallel those concerning drug use. Whether the three-decade increase in American crime rates was a perturbation in the centuries-long decline in violent crime, or not, rates have declined sharply since at least the early 1990s. Applying Musto's model to crime generates hypotheses that attitudes would become harsher, policies severer, law enforcement more vigorous, and minorities more ensnared in the justice system. All of that happened.

The principal questions are whether the drug use, drug policy pattern Musto first described in 1973 occurred during the current drug wars, and, if so, whether the same pattern characterizes crime rates and crime control policies. Yes, and yes, are the answers. First, though, a look at recent crime rate declines, and whether they are likelier to result from long-term social forces or short-term policy innovations, is in order. Then I turn to the central questions.

Short-Term Crime Trends

The recent fall in U.S. crime rates is much likelier to result from underlying social and normative changes than from recently adopted crime control policies such as three-strikes laws, zero-tolerance policing, or mass incarceration. That so many people believe, or purport to believe, the latter is a product of contemporary penal sensibilities that predispose such beliefs. There are two major, and several lesser, reasons for so concluding.

The place to begin is to look at crime rates from the Uniform Crime Reports (the "UCR") for the last forty years. Figure 5.6 shows rates of crime reported to the police for murder, rape, robbery, motor vehicle theft, and burglary from 1960 to 2000. In order to show rates for those five crimes on one figure, rates for burglary and motor vehicle theft have been divided by ten and those for rape and murder have been

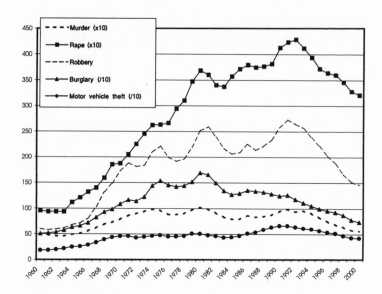

Figure 5.6 Reported crime rates, United States 1960–2000 (per 100,000 population), murder, rape, robbery, burglary, and motor vehicle theft
Source: Sourcebook of Criminal Justice Statistics Online, Table 3.120.

multiplied by ten. This does not distort the figure's message because its aims are to show trends for particular crimes and allow comparisons between trends for different crimes.

The Uniform Crime Reports, which are compiled and published annually by the FBI from data provided by police forces, classify those five crimes plus aggravated assault, theft, and arson as Index Crimes. I excluded arson from figure 5.6, because of its relatively low incidence. Aggravated assault is excluded, because we know that the percentages of assaults reported to the police steadily increased during the past twenty years, and rising rates partially reflect major changes in citizen reporting rather than changes in the occurrence of assaults. Rising rates of aggravated assault partly result from declining tolerance of violence, which means that assaults previously seen as too minor to record are recorded, and partly from reduced tolerance of domestic violence, which means that acts of family violence once seen as primarily private matters are recorded as crimes (Blumstein 1993). Rape reporting patterns have also changed in recent decades because alleged acquaintance, date, and marital rapes are much more often reported and recorded than in earlier times. I nonetheless include rape in figure 5.6 because of its seriousness and policy importance and because reporting and recording patterns are more likely than those for aggravated assault to have stabilized and less likely to create serious distortions.

Several things stand out from figure 5.6. The trends for all five crimes are broadly similar. Rates for all five rose steeply from the 1960s to the early 1980s, reaching their highest levels since 1960. Then they fell for five years. Beginning in 1986, they began another rise that lasted for five years and topped out in 1990–91. After that, rates fell sharply and consistently. Some people date the crime rate declines from the first peak in the 1980s, others from the early 1990s highs. It does not really matter. Rates may have begun a long-term decline around 1980 and then temporarily changed direction before resuming. Or the climb may have begun in earnest in 1980 but temporarily been obscured by the effects of the crack cocaine epidemic beginning in the mid-1980s. Alfred Blumstein (1993) has argued that the rapid expansion of new crack cocaine markets, at a time when youth gangs were spreading rapidly and ever-more-lethal firearms were becoming readily accessible, produced an explosion of violence and related crime, which in a few years abated when the markets matured and turf battles ended. Either way crime rates have been falling substantially for a considerable period. Sooner or later they will stabilize, and inevitably they will at least for a time rise again. As yet though, there have been no signs of steep upward movements.

The timing of the major shifts in direction is the same whether the increases of the late 1980s are taken into account or not. Rates for all five offenses peaked around 1980, and have fallen since, or peaked twice, and each time fell sharply thereafter, but in either case, rates for all five changed at about the same times. Something fundamental was changing in the United States and it affected each of these major crimes in the same ways.

Two other sources of information about crime trends, the U.S. National Crime Victimization Survey (the "NCVS") and the International Crime Victimization Survey (the "ICVS"), tell the same story. Victimization surveys, which ask respondents to answer questions about crimes they have suffered, provide a crosscheck on official crime data. Victimization surveys generate much higher estimates of the amount of crime than do official data. That is because they include minor and uncompleted crimes that people do not consider worth reporting or about which it appears unlikely the police can do anything. However, the proportions of each type of victimization that are reported to the police are known, and change little from year to year. Thus, though the absolute levels of crime reported by the UCR and the NCVS should be different, the trends they show should be the same.

The NCVS, conducted by the U.S. Bureau of the Census for the U.S. Bureau of Justice Statistics, has since 1973 published data from interviews conducted every six months with members of 40,000 to 60,000 households. It is the world's largest, longest running, and most technically sophisticated national victimization survey. Figure 5.7 shows reported victimization rates for assault, rape, robbery, and theft per 1,000 persons aged 12 or over, burglary rates per 1,000 households, and motor vehicle theft per 1,000 vehicles for the years 1980 to 2000. Rates for burglary and theft are divided by 10. These are four of the five crimes shown in figure 5.6, plus theft and assault. The victimization trends for rape, robbery, and motor vehicle theft follow the same twin-peaks-followed-by-steady-decline pattern as the official crime data shown in figure 5.6. So does aggravated assault, which I have included in this figure, since victims' reports are not distorted by official reporting and recording practices. Burglary and theft show continuous declines.

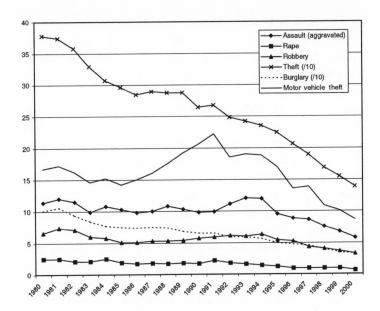

Figure 5.7 U.S. victimization rate as measured by the NCVS, 1980–2000

Source: National Criminal Victimization Survey, 1980–2000.

The ICVS is a smaller, newer, and less frequent victimization survey than the NCVS. It has been conducted four times beginning in 1988–89 by varying numbers of countries, but always including England, Holland, Germany, and the United States. Its goals include cross-national comparisons of crime trends and rates. To do this, and avoid the complicating effects of national differences in how crimes are defined, reported, and recorded, the ICVS employs standardized questionnaires and methods in each country. Rather than ask respondents whether they have suffered particular crimes, the definitions of which vary between countries, the ICVS asks such things as, has anyone taken anything from you? When the response is "yes," follow-up questions pinpoint exactly what happened. For that reason, and because in various ways it is less sophisticated than the NCVS, the ICVS differs substantially from the NCVS in many technical respects. It also uses a much smaller sample of respondents. And yet, as table 5.1 shows for robbery, assault, burglary, and auto theft, the American victimization rate trends for the ICVS parallel the victimization rates reported by the NCVS and the crime rate trends of the Uniform Crime Reports.

U.S. crime rates, however measured, have been falling for more than a decade. Year-to-year changes may result from random variation or, in the Uniform Crime Reports, changes from one year to another in which jurisdictions fail to submit data on time or at all. Trend changes for a single crime such as notably rape, aggravated assault, or auto theft may result from changes in citizens' reporting or police recording patterns. But when all credible sources of data on crime trends show the same trends for a decade, when the rate declines are steep and nearly continuous, and when they are the same for murder, the most reliably reported crime, as they are for other crimes, something has happened and crime has fallen as a result.

Why Have Crime Rates Fallen?

The most obvious explanations for why crime rates have fallen, and the most widely believed—that sentencing poli-

Table 5.1 U.S. assault, auto theft, burglary, and robbery rates per 1,000 Americans 16 and over, International Crime Victims Survey, 1989, 1996, 2000

	1989	1996	2000
Assault	101	100	65
Auto theft	29	20	6
Burglary	56	39	33
Robbery	28	16	6

Source: John van Kesteren, Pat Mayhew, and Paul Nieuw-beerta. 2000. *Criminal Victimisation in Seventeen Industrialized Countries—Key Findings from the 2000 International Crime Victims Survey.* The Hague: Netherlands Ministry of Justice.

cies became tougher, police became more aggressive and more efficient, and many more people were sent to prison—are almost certainly wrong. These policy changes no doubt influenced the fall in crime rates, but they were not the major explanation. This can be shown in two ways.

First, crime trends in cities and states that adopted especially celebrated crime control policies can be compared with trends in comparable cities and states that did not. When such comparisons are made, it becomes clear that comparable trends occurred everywhere, including in cities that did not adopt aggressive zero-tolerance policing styles, and in states that adopted neither truth-in-sentencing nor three-strikes laws.

Second, crime trends in the United States in the 1990s can be compared with those in other Western countries that did not adopt harsh American-style crime control policies. Incarceration rates and trends can be used to show that U.S. policies were more punitive than those elsewhere and that the increase in punitiveness was unmatched elsewhere. The U.S. imprisonment grew by half between 1990 and 2002, rising from 450 per 100,000 to over 700. By comparison the highest rates in other Western countries in 2000 were around 150 per 100,000 (Portugal, New Zealand) and for most were below 100 (France, Germany, Italy, all the Scandinavian countries) (Barclay and Tavares 2002).

In addition, there were substantial country-to-country variations in imprisonment rate patterns (Tonry 2001). They went up about as rapidly in Holland as in the United States, rose significantly in England, New Zealand, and Portugal, fell steeply in Finland, were broadly stable in Germany and Canada, and fluctuated widely in France. Yet crime rates fell in the 1990s in every Western country. Once cross-national comparisons are made, it is not obvious why harsh policies should be seen as explaining the U.S. crime rate declines when similar declines occurred in many countries that did not adopt U.S.-style policies.

Zero-Tolerance Policing in New York City Not everyone knows about historical crime trends or how U.S. trends compare with those elsewhere. So it is not unreasonable that many people wrongly believe that tougher crime control policies are the primary reason American crime rates fell in the 1990s. After all, New York City in 1994 introduced policy changes popularly known as zero-tolerance policing and New York City crime rates fell in 1995. California enacted its three-strikes law in 1994 and crime rates fell in 1995. Nationally, the number of people in state and federal prisons quadrupled from 316,000 in 1980 to 1,300,000 in 2000 and the violent crime rate in the Uniform Crime Reports fell substantially during the same period. Unfortunately, all of those appearances are misleading.

Consider, first, the effects of zero-tolerance policing in New York and California's three-strikes law. In each place, crime rates fell the year after the innovation took effect, and New York's Mayor Rudolph Giuliani and California's Governor Pete Wilson were quick to take credit. Neither of them, however, nor many other observers, took account of the familiar phenomenon of the pre-existing trend. If, for example, all the 9-year-old children in a town are given a banana-a-day as part of their regular diet for a year following the ninth birthday, they will on average gain a measurable number of pounds and inches. Anyone who claimed that eating bananas was the principal reason they grew would be ridiculed. Ten-year-olds are bigger and taller than 9-year-olds. Though eating bananas might be part of the reason, it would be but a small part.

It turns out that both New York City and California had been experiencing crime rate declines for several years before their self-heralded policy changes occurred. Continuation of the pre-existing trends is as likely an explanation for the crime rate drops as were zero-tolerance policing and three strikes.

New York's innovations go under other names—order maintenance policing, misdemeanor policing, broken windows policing (Harcourt 2001). The core elements, whatever name is used, were increased arrests of misdemeanants and aggressive patrol. Since zero-tolerance policing is the term in widest use, I use it here. Sharp reduction in the homicide rate was the most often claimed evidence of the crime-reducing effects of zero-tolerance policing, but in retrospect that evidence is not very compelling. Franklin Zimring and Jeffrey Fagan showed that non-gun homicides began a steady decline in 1987. Gun homicides increased rapidly in the late 1980s and early 1990s and then began their steep decline. This contrast is important because non-gun homicides are typically associated with powerful emotion, alcohol, domestic violence, and the structures of everyday life. The social conditions that give rise to these homicides change slowly. Gun homicides, by contrast, are associated with street crime, gangs, and drug markets, and as gangs and markets change, homicide patterns change with them. Thus, if evidence is wanted of crime rate changes associated with fundamental changes in values, non-gun homicides are the place to look, and their decline predated zero-tolerance policing by almost a decade.

What needs explaining is why gun homicide rates went up in the late 1980s rather than why they went down in the mid-1990s. Benjamin Bowling (1999) showed, as Alfred Blumstein (1993) had earlier proposed, that explosion of the crack cocaine markets in the mid-1980s, and their stabilization in the 1990s, parallels the national and New York City crime trends of that period.

One way to assess whether New York homicide rates were reduced as a result of zero-tolerance policing is to compare New York's homicide rate trends with those of other large American cities during a comparable period. Here again, the data urge caution about claiming too much from zero-tolerance policing. Figure 5.8 shows homicide rates for ten American cities from 1990 to 2000. The rates have been standardized to the 1990 rates. That means that the 1990 rate, whatever it was, is assigned the value 100 and subsequent changes are shown as percentage changes from 100. This makes trend comparisons easier to see.

The patterns shown in figure 5.8 vary in detail, partly because the numbers of homicides in some cities are small enough that random statistical variations can produce sig-

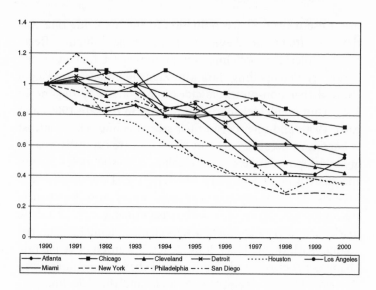

Figure 5.8 Homicide rates for ten American cities, 1990–2000, standardized to 1990 = 100
Source: Sourcebook of Criminal Justice Statistics.

nificant year-to-year shifts. Nonetheless, the broad patterns are similar. Homicide rates in every big city, including New York City, began to drop before zero-tolerance policing was initiated in 1994. New York's 1990s decline in homicide rates is among the steepest, but, perhaps ironically, it shares that distinction with San Diego, a city whose police department publicly rejected the zero-tolerance model and prides itself on its community policing approach. Homicide rates in Houston, a city not notorious for innovativeness in policing, fell just about as much. Judy Greene, analyzing the city-by-city data in a different way, reached much the same conclusion (Greene 1999). Bernard Harcourt, in the most exhaustive analysis of the evidence for what he calls broken windows policing, concludes: "After reviewing the social-scientific data, replicating a key study, and closely scrutinizing the empirical evidence in New York City, Chicago, and other cities, I find there is no good evidence to support the broken windows theory" (2001, p. 7). John Eck and Edward Maguire, in an exhaustive survey of evidence on the effects of policing on crime rates in the 1990s, concluded zero-tolerance policing "cannot be given credit for the decline in homicides in New York City" (2000, p. 235). So the evidence for the crime-reducing effects of New York's zero-tolerance policing is much weaker than is generally recognized.

Three-Strikes in California Likewise the evidence for California's three-strikes law. Figure 5.9 shows homicide, rape, robbery, motor vehicle theft, and burglary rates for California from 1980 to 2000, with some multiplied and others divided by ten. Declines in rates for all those crimes began long before the three-strikes law took effect and continued long afterward. The pattern is the same as figure 5.6 showed for the entire country: rates for all offenses fell from 1980 through

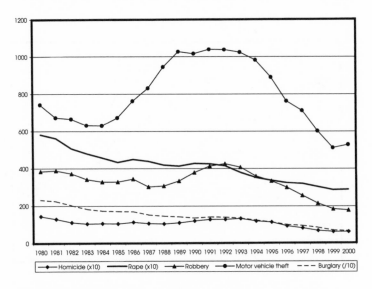

Figure 5.9 Crime rates (per 100,000 population), selected offenses, California 1980–2000
Source: Sourcebook of Criminal Justice Statistics.

1985–86, rose through 1990–92, and fell steadily thereafter. Figures 5.10 and 5.11 show homicide and robbery rates for the five most populous states including California, standardized to 100 in 1980, for the period 1980–2000. Those states vary widely in their sentencing policies and only California enacted a widely drawn three-strikes law. Compared with the other four most populous states, figures 5.10 and 5.11 show nothing special about California crime rates before or after the three-strikes law took effect. In both figures, crime rates declined in all five states with Illinois showing lesser declines and the patterns for the other four being indistinguishable.

This conclusion that the three-strikes law had little effect on crime rates in California is consistent with most assessments. Experience through 2000 has been summarized by Franklin Zimring and colleagues. Application of the three-strikes law depended on discretionary decisions by prosecutors to charge defendants under its provisions. In some counties, prosecutors seldom filed three-strikes charges. Others

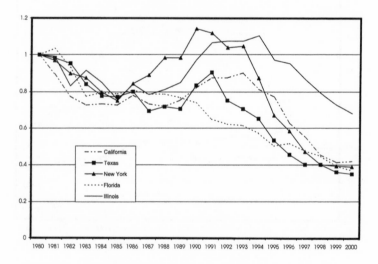

Figure 5.10 Homicide rates, standardized to 1980 = 100, five most populous states, 1980–2000
Source: Sourcebook of Criminal Justice Statistics.

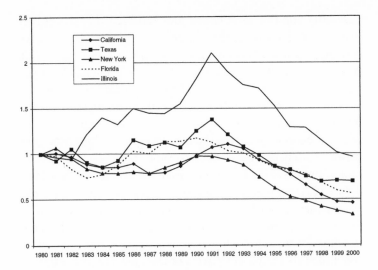

Figure 5.11 Robbery rates, standardized to 1980 = 100, five most populous states, 1980–2000
Source: Sourcebook of Criminal Justice Statistics.

did so often. The counties where charges were least often filed had the largest crime rate drops, those where they were most often filed had the smallest. Zimring and his colleagues conclude: "The decline in [California] crime [rates] after the effective date of the three-strikes law was not the result of the statute" (2001, p. 101). A sizable number of other studies have reached similar conclusions (Males and Macallair 1999; Turner et al. 1999).

This conclusion that changes following adoption of major new crime control initiatives are largely attributable to continuation of preexisting trends is not novel. One of the best-known demonstrations of that phenomenon occurred in California in connection with the 1976 adoption of its Uniform Determinate Sentencing Law. In enacting this law, which abolished parole release, California became the first large state to adopt "determinate sentencing." The earliest evaluations compared sentences imposed during the year before and the year after the law took effect, and reported that the effects included an increase in the proportion of convicted felons receiving prison sentences (e.g., Lipson and Peterson 1980). This is what conservative proponents of the law wanted (Messinger and Johnson 1978), and it was hailed as a sign of success.

When another research team looked at sentencing patterns for three years before and three years after the law took effect, it became clear that the percentages of felons receiving prison sentences had increased each of the six years. The rate of increase was no greater after the law took effect than before (Casper, Brereton, and Neal 1983). The law's apparent effects turned out instead to be merely the continuation of preexisting trends. A few years later, evaluators of North Carolina's Fair Sentencing Act, which took effect in 1981, concluded that apparent effects of that law's implementation were instead the continuation of preexisting trends (Clarke 1987).

The simplest, and therefore best and likeliest, explanation for California's experiences with determinate sentencing in the 1970s and the three-strikes law in the 1990s is that broad-based changes were underway in values and norms that caused both the changes in laws and the behaviors that the legal changes appeared to produce. A rising tide lifts all boats.

Here is what likely happened. Beginning in the 1970s, Californians began to become less sympathetic to offenders and more moralistic and judgmental about wrongful behavior. As a consequence, prosecutors became more aggressive in their handling of cases, judges became more severe in their sentencing, sending increasing percentages of offenders to prison, defense lawyers became less sympathetic to their clients, and probation officers became less likely to look the other way when probationers violated conditions. Once these changes started, they became a trend, and the percentage of offenders receiving prison sentences grew each year. In the midst of these normative and behavioral changes, both sensing the shifts in their constituents' attitudes, and feeling the same way themselves, legislators enacted laws that were less sympathetic to offenders' interests. In the following years the percentages of offenders sent to prison went up, seemingly as a result of the law change but actually as a result of the underlying normative changes and the associated behavioral changes. The changes in sentencing patterns would have happened even if the Determinate Sentencing Law had not been adopted. That is what happened in the 1970s in many other states that did not radically overhaul their sentencing laws. Figures 5.10 and 5.11 tell the same story about the 1994 three-strikes law.

International Crime Trend Comparisons

In the preceding subsection I showed that there are good reasons to doubt that harsh crime control policies caused recent falls in the American crime rate. One way to test whether that is right is to compare U.S. crime trends in the 1990s with those in other countries. This can be done in two ways, and both suggest that U.S. crime trends correspond to those of other countries that did not adopt U.S.-style policies. Crime trends can be compared using trend data from the International Crime Victimization Survey. Crime and imprisonment rate data from the United States and Canada can be compared. Both these comparisons support the same two conclusions: U.S. crime rate trends closely parallel those of other Western countries, and crime rates move independently of imprisonment rates.

Figure 5.12 shows trends in total crime rates for five countries as shown by the International Crime Victimization Survey. Because the ICVS is repeated at three- and four-year intervals, the only data available are for the four surveys to date. Nonetheless, they show exactly the same trends as official data from these countries show. For the United States, rates rose from 1988 to 1991 and fell in 1995 and again in 1999. Other countries' downturns as shown in official data began later but by the mid-1990s crime rates were falling almost everywhere. And so figure 5.12 shows.

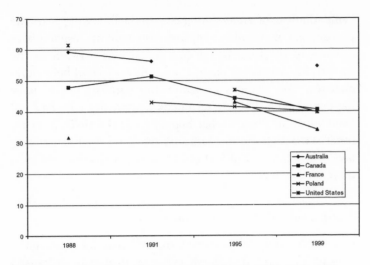

Figure 5.12 Trends in crime as measured by the ICVS, 1988, 1991, 1995, 1999 (offenses per 100 inhabitants)
Source: International Crime Victimization Survey, 1989, 1992, 1996, 2000.

Figure 5.13 shows homicide, robbery, and imprisonment rates per 100,000 population in Canada and the United States since the early 1980s. A 2001 report of the Canadian government statistics agency on "Crime Comparisons between Canada and the United States" observes in its opening paragraph: "Despite differences in rates, trends in crime between the two countries have been quite similar over the past twenty years" (Gannon 2001, p. 1). Violent crime rates in Canada are generally lower and property crime rates higher. Figure 5.13 shows homicide and robbery trends because both are serious offenses and trend data are not especially vulnerable to distortion by changes in recording practices. The patterns for the two offenses are the same in both countries: an early 1980s peak followed by a mid-1980s trough, followed by a second peak around 1990 and steady declines afterwards. Imprisonment rates, however, are starkly different. The Canadian rate was flat throughout the 1990s, falling to its lowest

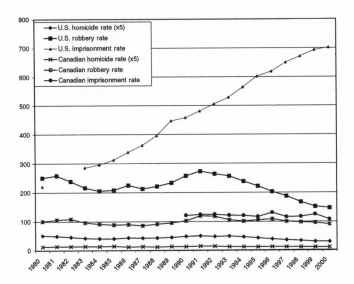

Figure 5.13 Violent crime and imprisonment rates for the United States and Canada (per 100,000 inhabitants)
Source: FBI: Uniform Crime Reports and Bureau of Justice Statistics; Canadian Centre for Justice Statistics.

level of the decade in 2000. The U.S. rate rose continuously. In 1990, the Canadian imprisonment rate was about a quarter of the American rate. In 2000 it was a seventh. And yet both countries experienced a decade-long decline in crime rates. It makes you wonder.

I draw two lessons from this survey of evidence on the effects of changes in crime control policy on crime rates and patterns, both consistent with this book's sensibilities theme. The first is that policy changes, and their putative effects, are both often the consequences of previous broad-based changes in social norms and attitudes. Such underlying changes in California in the 1970s explain why some people proposed and others enacted particular policies, and they explain why practices changed in particular ways before and after the law took effect. The three-strikes law was adopted in California and zero-tolerance policing in New York when they were because shifts in attitudes and norms made their adoption seem sensible and right and produced their effects.

The second lesson is that people were predisposed to believe the changes would produce their sought-after effects. Even though the continuation of preexisting trends hypothesis was at least as plausible as the hypothesis that the innovations "worked," only the latter seems to have occurred to those involved.

Put differently, changes in relevant sensibilities made the policy changes appear desirable, made achievement of their intended effects likely, and made critical assessment of the cause-and-effect processes unlikely.

Does Crime Policy Follow
Drug Policy Cycles?

Crime policies and practices are affected by changes in sensibilities in much the way drug policies are. Because, however, U.S. drug policy historians have documented three cycles in the past two centuries and crime historians describe only a single U- or reverse-J crime rate curve in the same period, followed by the 1960–90 crime rate rise, the analysis must be by analogy.

The validity of Musto's drug policy cycles analysis, first offered in the 1973 edition of his classic book *The American Disease*, can be tested against the events that followed. Here, again, are Musto's predictions of what happens after drug use peaks and begins to decline:

> [1] Public opinion turns against drugs and their acceptability begins to evaporate. [2] Gradually, drug use becomes associated, truthfully or not, with the lower ranks of society, and often with racial and ethnic groups that are feared or despised by the middle class. [3] Drugs become seen as deviant and dangerous and become a potent symbol of evil. [4] Trailing behind this decline come large-scale legislative and law enforcement efforts . . . aimed at cur-

tailing drug sales and use through energetic prohibition and enforcement and ever-harsher punishments against sellers and users. (Kagan 1989, p. 7)

Viewed as hypotheses, no informed person can seriously disagree that the four numbered propositions were confirmed. Here I pithily summarize.

Hypothesis 1: After drug use in the United States began a steep long-term decline in 1979–80, public opinion, evidenced by poll results and support for the War on Drugs, turned decisively against drugs and their acceptability.

Hypothesis 2: The disproportionate focus of antidrug efforts on racial and ethnic minority groups is shown by targeting of street-level drug law enforcement on minority, principally black, inner-city dealers, by stereotyping in the entertainment media, by a focus on crack cocaine sold by blacks rather than powder cocaine sold by whites, and by the disproportionate presence of blacks and Hispanics among imprisoned drug dealers.

Hypothesis 3: The hype and emotionalism of antidrug efforts demonstrate how drug use increasingly was perceived and portrayed as deviant and dangerous.

Hypothesis 4: Long after drug use began a steep decline in 1979–80, the federal Anti-Drug Abuse Act of 1986 established decades-long mandatory minimum sentences and the 100-to-1 crack/powder cocaine rule, in 1988 the first federal Drug Czar was authorized and the War on Drugs was declared, and in 1989 the arrest rate for drug crimes reached six times the 1980 level.

Figure 5.14 shows self-reported drug use data for people aged 12 to 17, and 18-to 25-year-olds from annual surveys sponsored by the federal government. The six curves represent the percentages of people in those two age groups who, over a quarter of a century, said they had used heroin, cocaine, or marijuana in the preceding year. For marijuana and heroin (and also, though not shown here, for amphetamines,

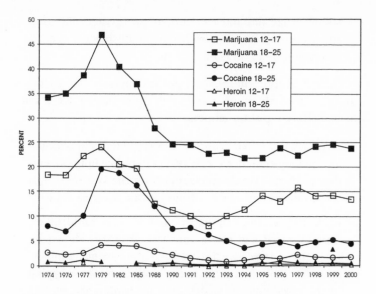

Figure 5.14 Estimated drug use by age group, selected years, 1974–2000

Source: Sourcebook of Criminal Justice Statistics.

alcohol, and nicotine) self-reported use peaked around 1980 and declined rapidly thereafter, eventually settling at much lower plateaus. The cocaine pattern is similar though the peak was a little later. Since the mid-1990s, rates have stabilized well below the peaks, and there were slight downturns in 2000.

That use of so many different addictive or dangerous substances peaked at about the same time is striking. Something in American sensibilities changed in the late 1970s. The effects of that change affected consumption not only of dramatically dangerous and deviant substances like cocaine but of butter, eggs, and whole milk, all things traditionally associated in American popular imagery with health and sturdiness. The sensibilities change certainly reflected heightened concern about personal health. Probably also it included a growing sense of the importance of personal responsibility for one's life and well-being, and growing judgmentalism about the weakness or irresponsibility of people who are dangerously self-indulgent and personally irresponsible.

All of these changing attitudes and beliefs fit Musto's model of changing sensibilities toward drug use, and they help explain both why hard drug use peaked when it did and began to decline, and why the predicted changes in beliefs and policies occurred. And they did occur. The harshest policies were not adopted until 1986, three-to-six years after use peaked, the first Drug Czar was appointed only in 1988, and the highest arrest rates for drug offenses were reached only in 1989.

If reduction in drug use, and its related social ills, were the primary aims of drug policy, America turned the corner in its drug war in 1979–80, nearly ten years before the Drug Czar arrived and policies became harshest. All of this is as Musto predicted, and it is not surprising if the drug war is seen not in instrumental terms but in expressive terms. Sensibilities affecting drug use changed, and the new policies expressed, reinforced, and celebrated the changes.

But there is more to figure 5.14, also consistent with Musto's predictions. He predicted that, after a period of increasing self-righteousness in public attitudes and zealousness in law enforcement, the tension would ease. Laws would be enforced less vigorously, policies become less stereotyped, and voices expressing concern about the side effects of antidrug policies or about the issues raised by drug use become louder.

Figure 5.14 shows this too. In 1988 Baltimore Mayor Kurt Schmoke began openly to call for reconsideration of U.S. drug policy and soon was followed by conservative intellectuals like Milton Friedman and William F. Buckley. More recently, and more vocally, conservative Republican New Mexico Governor Garry Johnson repeatedly called for fundamental reconsideration of U.S. drug policies. In 1995 the U.S. Sentencing Commission called for repeal of the 100-to-1 policy that punished mostly black sellers of 10 grams of crack

cocaine as severely as dealers of 1,000 grams of powder cocaine. In 1994 conservative Utah Republican Senator Orrin
Hatch began to call for reconsideration of mandatory minimum sentences, and in 1994 the U.S. Congress enacted
"safety-valve" legislation that reduced the severity of federal
drug law penalties for many first offenders; states such as
Washington enacted comparable laws.

Drug courts, premised on the ideas that treatment can work
and that drug dependence is a chronic relapsing condition,
were established in many states. Though most began as diversion programs for non-violent first offenders, as the decade
progressed many began to work with people with lengthy
records or charged with serious crimes. From the mid-1990s
onwards, referenda were adopted, initially in conservative
states like Arizona and California, permitting medical use
of marijuana, and in 2000 California again by referendum
adopted policies preferring referral of first- and second-time
drug offenders to treatment rather than to prosecution. Conservative New York Republican Governor Pataki has called
for and proposed substantial weakening of New York's notorious Rockefeller Drug Law. The tide, as Musto predicted
thirty years ago would happen, is turning.

So much for drugs. The question is whether patterns like
those Musto foresaw for drug policy are likely also to affect
crime policy. The answer is "yes," as figure 5.15 shows. Figure 5.15 presents the same data as figure 5.6 for homicide,
robbery, motor vehicle theft, and burglary rates from 1960
to 2000, except that it also shows high points in the toughening and softening of U.S. crime policies. It may be right to
consider U.S. crime rates to have peaked around 1980, perhaps not coincidentally when drug use peaked, even though
there was a five-year reversal in the late 1980s. The harshest
policies were adopted in the fifteen years after 1980. The
prison population grew unremittingly, initially because more
drug offenders were sent to prison but also because the
chances that offenders received a prison sentence grew enormously, and more recently because prison sentences became
much longer (Blumstein and Beck 1999). The federal manda-

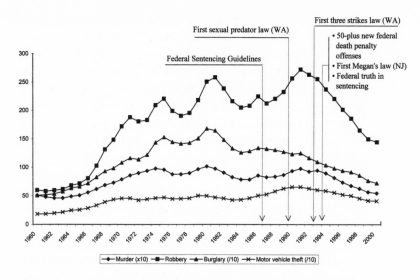

Figure 5.15 American violent-crime-rate pattern with policy changes

tory sentencing guidelines took effect in 1987. Under federal financial pressures more than half of the states adopted truth-in-sentencing laws requiring many violent and drug offenders to serve at least 85 percent of their sentences. In 1993 Washington State passed the first three-strikes-and-you're-out law. California's much broader law followed in 1994 and nearly half the remaining states followed within a year or two. In 1994 the U.S. Congress made the federal death penalty applicable to more than fifty additional offenses. Megan's laws requiring registration of sex offenders and providing notification of their presence spread across the country in the mid-1990s.

So the first part of Musto's post-peak model appears also to apply to crime. That is not surprising. It is easy to imagine parallel psychological, social, and political developments and comparable changes in sensibilities. Through the 1970s, for crime as for drugs, there was spirited debate about causes of unwanted behavior, about the comparative merits of treatment or punishment, and about the competing values that underlie policy choices, and there was deep pessimism about the likely effectiveness of state action. I describe in chapter 7 how now-nearly-forgotten debates raged in the 1970s about issues such as preventive detention and prosecutorial appeals of sentence that seem in retrospect almost quaint. Today it seems obvious to most people (though in both cases not to me) that offenders may fairly be held before trial because of additional crimes they might commit and that it is fair for prosecutors to appeal sentences they do not like.

During the 1970s, due process liberals were still arguing in the courts for greater procedural fairness for criminal defendants and still winning respectably often. The prisoners' rights movement was winning numerous victories in the courts. Sentencing reform initiatives were concerned primarily with equal and consistent treatment of offenders and proponents only occasionally claimed that changes would reduce crime rates. In other words, people were spiritedly disagreeing about the timeless questions of how collective interests in security and safety can be pursued while taking account of the legitimate interests of alleged offenders. That does not mean that due process liberals were winning most of the legislative and court battles or that law-and-order conservatives were mostly losing, but that disagreements were vocal and vigorous and it often was not obvious which side would win.

By the mid-1980s and continuing into the mid-1990s, the picture was very different. Open political debate on crime issues stopped. "Soft on crime" became the most damaging and dreaded epithet with which one electoral candidate could tar another. Rather than risk the near-certain defeat that label—if successfully attached—would bring, candidates competed to assure voters of their toughness. President Bill Clinton was one of many Democrats who eventually won congratulations for deciding not to let the Republicans get to his right on crime (S. Walker 1998; Friedman 1993). The effect of all this was that voices were stilled and opposition to policies that were seen as ham-fisted, cruel, or misconceived moved behind the closed doors of legislative committee rooms.

Capturing the ethos of the time, a senior U.S. Justice Department official, whose position gave her influence over funding of *Crime and Justice*, a scholarly journal Norval Morris and I started, once told us, "People are either for victims or for criminals," and, chillingly at the time, "you're for criminals." That forced choice is nonsense, but it was widely held to be necessary in the 1980s and early 1990s.

A human mind can coherently and responsibly contain the ideas that the fears and sufferings of victims should be recognized and sympathetically addressed, that alleged offenders should be treated fairly and sympathetically, and that both groups are entitled to be treated with concern and respect. Nonetheless, saying that in election campaigns and on legislative floors, and acting as if it were true, exposed politicians to the accusation that they were "for criminals," and few would take that risk.

The second half of Musto's post-peak hypothesis seems also to apply to crime. Just as is happening with drugs, monolithic anticriminal views are breaking down, and competing values are again being urged. In 1996 in *Koon v. United States*, 518 U.S. 81, the U.S. Supreme Court made application of federal guidelines less rigid and returned discretion to federal judges. In 1997 the California Supreme Court, all of its members appointed by conservative Republican governors, in *People v. Alvarez*, 14 Cal. 4th 968, fundamentally weakened California's three-strikes law by giving judges authority to decide it ought not to be applied in any particular case. In 2001 in *Andrade v. State*, 270 Fed. 3rd 743, a federal court of appeals held California's three-strikes law unconstitutional when applied to the case of a man convicted of a $150 theft from K-Mart. In July 2002 the California Supreme Court in *People v. Mower*, 122 Cal. Rptr. 2d 326 (200), held that California's medical-use-of-marijuana law precluded prosecution for possession or cultivation of marijuana by a qualified patient or physician. Throughout the criminal justice system, rehabilitative programs, especially concerning drugs, rapidly gained support and funding. Throughout the country, restorative and community justice programs were established at grassroots levels and within state and county bureaucracies. Most were concerned more with problem solving and dispute resolution than with punishment and blaming. Sentencing and sanctions systems are fragmenting in the United States.

Musto's cycles model thus equally well predicted the drug and crime policy progressions of the past century. If past be prologue, the model is likely also to predict future policy trends, if we let it. But, if we can learn from the distant and recent pasts, and come to a better understanding of the ways sensibilities are shaped, we may be able to do better and avoid the excesses that inevitably future generations will come to regret.

Moral panics had a role to play in the recent evolution of crime control and penal policy. Overall, the principal background to policy changes was the interaction between cycles, sensibilities, and policy. Against that backdrop, however, moral panics had much greater power, and longer term effects, than otherwise they might. Prevailing sensibilities provided especially rich soil in which to plant the most emotion-based crime control ideas of the past two decades.

In our time, cycles, sensibilities, and moral panics coincided in ways that produced current crime control and penal policies. Crime rates rose, and steeply, for an extended period. The world changed with globalization, economic restructuring, fundamental social changes, and increased population diversity. All these things raised fears and anxieties that were in part displaced to people (criminals) and things (crime and disorder) that were ready objects of hatred and derision.

How events would have unfolded had American crime rates not begun their sharp rise in the 1960s and their sharp fall more recently is unknowable. We do know, however, that horrible crimes have been committed in all periods and that moral panics and sustained periods of extraordinarily harsh crime and punishment policies have not always followed. Examples that come to mind in my no longer short life include Richard Speck's 1966 killings of eight nurses in Chicago, Richard Gacy's and Jeffrey Dahmer's separate killings of tens of vulnerable young men, the Tate-LaBianca killings by Charles

Manson and his followers. All of these were horrible crimes that filled people with horror and revulsion, but none has been memorialized in policy as Len Bias, Polly Klaas, and Megan Kanka have been.

Whatever did or did not happen in other times, we know what happened in our time and we have a good sense of why. Knowing these things, we should be able to devise ways to undo the excesses of recent crime control and punishment policies.

Contemporary penal sensibilities have led public officials to propose and support policies that would have been unthinkable in other recent times and in other countries today, even though they are commonplace in the United States, and have been enthusiastically supported by public officials, policy intellectuals, and the general public.

One way to show how much modern American policies differ from those in earlier times and other places is to note how often they call for imposition of disproportionate punishments. Most normative theories of punishment, and the punishment jurisprudences of most Western countries, attach importance to the ideas that more serious crimes warrant harsher punishments than do less serious crimes and that comparably serious crimes warrant comparably severe sanctions. This is often in shorthand referred to as the proportionality principle: punish like cases alike and unlike cases differently.

Proportionality in punishment is not a modern idea. From retributive and utilitarian premises that are often seen as nearly opposite, Immanuel Kant and Jeremy Bentham, the archetypes of the two principal contending modern views about punishment, both proposed that just punishments should be proportionate to the seriousness of crimes. Kant favored proportionality on a *lex talionis* principle. There is a moral imperative to punish wrongdoers in proportion to the nature of the wrong they have done. Bentham argued for proportionality as a way to optimize the deterrent effects of punishments. It was not only philosophers who thought proportionality important. Thomas Jefferson in 1776 averred:

"Punishments I know are necessary and I would provide them, strict and inflexible but proportioned to the crime," and proposed legislation to that end in the Virginia Assembly (N. Walker 1999, p. 39). Blackstone in his *Commentaries on the Laws of England* insisted that "punishment ought always to be proportioned to the particular purpose it is meant to serve, and by no means to exceed it" (N. Walker 1999, p. 40).

The principal disagreements in our time have been about details. People such as Andrew von Hirsch (1993) think that proportionality is the central moral value underlying any just punishment system and that the seriousness of the crime should be the primary determinant of punishment. Others such as Norval Morris (1974) think it is one among several important values and sets outer limits on justifiable punishments. Still others such as H. L. A. Hart (1968) think that proportionality ideas are important for practical reasons; a system that regularly imposed disproportionate punishments would defy conventional morality, create a sense of public insecurity, and lose credibility.

Classical utilitarians such as Jeremy Bentham (1843) argued that human rights claims based on moral ideas were "nonsense on stilts," that human happiness should be the measure of good policies, and that pursuit of abstract ideals like proportionality was not inherently important. Nonetheless, he urged that more serious crimes merit harsher punishments, to give offenders an incentive to choose to commit the less serious of possible alternate crimes, and that punishments should increase with the value or seriousness of the crime, so that the penalties for crimes would outweigh the likely benefits. He also urged a punishment-limiting principle of "parsimony": no punishment can be justified unless, taking account of both the criminal harms it might avert and the suffering it imposes on the offender, it produces net happiness or utility (Morris 1974; Tonry 1994).

Yet modern American punishment policies regularly require imposition of disproportionate penalties, and many policy makers and some influential scholars (Wilson 1995; Bennett, DiIulio, and Walters 1996) support them. Sentencing laws and guidelines in the federal system and in many states require harsher penalties for drug crimes than for many assaults, rapes, and homicides. California's three-strikes law demands twenty-five-year and longer sentences for some people convicted of trivial third felonies even though first-time rapists and robbers receive much shorter sentences.

Some people justify these policies on the rationale that punishments may legitimately reflect popular demand for vindictive and shaming punishments (e.g., Kahan 1998a, b), others (Bennett, DiIulio, and Walters 1996) on the rationale that public opinion demands harsh punishments and so be it. Putting Kahan's rationale differently, the important relationship is not between crime and punishment, or between punishment and public safety, but between punishment and public edification. This is a profoundly radical idea that removes any considerations of proportionality, fairness, or justice to the offender from the calculus. The public opinion argument is little less radical because, as the cycles and moral panic literatures discussed earlier make clear, public opinion can be impulsive, ill-considered, and cruel. Philosopher Ronald Dworkin argues that justice requires all people to be treated with "equal concern and respect" (Dworkin 1986). Punishment policies premised either on public appetites for debasement of offenders or on knee-jerk responses to opinion polls do not do that. Nor do policies that ignore proportionality concerns.

There is nothing inherently wrong with laws that punish repeat violent offenders more severely than first-timers, monitor the whereabouts of sex offenders, or treat one kind of drug trafficking more harshly than another. Reasonable people can differ about their desirability and their detailed provisions. However, during moral panics and the downswings in cycles of intolerance, many people tend to exaggerate the scale of problems, become self-righteous and intolerant, and support views and policies that in less hysterical times they would reject. Many people come to believe things that at other times they would not believe, and to say things that at other times they would not say.

We live in a time when a series of moral panics about sexual and violent crimes and about drugs have coincided with downturns in crime rates and drug use, which has meant that the short-term effects of moral panics have interacted with the effects of intolerant attitudes associated with periods of long-term decline in drug use and crime. Repressive contemporary policies are the result. The hitherto unthinkable became not only thinkable but also acceptable.

Law professor Dan Kahan, for example, has offered a number of policy proposals that would have been close to unthinkable thirty years ago. Below I discuss one of these—deliberate humiliation and debasement of offenders serving community penalties—at some length. Here I sketch another. Kahan has argued that the ex post facto principle, the idea that people should not be subject to criminal prosecution and punishment for actions that were legal when they occurred, is wrong and ethically unnecessary. The ex post facto principle has been uncontroversially accepted in Western countries as an ethical necessity since the Enlightenment. It has been embedded in every major human rights protocol, including the U.S. Constitution, most American state constitutions, the European Convention on Human Rights, and the United Nations Declaration on Human Rights. Kahan (1997) proposes that judges should be able to reinterpret existing laws so as to punish behaviors that were not criminal when they were committed. The logic is that a person who does something morally wrongful knows it, and if a judge retroactively decides to treat that act as a crime, so be it; the defendant should have known better and deserves what happens to him.

Kahan uses sexual exploitation—"sleep with me and I will support you and your children; otherwise, leave"—to illustrate his argument. Such stories strike emotional chords. It is not fair for people to manipulate others to obtain sexual intimacies, even though legislatures may not have made it criminal. And it is easy to empathize with vulnerable people. Kahan's logic, however, applies equally to retroactive criminalization of homosexuality, adultery, drug use, blasphemy, or sedition. Just as one judge could decide that use of economic pressures to win sexual favors is wrong, that the person exerting pressure should know it is wrong, and that laws should retrospectively be reinterpreted to make it criminal, another judge could decide that homosexual acts are wrong, known to be wrong, and should be treated as crimes. Few people would want to live in a society where judges held such powers.

The realms of right, ethical, moral, and legal conduct have never been perfectly congruent. If legislatures want to criminalize sexual intimacies with people subject to unusual psychological or economic pressures, that can be done. Legislative definition of wrongful conduct as criminal is the critical moment only after which citizens can fairly be presumed to know what actions constitute crimes.

Why have proposals such as Kahan's taken shape now? Because the sensibilities of our times have made it easier to be judgmental, to stereotype wrongdoers, and to look for punitive and authoritarian solutions to difficult problems. The past few decades have been a time of harsh penal sensibilities associated with declines in drug use and crime. With the passage of time, such proposals will again become unthinkable.

Changing sensibilities affect the ways we see and react to things, and how we think about them, but that does not necessarily mean that things we do under their influence will be bad or inhumane. Contemporary penal sensibilities may foster excessively vindictive and uncaring responses to crime and criminals, but they may also have made more constructive policy changes possible. Contemporary programs to address victims' interests and needs, for one example, and the move to criminalize domestic and marital violence, for another, may be products of contemporary penal sensibilities. I return to these more positive effects in the final paragraphs of this chapter. Here, however, my focus is on vindictive and inhumane policies.

What is "unthinkable" to one person may not be to another, so I offer examples in this chapter of modern policies that reject conventional views in the United States at other times and in other countries today. The first is the federal sentencing guidelines' "real offense sentencing" provision under which people are punished for crimes of which a jury acquitted them. Few people in other times and places would approve of punishing people for crimes of which they had been found "not guilty."

The second is a provision of the Virginia sentencing guidelines that, all else being equal, punishes young offenders, for example, 18-year-olds, more harshly than 35-year-olds. In all other Western countries today, and in every U.S. jurisdiction until recently, comparatively gentler handling of young offenders is or was generally believed to be wise and just.

The third is Professor Kahan's "punishment incommensurability" theory of punishment as debasement (Kahan 1997, 1998a, b). Kahan argues that community penalties cannot substitute for prison sentences because they are insufficiently debasing. Few informed people in other times and places would find such a proposition congenial.

The three examples are merely illustrative and were picked because they are largely unknown except among specialists. In discussing them I first describe them and then summarize the relevant scholarly literatures that might arguably support them. Lest it be thought that the three examples are aberrations or anomalies, of which every era has some, do not forget that they have occurred in a time when the United States is awash in overbroad and indiscriminate three-strikes, sexual psychopath, and truth-in-sentencing laws, innovations that have been widely emulated in no other countries (Tonry and Frase 2001).

Real Offense Sentencing

The real offense sentencing provisions of the federal sentencing guidelines direct judges to calculate sentences on the basis not only of offenses of which the defendant was convicted but also of offenses with which the defendant was not charged, for which charges were dropped or dismissed, and of which the defendant was acquitted. All these other offenses are to be taken into account if the judge decides the defendant committed them. In making this decision, the judge is not bound by the general criminal law standard that people can be found guilty only on the basis of proof "beyond a reasonable doubt." The decision need be made only on the basis of the much lower standard that applies to civil law matters, "more probably than not." This means the judge must punish a person even if the judge believes there is only a slightly better than fifty–fifty chance that he or she committed a crime at all.

Eighth Circuit Federal Court of Appeals Judge Philip Heaney described how real offense sentencing works:

> Under the guidelines, however, sentencing judges are routinely required to sentence offenders for "relevant conduct" which was not charged in an indictment or information and which was not admitted in a guilty plea or proved at trial. Indeed a court may also increase an offender's sentence for acts of which the offender was acquitted. Uncharged conduct need not be proved beyond a reasonable doubt, but only by a preponderance of the evidence. (Heaney 1991, p. 209)

Judge Heaney slightly understated the provision's force. Under the relevant guidelines, the judge, not "may," but "shall" take account of uncharged and acquitted conduct in setting the sentence.

Three things about this policy stand out. First, real offense sentencing involves a radical rejection of basic ideas of fairness. Affected offenders lose the benefit of the criminal law's requirement of proof beyond a reasonable doubt, the rules of evidence, and constitutional procedural protections. These are all devices created and intended to protect against the possibility, or at least reduce the likelihood, that innocent people will be convicted of crimes and made vulnerable to the consequent stigmatization and punishment. The safeguards for defendants in federal sentencing hearings, in which loss of liberty is in issue, are fewer and weaker than those for defendants in lawsuits about minor car accidents where, at most, money is at stake.

Second, a real offense sentencing policy exists in the federal sentencing guidelines and nowhere else in the United States or any other Western country. Every other American sentencing commission that considered adopting such a policy rejected it, sometimes as in Washington State (Boerner and Lieb 2001), expressly forbidding judges to take account of such alleged but unproven crimes. In other countries, including Australia (Freiberg 2001), appellate courts have explicitly forbidden sentencing judges to take such information into account.

This is not to say that judges do not sometimes take account of unproven criminal conduct when they impose sentences. Under the indeterminate sentencing systems that were common in the United States before 1980, judges were supposed to individualize sentences, and doing that was seen to require consideration of any information about the offender that the judge thought relevant. And it would be hard not to expect that a judge who thought one defendant had assaulted a spouse just once under great stress and another had done so many times would take that difference into account in deciding what to do. The critical difference is that the federal guidelines require judges to do so. Indeterminate sentencing allowed them to do so.

Third, despite real offense sentencing's radical nature, neither the U.S. Sentencing Commission nor the federal appellate courts have shown much ambivalence about it. Objections to real offense sentencing have been frequent and vocal since the U.S. Sentencing Commission issued its first proposed draft guidelines, but the commission has never indicated that the policy might or would be reconsidered. Federal appellate courts, including the Supreme Court, have squarely upheld it, even in relation to offenses of which defendants had been acquitted.

Section 1B1.3 of the federal guidelines provides that sentences "shall" be calculated on the basis of the offender's "relevant conduct," or as the commission called it in explaining the provision, his "actual offense behavior." The rationale was that the relevant conduct approach would offset efforts by prosecutors to manipulate the guidelines. The federal guidelines are expressed in a two-axis grid. One axis is a scale of offense severity, the other of past criminal record. The sentence should be selected from within a narrow range indicated in the cell at which the two scales intersect. The prosecutor's ability to select and dismiss charges can determine which cell in the grid governs a particular case and thereby can greatly narrow the judge's choices. If, however, because of the real offense sentencing policy, neither filing nor dismissing charges necessarily affects the sentence that may be imposed, the prosecutor in theory will have less influence. In practice, the commission's sacrifice of defendants' protections did not work; prosecutors gained power under the federal guidelines (Heaney 1991; Schulhofer and Nagel 1997).

Statutory sentence maxima are the only absolute constraint on the relevant conduct provision. If, for example, the statutory sentence maximum for the charge of conviction is sixty months, the applicable guideline range for that offense is forty to forty-six months, and the applicable guideline range for all relevant conduct is 108 to 110 months, no sentence longer than sixty months may be imposed.

The U.S. Supreme Court has upheld the constitutionality of real offense sentencing in general (*Witte v. United States*, 515 U.S. 389 [1995]) and in the case of offenses of which the defendant was acquitted (*United States v. Watts*, 519 U.S. 148 [1997]). The rationale in *Witte v. United States*, on the basis of *Williams v. New York*, 337 U.S. 241 (1949), is that it was always so. In the rehabilitation-premised era of indeterminate sentencing, judges could take account of anything they deemed relevant in making an individualized decision in a particular case. That was the rationale of *Williams v. New York*. The Supreme Court, however, seemed untroubled by the segue from the court *may* take account in order to individualize, to the court *shall* take account even though it may not individualize.

Every state that adopted sentencing guidelines, and the American Bar Association's Standards on Sentencing, rejected real offense sentencing. There were two reasons: the Caesar's wife notion that justice should not only be done but be seen to be done and the practical objection that it would not reduce the power of prosecutors—plea bargaining prosecutors and defense lawyers will devise ways to defeat it (Tonry 1996, chap. 3). The evidence on the latter point is clear. From the guidelines' earliest days (Federal Courts Study Committee 1990) through their early maturity (Nagel and Schulhofer 1992) to their maturity (Schulhofer and Nagel 1997), observers have agreed that the federal guidelines shifted power to, not from, prosecutors. Most cases are disposed of by negotiated plea agreements and various features of federal sentencing law and policies have strengthened the prosecutors' hand. In other words, real offense sentencing was unlikely to work and has not worked. When I describe federal real offense sentencing to U.S. lawyers who are unaware of it, or to lawyers and judges outside the United States, the reaction is always a combination of disbelief, disapproval, and disdain.

Youth as an Aggravating Circumstance

In Virginia, youth is an aggravating circumstance that increases the likelihood that a convicted person will be sentenced to imprisonment. This stands on its head the mainstream view for most of this century in the United States and most Western countries that youth is a mitigating circumstance. The juvenile court, however beleaguered in our time by changes in age eligibility and waiver-to-adult-court laws, still exists in every American jurisdiction and is premised on notions that kids are different and should be treated differently (Feld 1999). In Sweden, Finland, and much of Northern Europe, the age of criminal responsibility, the age at which acts can be treated as criminal, is 15 (Janson 2004; Kyvsgaard 2004). Older teenagers are dealt with by the regular criminal courts, but most are sentenced to special programs for young offenders and all are entitled to have the severity of their sentences reduced because of their age. Social welfare agencies deal with what would otherwise be crimes by youngsters under 15; as a legal matter, their wrongful acts are not crimes. In New Zealand, most juvenile cases must be handled by means of consensual restorative processes (Morris 2004). In Scotland, youth justice remains a branch of the social welfare system (Bottoms and Dignan 2004). Virginia's approach is unique.

Rationales for why children should be treated more sympathetically and gently than adults have varied over time and space and between people. Sometimes the argument is that young people are morally immature and, for that reason, less fully responsible for their actions. Sometimes it is that young people are developmentally immature and thus more malleable and "amenable to treatment." Sometimes it is that many people do things as teenagers, because they are teenagers, that they will later regret, and that aging is all that is needed to turn most into law-abiding citizens. Criminal records would damage them and their life chances for no good reason. Whatever the rationale, even the most aggressive attacks on the juvenile court—in laws that make it easier for juvenile court judges or prosecutors to waive young offenders to the adult courts, laws that remove some offenses from juvenile court jurisdiction altogether whatever the defendant's age, and laws that reduce the maximum age jurisdiction of the juvenile court from 17 to something younger—leave a large majority of cases traditionally handled by juvenile courts within the courts' jurisdiction (Zimring 1982, 1989; Bishop 2000). Virginia's sentencing commission, however, rejected the view that young people should receive different and gentler handling.

Explaining what Virginia policy makers did requires a close look at Virginia's guidelines. The guidelines, like all U.S. sentencing guidelines, specify whether a prison sentence should be imposed and, if so, for how long. Like the federal guidelines, the Virginia guidelines can be set out in a grid.

The recommended sentence is shown in the cell at which the applicable offense severity row and criminal record column intersect.

However, for people sentenced for drug offenses (14,193 in 1997), larceny (8,817), and fraud (4,725), a separate scoring sheet indicated who among them should be sentenced to a community punishment like probation or community service rather than to a prison sentence. This is an important provision, since those three offenses constituted nearly three-fourths (71 percent) of sentenced cases in 1997 (Virginia Criminal Sentencing Commission 1997, p. 22). The scoring sheet assigned points to various of the offender's characteristics. Some, such as prior arrests, convictions, and incarcerations, relate to the offender's past criminality. Others, such as sex, age, marital status, and employment record, relate to personal characteristics. A number of Virginia policy choices might be questioned. Being male, unmarried, and unemployed warrant "points" that increase the likelihood of imprisonment. Many people might believe it unfair to punish someone more harshly for those reasons.

Age counts against a defendant's chances of avoiding prison in two ways. It is important to know that in 1997 "nine points" was the cut line above which the guidelines specify offenders should be sent to prison. First, the younger the offender, the more points. An offender who is 19 or under receives six points, and the number of points then declines with advancing age: 20 to 27 (four points), 28 to 33 (three points), 34 or older (no points). Second, any prior juvenile commitment or incarceration counts four points. Thus, a 17-year-old (six points) who previously was committed to a juvenile institution (four points) receives ten points and should go to prison. Being unemployed (one point), unmarried (one point), and male (one point) also add points, so the 17-year-old described in the preceding sentence with those characteristics (most will have them), receives thirteen points, well above the nine-point cutoff. Even without a prior juvenile commitment or incarceration, most 17-year-old drug or larceny defendants will be unemployed, unmarried, male, and pointed by the guidelines toward prison. So much for any ideas in Virginia that young offenders deserve special tolerance, solicitude, or the benefit of the doubt.

The juvenile aggravators are even more striking when compared with other factors that get scored. No other factor is weighted more heavily than being under age 28 and few as heavily as a prior juvenile court record. The four points assigned for a *single* juvenile commitment dwarfs those for more serious records. Having *four or more* felony convictions, for example, counts for three points. Having been incarcerated as an adult *five or more times* counts as three points.

Compare two hypothetical offenders. An unemployed (one point), male (one point), 18-year-old (six points) drug offender who served a one-week juvenile commitment when 15 (four points), totals twelve points, and should go to prison. An unemployed (one point), male (one point), 35-year-old (no points), drug offender with four prior felony convictions (three points) and five prior adult incarcerations (three points) totals eight points and should be diverted from prison. Most people, knowing no more, would doubt that most 18-year-olds with a minor juvenile record should be sent to an adult prison, but acknowledge that some possibly should. My guess, however, is that few people would have equal ambivalence about a 35-year-old with the record described.

There is a logic to the Virginia policies that derives from the Virginia guidelines' "selective incapacitation" rationale (Virginia Criminal Sentencing Commission 1997, pp. 41–52). If the only concern at sentencing were prediction of future offending, if matters of fairness, justice, and youth policy were deemed not relevant, Virginia's antiyouth policies might make sense. At least three robust research findings are relevant.

First, criminal careers research instructs that most active offenders age out of criminality by their mid-thirties (Blumstein et al. 1986). Thus, 35-year-olds are less likely than younger offenders to reoffend. This "justifies" the seeming anomaly that older offenders with lengthy records receive no aggravating points.

Second, developmental research in the United States and other countries instructs that there are distinct age-crime curves, with the prevalence of offending peaking in the mid-teens for property offending and in the late teens for violent offenders, with rapid drop-offs after the peaks (Farrington 1986). Thus, the older the (young) offender, the more likely that he or she will soon desist from crime. This "justifies" the anomaly that the aggravating points are inversely related to the offender's age.

Third, developmental research also shows that early onset of serious delinquency is a strong predictor of both seriousness and continuation of offending (Tremblay and Craig 1995). The specialized vocabulary of this literature distinguishes between "adolescence-limited" offenders and "life-course persisters" (Howell and Hawkins 1998). The former are wild-oats teenagers for whom delinquency is a short-term developmental phase and the latter are more persistent offenders whose delinquency extends into adulthood. For young offenders believed to be "adolescence-limited," the smartest course often is to let them alone, turn them over to their parents, or deal with them informally. They will most likely grow up to be law-abiding. Stigmatizing them with a juvenile or criminal record may lessen the odds that will happen. An early onset of delinquency, however, is one characteristic that often distinguishes life-course persisters from adolescence-limited offenders, even though many people who commit offenses when young soon stop. This, arguably, "justifies" the heavy weight given to a juvenile record.

Many objections could be raised to the Virginia scheme. Punishing people more severely because they are male violates gender-neutrality norms. Punishing people more severely because they are unmarried penalizes people as a consequence of an inherently personal choice that most people would ordinarily insist is not the state's business. Punishing people because they are unemployed may injure those already disadvantaged by lack of marketable skills, mental disabilities, or high unemployment rates. Giving greater punitive weight to offenders' ages than to their past criminality violates basic and widely shared culpability notions.

But most strikingly, counting peoples' youth against them rather than for them sacrifices individual lives and futures in the interest of aggregate statistical predictions. None of the three bodies of knowledge on which Virginia's policy ostensibly rests supports it. First, criminal careers research shows that the vast majority of offenders desist from crime by their mid-twenties, so Virginia's guidelines will result in many offenders being held long after they would have ceased offending anyway.

Second, the age-crime curves tell us that the highest offending rates are in the mid- to upper teenage years and that most young offenders soon desist.

Third, the distinction between adolescence-limited offenders (the large majority of young offenders) and life-course persisters (a handful) is real, but based on hindsight. Examinations of the records of 25-year-olds who committed crimes as 16- and 17-year-olds make it clear that most desisted from offending and a few did not. Looked at from the other way round, we can not know who among current 16- and 17-year-old offenders will persist and who will not. We can make predictions, based on individuals' personal characteristics, but those predictions are not very good. Among those predicted at 16 to be persisters, most will not be (Blumstein et al. 1986).

It is important to remember that Virginia's distinctive youth-as-an-aggravating-circumstance sentencing policy has nothing to do with moral ideas about offenders' culpability or the seriousness of their crimes. All else equal, including the crimes people commit and their past records, the Virginia policy treats younger people more harshly. In adopting it, the Virginia commission was interested only in incapacitation, and considerations of just treatment of offenders were beside the point. The policy premise for punishing teenagers more harshly than middle-aged adults was "selective incapacitation."

Selective incapacitation was an idea that was promoted in the early 1980s on the basis of RAND Corporation research headed by Peter Greenwood (Greenwood with Abrahamse 1982) that claimed to show that researchers could successfully identify high-rate serious offenders. If true, adoption of selective incapacitation policies would have permitted jurisdictions to increase sentence lengths for high-rate offenders while reducing sentence lengths for other offenders and, overall, reducing prison populations and costs. The only difficulty, as the National Academy of Sciences (Blumstein et al. 1986) soon showed, was that his predictions were based, like those concerning "life-course persisters," on hindsight. Used prospectively, the predictions were too inaccurate to be relied upon and would have resulted in lengthy confinement of many people who would not have committed serious crimes in the future.

How could Virginia policy makers have adopted so regressive a policy and one so unjustifiable on the basis of available knowledge? Part of the answer is political ideology. The commission's initial chair was former U.S. Attorney General William Barr, an outspoken proponent of harsh punishment policies. But why would such a person have been made chair of a state sentencing commission, and why would other members of the Virginia Sentencing Commission have allowed such policies to be adopted? The temper of the times, the prevailing penal sensibilities, permitted Virginia policy makers to ignore the demonstrated failures of selective incapacitation as a policy option, to ignore traditional notions about appropriate handling of young offenders, and to adopt policies that treat children more severely than adults.

Disintegrative Shaming

Professor Kahan's "shaming" (1998a, pp. 1639–43) or "punishment incommensurability" (1998b, pp. 691–708) argument is the strangest of the three examples. Twenty years ago, Kahan's arguments on disintegrative shaming, like those mentioned earlier on ex post facto laws, would have been widely considered bizarre. In our time, they won him appointments at two of America's pre-eminent law schools, the University of Chicago and Yale. Though he has written about shaming repeatedly and at great length, the basic argument can be briefly summarized. Punishment is not, as most people who write about punishment theory suppose, primarily about attributions of culpability and imposition of deserved punishments, or primarily about crime prevention, but about shaming. Most writers about punishment do not understand this, he says, and if they hope ever to influence policy must accept that punishments should "unambiguously express disgust" of the offender (Kahan 1998a, p. 1656). Explaining, for example, that community penalties will not win public favor until they are made more debasing, he compares them unfavorably with imprisonment:

> Prison, in contrast, does unequivocally evince disgust. . . . By stripping individuals of liberty—a venerated symbol of individual worth in our culture—and by inflicting countless other indignities—from exposure to the view of others when urinating and defecating to rape at the hand of other inmates—prison unambiguously marks the lowness of those we consign to it. (Kahan 1998, p. 1642)

Elsewhere, he writes that offenders should be subjected to "intrinsically repulsive," "degrading," or at least "effectively stigmatizing" punishments and that, for example, community service should be renamed "shameful service" (1998a, p. 706).

So far as I can tell, these ideas derive from two intellectual developments of recent decades, both of which Kahan misunderstands or misinterprets. The first is increased attention to the norm-reinforcing, moral-educative, and expressive effects of punishment that in earlier chapters I associated with Émile Durkheim. Until the last ten years, most scholarly writing on punishment was by lawyers and philosophers, and they tended to concentrate on procedures and policies as they affected the convicted offender standing before the judge, or on the possible crime-reductive effects of particular sentences or policies. Since then, precipitated by sociologist David Garland's (1990) writing on the sociology of punishment and psychologist Tom Tyler's work on procedural justice (1990, 2003), much more attention has been given to the broader normative and social-psychological effects of punishment.

The second development Kahan apparently misconceives is the growing and increasingly subtle literature on public understanding and opinion about punishment (Roberts et al. 2002). This shows broadly that the general public believes sentences are too lenient, but it also shows that public opinion is based on misconceptions of crime and punishment attributable to media concentration on exceptional cases, that judges' sentences are harsher than the public realizes, that the sentences citizens say they would prefer are less severe than are actually imposed, and that there is widespread support for rehabilitative programs and community penalties.

Kahan is an appropriate figure on whom to focus because, more than any other contemporary American writer, he offers views about criminal justice policy that seem best understood in terms of prevailing penal sensibilities. It is hard to imagine how else they could be explained. Besides his proposals concerning abrogation of the ex post facto doctrine and degradation as a penal strategy, he has offered two other equally radical proposals. First, he proposed elimination of the centuries-old doctrine of strict construction of penal statutes (Kahan 1997). That doctrine, because of the importance of individual liberty, requires criminal statutes to be narrowly construed, with all interpretive ambiguities construed in favor of the individual. The maxim that it is better that ten guilty people go free than that one innocent be convicted is another emanation of the same underlying idea. Second, Kahan has vigorously and outspokenly supported efforts to give police authority to forbid poor young inner-city blacks from gathering peacefully on the streets (Kahan and Meares 1998; Meares and Kahan 1997).

I discuss the intellectual backdrop to Kahan's disintegrative shaming analysis in some detail to make a general point and a specific point. The specific point is that, looked at with any care, existing systematic knowledge and research findings provide no credible evidentiary base for Kahan's proposals. The general point, however, is that proposals such as Kahan's make perfect sense, of a sort, in the context of the penal sensibilities of the last ten years.

Expressive Punishments

Three major literatures—in philosophy, criminal law theory, and sociology—have revived interest in expressive punishments. Philosophers have developed communicative theories in which a central aim of punishment is to express to the offender the wrongfulness of his or her behavior. Criminal law theorists have emphasized the role of criminal punishments in reinforcing or undermining social norms. Sociologists have investigated ways in which official responses to crime shape the ways offenders perceive the integrity of the system and have argued that more respectful, nurturing, and holistic approaches may increase offenders' prospects for achieving law-abiding lives.

Communicative Theories of Punishment The first is the development in the philosophical literature, exemplified by the writings of Antony Duff (2000), Joel Feinberg (1970), Jean Hampton (1984), and Jeffrie Murphy (1985), of "communicative" theories of punishment. All of these are moral theories, premised on respect for the moral autonomy of the offender, in Dworkin's (1977, p. 227) terms showing "equal respect and concern" for each offender, and call in various ways for punishment to express to the offender the wrongfulness of his acts.

The prevailing image is of a judge, looking deeply into an offender's eyes, more in sorrow than in anger, and wanting to help her understand why what she has done is wrong. If it works, the offender will come to understand that she was temporarily distracted from right values by egoism, emotion, or impulse, and be ready to reclaim her place among right-thinking people. This will not happen because she was bullied, threatened, or brainwashed, but because as a morally autonomous person she now understands that, and why, her actions were wrong.

There are differences in view among philosophers working within the communicative punishment tradition as to whether the aim is solely to express norms to the offender, so that she as a morally responsible actor can come to understand the wrongfulness of her acts, or whether in addition there is a collateral aim through punishment to express norms to the general community as bystander. There are differences in view as to whether her regret, repentance, contrition, or remorse is a sufficient outcome or whether, for her sake or the larger society's, some material punishment should also be imposed or borne. There is also a question of how offenders who are insensitive, defiant, or impervious to moral reasoning should be handled. However, nowhere in this literature are there indications that the aim of punishment should be to express disgust of the offender or to debase her in order to placate public opinion. That, in the conventional Kantian language, would be to use the offender merely as a means, and that is something no mainstream moral theory would allow (N. Walker 1991).

Moral-Educative Theories of Punishment A second relevant punishment literature derives from the Durkheimian functionalist notion that the criminal law serves to identify and reinforce basic social ideas about right and wrong, that "crime brings together upright consciences and concentrates them." The Norwegian writer Johannes Andenaes (1974), who wrote about the "moral-educative functions" of the criminal law, was influential in reviving interest in such views. The criminal law is seen as performing a dramaturgical function, with punishment directed primarily at the community and not at the offender. Crime is a part of every human society, possibly a necessary part, a functional mechanism that helps set and then illuminate and reinforce the boundaries of acceptable behavior. The primary aim of punishment is to restate and reinforce prevailing norms: "[Punishment] does not serve, or else serves only secondarily, in correcting the culpable, or in intimidating possible followers. From this point of view, its efficacy is justly doubtful and, in any case, mediocre. Its true function is to maintain social cohesion intact" (Durkheim 1933 [orig. 1893], p. 108).

There has been a revival of interest in Durkheimian ideas about punishment in Germany and Scandinavia, as an alternative to retributive and utilitarian ideas. Influential elaborations of such views have been offered by Finnish writers Patrik Törnudd (1997) and Tapio Lappi-Seppälä (2001) under the name "general prevention," and in Germany by Bernd Schünemann under the name "positive general prevention" (Schünemann 1998). Both traditions distinguish their neo-Durkheimian ideas from Anglo-American "(negative) general prevention," which operates through the utilitarian processes of deterrence, incapacitation, and rehabilitation (Hart 1968).

The German and Scandinavian ideas emphasize that punishment has an important role to play in setting and reinforcing norms, but it is a secondary role. For the most part, extraordinary circumstances aside, people do or do not commit crimes because of the socialization they do or do not receive from primary institutions such as the home, the family, the church, the school, and the community. The primary work of crime prevention must be done in those places. It is important that the criminal law confirm basic behavioral norms, and be seen to do so, but the primary work must be done elsewhere. This has important, perhaps to most Americans surprising, implications.

First, because the law should perform its back-up role, it is important that criminal acts have penal consequences. As a result, although the Finns, Swedes, and other Scandinavians have among the lowest imprisonment rates in the world, expressed in terms of people in prison on an average day per 100,000 residents, they have among the highest prison admission rates in the developed world, expressed in terms of the number of people per 100,000 admitted to prison in a year (Young and Brown 1993; Kommer 1994).

Second, because the law should perform its back-up role, it is important that punishments be commensurate with the gravity of the offenses for which they are imposed. Put differently, proportionality is a first principle; unless more serious crimes receive harsher penalties and less serious crimes lesser ones, the law's normative messages will be morally incoherent and contradict the primary norm-setting processes (Lappi-Seppälä 2001).

Third, there is no reason to expect changes in the severity of penalties to be effective or desirable. If primary institutions play the major socialization roles, and punishment can only marginally reinforce or undermine prevailing norms, it would be unrealistic to imagine that changes in the severity of sanctions can have much effect. Patrik Törnudd (1997, p. 190) thus observed, "A strong belief in general prevention as the guiding rationale of the criminal justice system thus does not imply that changes in policy, such as increases in the severity of punishment, would widely be seen as an appropriate or cost-effective means of controlling crime."

Once again, there is nothing here, express or implied, about debasement, disgust, or stigmatization. Indeed, since Northern European countries take seriously the European Torture Convention's prohibition of inhumane and degrading punishments (Evans and Morgan 1998; Morgan 2001), it would be surprising if there were.

Reintegrative Shaming "Reintegrative shaming" is a reconceptualization of punishment proposed by Australian criminologist John Braithwaite (Braithwaite 1989, 2001). The proposal is simultaneously a hypothesis that restorative responses to criminal offenders might have greater crime-reducing effects than criminal justice responses and a normative argument that reintegrative processes are more humane and respectful of human dignity.

Braithwaite's notion is that reactions to crime should simultaneously express disapprobation and support, in much the same way as parents communicate to children that they have misbehaved but that they are still loved. The "shaming" communicates through disapproval the importance of the norms or expectations that were violated but in a way that also communicates respect for the individual and concern for her well-being, and is therefore "reintegrative." This is contrasted with the destructive shaming of the traditional criminal justice system that ostracizes, alienates, and often breeds defiance or leads to rejection of pro-social norms and attachment to antisocial ones. Braithwaite (1999, 2001) has proposed a number of reasons why traditional criminal justice approaches are likely to be less effective at socializing offenders and preventing crime than are reintegrative approaches.

Even this brief summary should make it clear that Braithwaite's affirmative theories of shaming have nothing in common with Kahan's proposals which, to the contrary, embody, even celebrate, the kind of destructive processes that Braithwaite decries.

Public Knowledge and Opinion

The second growing literature that might support Kahan's ideas, but does not, concerns public knowledge and opinion about punishment. In particular, Kahan cites a study by Canadian psychologists Anthony Doob and Voula Marinos (1995) of Canadians' support for the use of fines as punishments for various crimes. A majority of respondents indicated that, for many crimes, a fine would not be a normatively appropriate substitute for imprisonment. Tom Tyler and Robert Boeckmann's (1997) study of reasons (primarily "expressive") why ordinary people support three-strikes laws even though there are sound reasons to doubt their instrumental effectiveness offers comparable findings: imposing a lengthy prison sentence for a third violent crime sends a message people believe should be sent. Hans Boutellier (2000) and Joseph Kennedy more recently (2000) argue that punishment and crime control policy should be understood in our time as having primarily expressive functions. Kahan (1998b), drawing on a hodgepodge of newspaper clippings and letters to the editor as authority, makes similar arguments about community service.

There are serious problems with Kahan's claim that public support for punishment practices requires disintegrative shaming. It is poorly informed. A large literature shows that public attitudes are much more complex and less single-mindedly vengeful than he suggests (Roberts et al. 2002). It is overbroad. Even if nonincarcerative punishments for some very serious crimes would, in Model Penal Code language, "unduly depreciate the seriousness of the offense," most crimes are not that serious. It is parochial. In many Western countries, fines and community service are commonly used as sanctions for quite serious, including violent and sexual, crimes (Albrecht 2001; Lappi-Seppälä 2001; Tak 2001).

Under-Informed The large multinational public opinion literature offers much more complicated findings than Kahan suggests (Roberts 1992; Hough and Roberts 1997; Roberts et al. 2002). Surveys consistently show that the general public believes that the average crime is more serious than it is, substantially underestimates the severity of punishments imposed, and generally supports punishments less severe than are now imposed. The public has ambivalent views about punishment, wanting offenders to be punished for their crimes but, believing that social disadvantage and drug dependence are primary causes of offending, also wanting (and being willing to pay for) offenders to be rehabilitated. Finally, for all but the most serious crimes and the most incorrigible criminals, the public is willing to have criminals sentenced to community penalties in place of prison, so long as the community penalty is burdensome or restitutive (community service or work release coupled with restitution are okay, house arrest without more is not). Thus, while there is something to be said for Kahan's claim that the public wants symbolically appropriate punishments, that by itself is a partial and misleading summary of the evidence. None of the major scholars of public opinions and attitudes about crime interprets the preference for symbolically appropriate sentences as a demand for shaming punishments.

There is substantial evidence of public support for wider use of community services in place of incarceration for many kinds of offenders because it satisfies symbolic demands for punishments that are burdensome and express right values, and is in an important sense restitutive (Doble 1997; Doble and Immerwahr 1997; Farkas 1997; Begasse 1997). To the contrary, community service is a sanction that Kahan argues must be made "degrading," "stigmatizing," "shameful," and "intrinsically repulsive" if it is to win public support (1998*b*, p. 706).

Overbreadth Even if Kahan were right that the public insists on only prison sentences for violent crimes, most people now admitted to prisons have not been convicted of violence. In 1996, for example, of people committed to state prisons, 29.3 percent had been convicted of violent crimes, 29 percent of property crimes, 30.2 percent of drug crimes, and 11.3 percent of something else. In federal prisons the percentages, for the same categories in 1997 were 11.9 percent, 5.6 percent, 60.1 percent, and 22.4 percent. Among convicted jail inmates in 1996, the corresponding percentages were 21.8 percent, 28.6 percent, 23.7 percent, and 25.9 percent. The public opinion evidence summarized in the preceding paragraph shows that for the nearly 80 percent of people sentenced to prison for nonviolent crimes, there is broad support for increased use of nonincarcerative sanctions that do not debase.

Parochialism Experience in other countries suggests that the public would be willing to accept fines and community service as prison substitutes for all but the most serious crimes. Throughout Scandinavia and Germany, for example, day fines are the modal sanction. Day fines are penalties that take into account some measure of the offender's earnings or wealth, usually a day's net pay, and the seriousness of his crime. A moderately severe crime might generate a fine of thirty days' net pay. Day fines are used in these countries as punishments for most crimes, including many violent and sexual crimes and especially property crimes (Weigend 1997; Jareborg 2001; Albrecht 2001). In England, Scotland, and Holland, community service was established to serve as an alternative to prison sentences for moderately severe crimes and is used in that way (Pease 1985; McIvor 1995; Tak 2001).

Kahan's arguments for disintegrative shaming are not deducible from any of the important recent developments concerning expressive punishments or research on public opinion about crime and punishment. What is left is an idiosyncratic argument that offenders should be subjected to debasing, degrading punishments because, Kahan apparently believes, offenders have "failed to internalize society's moral norms" and populist appetites, however well- or ill-informed, would thereby be appeased or gratified.

All the consequences of penal sensibilities such as characterized the 1980s and 1990s need not be bad. Heightened willingness to adopt moralistic postures, harnessed properly, can be used to achieve positive social goals. The feminist movement has greatly sensitized Americans to issues of sexual exploitation and urged greater use of the law to address gender-related abuses of power and violence. Before the 1970s, people who were social policy liberals, and hence likely to be concerned with gender equity issues, were also likely to be due process liberals, and hence uncomfortable with criminal justice solutions to social policy problems that treated offenders harshly. By the 1980s, criminalization of domestic violence became a central plank in the feminist platform (Zimring 1989) and led to calls for mandatory arrest policies for alleged domestic assault misdemeanors. Reasonable people can differ, of course, as to when the criminal law should be invoked and for what kinds of cases. Since contemporary penal sensibilities make overreliance on the criminal law a recurring risk, it is possible that criminal law is being overused in our time as a response to domestic violence and that other, more nuanced, approaches in many cases would do more good and less harm.

Likewise, the modern victims' movement may owe much of its success to prevailing penal sensibilities. No informed person doubts that the victims' movement has enhanced attention to victims' interests and mobilized new resources to address victims' needs. There is no good reason why concern for fair handling of offenders implies lack of concern for victims, but it is clear that the contemporary victims' movement dates only from the 1970s. Before that, little programmatic or policy attention was given to victims issues. The overreactions associated with contemporary penal sensibilities predisposed advocates to the nonsensical view that they must be both "for" victims and "against" criminals. That dualism is not inexorable and may be moderating. As with the domestic violence movement, contemporary sensibilities appear to have mobilized and energized the victims' movement.

On balance, though, the most dramatic products of contemporary sensibilities have been negative. None of the three policies and proposals principally discussed in this chapter could have been seriously put forward in the 1950s or the 1960s. The penal sensibilities of those decades were, as the next chapter demonstrates, radically different. These three policy ideas, however, stand as a stark warning about what can happen when, during a cyclical period of heightened intolerance of offenders and drug users, policy makers lose their senses of humility and proportion and lose sight of timeless values.

7

Unthought Thoughts

Just as there are bad ideas and regrettable policies in contemporary America that are best understood as underconsidered outgrowths of contemporary penal sensibilities, there are ideas and policies, formerly so mainstream as not in their own times seriously to be questioned, that have all but disappeared. There are also ideas that are so much a part of contemporary sensibilities as seldom to be questioned, yet they seem nearly absent in other times.

Lots of examples could be offered of issues and ways of thinking that are common in particular times and conspicuously absent in others. Two issues, preventive detention and prosecutorial sentence appeals, which due process liberals and crime control conservatives fought over in the 1970s, provide examples. The preventive detention question was whether people charged with crimes could be held in jail until trial because they were believed to be dangerous and likely to commit an offense while free on bail. Until the 1970s, the conventional view was that, with one legitimate and one illegitimate exception, the only reason to deny bail was because the defendant was believed likely otherwise to run away. The legitimate exception was for capital cases, cases in which capital punishment was a possible punishment. The illegitimate exception concerned cases in which the judge wanted the defendant held in jail and, lacking a valid reason for doing that, purposely set the bail higher than the defendant could pay. The sentence appeal question was whether prosecutors should or constitutionally could be allowed to appeal sentences they did not like.

Most academic observers at the beginning of the 1970s would have expected due process liberals to win both debates. Both were issues in which individuals' interests in personal liberty conflicted with collective interests in public safety. Consistent with the penal sensibilities of that time, most academic observers believed that the nebulous and diffuse collective public safety interest should take second place to the concrete and particular liberty interests of individuals. The due process liberals lost both arguments. More to the point, though, few people in the early years of this new century would consider either issue particularly contentious. Penal sensibilities have changed and to most observers it is self-evident that dangerous offenders should be held before trial (and in some cases, if we believe they are dangerous, after their prison sentences have been completed), lest prospective victims unnecessarily suffer. Likewise to most people it seems self-evident that prosecutors should be able to appeal sentences they believe are not severe enough, lest offenders get off easy.

The rest of this chapter devotes more sustained attention to three other subjects—the Model Penal Code's treatment of purposes of punishment, how recidivism rates are measured, and how the costs and benefits of punishment should be measured. The first illustrates concerns whose centrality today is taken for granted but just a few decades earlier received little attention. Punitive ideas expressed in terms of just deserts, commensurability, retribution, and proportionality are predominant in modern discussions of punishment. Assertions that public opinion should or does guide setting of penal policies are common. Yet, during the decade-long development of the Model Penal Code, the most ambitious and successful criminal law reform ever undertaken in the United States, only passing mention was made of just deserts, proportionality, retribution, or placating the public mood as important aims of punishment or sentencing.

The second illustrates an empirical and policy issue that forty years ago seemed central and today is nearly forgotten: the curious disappearance from criminological research of interest in the recidivism of people released after serving a first prison term. Of people released from prison the first time, typically only about a third reoffend. Of all people released from prison, typically two-thirds reoffend. The former finding suggests either that prison sentences rehabilitate offenders, or that many people are sent there who need not be. Both were common beliefs in the 1960s. Conversely, the latter finding is consistent with widespread attitudes in more recent decades, when few believed prison sentences rehabilitate and many believed most offenders are incorrigible. The curiosity is not that each period seemingly unthinkingly employed recidivism measures that matched prevailing sensibilities, but that the earlier measure seems to have been forgotten entirely.

The third illustrates the collective amnesia or blindness that changing penal sensibilities can cause and, perhaps more optimistically, that there may be signs that the amnesia is wearing off as sensibilities become less harsh. Jeremy Bentham, the first great analyst of the costs and benefits of punishment, was clear that all costs and benefits counted—crimes, losses, and victim suffering prevented; costs to the state of administering punishments; and the suffering of punished offenders and their loved ones. Bentham's analyses and calculations were theoretical. Only in recent decades have specialized skills been available that permit sophisticated quantitative calculations of the costs and benefits of punishments. And in these decades, nearly everybody left the offender, and his family, and his community out of the equations. Costs of running the courts, jails, probation, and prison were calculated, and costs of law enforcement, and victims' property losses, lost earnings and productivity, medical costs, and pain and suffering. Few analysts thought about offenders' lost earnings and productivity, reduced life chances and life expectancies, or pain and suffering, much less the similar burdens borne by their partners, children, and other loved ones. It should not be too surprising, in an era when people were expected to be "for" victims or offenders, that politicians overlooked the effects of penal policies on offenders and their families. Were it not for the force of prevailing sensibilities, however, it would seem astonishing that academics were equally blind. In the last few years, analysts have remembered offenders (e.g., Cook and Ludwig 2001).

All three illustrations are like Holmes's non-barking dog. The absence of issues from an era offers important clues to the governing penal sensibility. And, if those times were blind to some things and acutely aware of others, in each case opposite to our own times, we are likely to be just as vulnerable to collective selective awareness.

Preventive Detention and Prosecutorial Appeals

In 2002 battles over preventive detention and prosecutorial sentence appeals are distant memories. Few people seem in principle opposed to either or to recognize the issues as in any way contentious. Due process liberals, judges, and just about everyone else has been socialized by the ethos of our time into accepting the public safety cases for both as self-evident. It was not so before and likely some day will not be again.

In the 1970s, there were heated and extended political fights over preventive detention. Due process champions for years successfully opposed federal adoption of legislation that would permit persons accused of crimes to be confined before trial because of dangers they might present to public safety. Defendants are presumed innocent, the argument went, and pretrial confinement is allowable only to assure defendants' presence at trial. Detention for any other reason except in the case of capital crimes is an unconstitutional invasion of citizens' liberty interests.

Crime-control conservatives by contrast argued that citizens' interest in public safety justified restrictions on the liberties of dangerous alleged offenders. Moreover, they argued, judges in practice sometimes set bail so high that people they believed to be dangerous offenders could not raise the money to pay it and accordingly had to remain in jail until trial. This is hypocritical, they argued, and probably resulted in judges detaining dangerous offenders less often than they should. The battle raged for years but finally the conservatives won and in 1973 Congress enacted the District of Columbia preventive detention law (D.C. sect. 23–1322-23–1331).

Preventive detention today is commonplace, authorized by federal law and the laws of most states, and repeatedly sanctioned by state and federal appellate courts. The Supreme Court long ago, in *Bell v. Wolfish*, 441 U.S. 520 (1979), held that the presumption of innocence is merely an evidentiary rule and does not by itself imply anything about pretrial commitment. In its most extreme form, sexual psychopath laws provide that states may hold convicted sex offenders after the expiration of their prison sentences if a court decides, by a civil law more-probable-than-not standard, that they are dangerous. The constitutionality of such laws was upheld by the U.S. Supreme Court in *Kansas v. Hendricks*, 521 U.S. 346 (1997). The federal real offense sentencing provision, discussed in chapter 6, also allows people to be sentenced to longer prison sentences on the basis of more-probable-than-not findings. The rationale is not preventive detention, but the practice resembles preventive detention in the sense that people's liberty is taken on the basis of scant evidence to achieve larger public purposes.

Here is another example of a long-forgotten but sharply contested issue of principle. Before the first sentencing guidelines were developed in the 1970s and 1980s, appellate review of sentences in the United States was close to nonexistent. This was because indeterminate sentencing, ubiquitous in the United States before 1975, accorded judges and other officials great discretion to individualize decisions. There were, in effect, no sentencing rules or standards whose correct application appellate courts could assess. The creation of sentencing guidelines, however, implied the right of defendants to appeal sentences (Frankel 1972). Guidelines created standards or presumptions that, if improperly or incorrectly interpreted or applied by the judge, could result in wrongful deprivation of an offender's liberty. Surely a defendant could seek appellate review of a trial judge's sentence when he or she reasonably believed the sentence was longer or otherwise harsher than applicable guidelines indicated it should be? But if defendants were to be allowed to appeal sentences they believed too harsh, should not prosecutors be allowed to appeal sentences they believed too soft?

There were two principal arguments for the prosecution: procedural symmetry, what is fair for the defendant is fair for the prosecution; and substantive symmetry, if the defendant has a legally enforceable interest in avoiding too much punishment, the state has a reciprocal interest in avoiding too little.

There was one principal argument against: the state should not be able to get on appeal what it could not get in court. Just as, under double jeopardy doctrine, an acquittal absolves a factually guilty defendant of the cost, stigma, and emotional turmoil of a second prosecution, so an anomalously slight sentence should insulate a defendant from the risk of a harsher one. The state gets but one bite at the defendant's apple, and the presumptions all run in favor of the defendant's autonomy and liberty interests. Such a position is also consistent with the principle of strict construction of penal statutes mentioned in chapter six. Just as ties in baseball go to the runner, ambiguities in criminal court benefit the defendant.

There was extended and spirited disagreement. Most criminal procedure scholars predicted that prosecutorial appeal would not withstand constitutional scrutiny. In *United States v. DiFrancesco*, 449 U.S. 117 (1980), regarding a "dangerous special offender," it did, and the issue has disappeared. Prosecution appeals of sentence are now commonplace in every American jurisdiction that allows defendants to appeal sentences.

One might suggest that the two preceding examples merely illustrate the legal doctrine of stare decisis in action. Litigants have accepted that the courts have ruled, and life has moved on. That could be, but not necessarily. When courts decide essentially arbitrary questions in civil law disputes, it should be no surprise that the choice is typically accepted. In contract law, for example, common law courts long ago were faced with the problem of acceptances of offers of sale that are lost in the mail. When the acceptance genuinely is lost, either party might be damaged. If the price of the goods goes up, the would-be buyer, believing he has already bought at a good price, will stand pat. If his lost acceptance prevents formation of a contract, he will have to pay more to buy the same goods elsewhere (or from the original seller). Conversely, the seller who did not receive the acceptance may sell the goods to another buyer and, if he is held to the original contract, may have to sell at a loss if the price of goods goes up, or pay damages. In the long run, it did not matter which way the courts resolved the issue of the acceptance lost in the mail. If the rule is clear, parties can plan around it by buying insurance or negotiating over who bears what risk of loss.

Disputes over civil liberties or other normative issues often are another matter. There are many normatively contested subjects about which people do not lambishly accept authoritative court decisions. Abortion, gun control, and capital punishment are examples. The difference may be that these are such deeply contested normative issues that proponents of polar positions are less likely to be worn down by the general penal sensibilities of an era, or those issues may be so normatively contested that there are no general penal sensibilities.

Issues imbued with less primal emotions may be more susceptible to the social and cognitive forces Musto (1973), Gusfield (1963), Gilmore (1974), Johnson (1976), and many other historians describe. Preventive detention and prosecutorial appeals, because they squarely involve deprivations of individuals' liberty for collective purposes, might have been expected to remain galvanizing issues akin to gun control or abortion. The sensibilities of our time, however, are such that they did not.

Desert and the Model Penal Code

It can be eye-glazingly tedious to encounter an nth recital of the variety of mainstream but often overlapping sets of punishment theories—retributive, utilitarian, consequential, hybrid, communicative, expressive—and the various ways they can be subpartitioned. Precursors, foreshadowers, and full statements of core ideas can be found in third-century Athens, and they have echoed and accreted throughout the centuries. This is a subject about which little that is new is likely to be found under the sun. Every post-Enlightenment period has its matched pair of preventive and moralizing debaters—Jeremy Bentham and Immanuel Kant, John Stuart Mill and James Fitzjames Stephen, Herbert Hart and Lord Patrick Devlin, Norval Morris and Andrew von Hirsch.

For the past quarter century, retributive "just deserts" ideas have been in the ascendant among philosophers, politicians, and practitioners. Philosophers and just deserts theorists generally put forward subtle and principled accounts that tie punishment to offenders' culpability and take their liberty interests seriously. In practical politics, the ascendancy of desert ideas is cruder and reduces to little more than an idea that offenders deserve to suffer. Often this is expressed in slogans—"Do the crime, do the time;" "Three strikes and you're out;" "Hard time for hard crime." And yet, the Model Penal Code, completed forty years ago, a decade in the making, rarely mentions desert, retribution, or proportionality in its text or original commentary, and echoes of such ideas only occasionally appear in the transcripts of the American Law Institute ("ALI") meetings at which successive drafts were discussed.

This wafting of ideas, even of particular ideas, in and out of eras, is nothing new. Nigel Walker (1999, p. xi) similarly observes of an earlier era in which utilitarianism was ascendant:

> In 1877 Edward Cox, Recorder of Falmouth, published the first English textbook on sentencing, *The Principles of*

Punishment. It preached a Benthamite version of utilitarianism, in which the only important consideration was the need for deterrence in some kinds of case, and the absence of this need in other kinds. Reformation was treated with scepticism. . . . Most remarkable, was the absence of any attention to retribution, let alone "just deserts."

The Model Penal Code's draftsmen began work early in the 1950s, and the final version was formally approved and published in 1962. The following paragraphs describe and quote from American Law Institute discussions of such things as purposes of punishment, presumptions against imprisonment and for parole release, and related subjects. The Code went through a series of tentative drafts. I mostly refer to these rather than to the final version, since my interest here is in the proposals and how they were discussed rather than in the Code per se.

The main themes are that offenders' prospects for law-abidingness are nearly always relevant to decision making, that officials should have broad discretion in making decisions, and that prison should be used as little as possible. A fourth theme could be offered—that public safety considerations be taken into account, in effect a co-equal goal with offender rehabilitation. An offender who is believed not to have been rehabilitated is an offender who may need incapacitation. In transcripts of debates, however, allusions to public safety often feel as if they are offered by rote and the Code's provisions clearly give primacy to the first three themes.

The ALI is an establishmentarian organization of lawyers, judges, and law professors. It has a self-perpetuating nominated membership and for much of its life has been preponderantly composed of members of major commercial law firms. At least in legal circles, one might suppose that "prestigious" were part of the organizational name, as in "X is a member of the prestigious American Law Institute." It was established in the 1920s with a law reform purpose and special emphasis on systematizing and rationalizing state laws (Goodrich and Wolkin 1961; Hull 1990; American Law Institute 1998; Elson 1998). Each American state and the federal government has its own legal system, and this led to the practical problem for businesses operating in national markets that legal provisions concerning basic features of contract, tort, insurance, and personal property law varied significantly from state to state. Initially ALI concentrated on descriptive summaries or "restatements" of existing law, as in the Restatement of the Law of Contracts, or on more prescriptive synthetic proposals for improvement, as in the Uniform Commercial Code. Particular ALI projects are carried out under the aegis of committees, and under the direction of "reporters," but proposals receive official ALI imprimatur only upon positive votes of the membership at annual meetings.

The Model Penal Code exemplified later and more prescriptive attempts to develop model codes which, if successful, might serve as the bases for comprehensive refashioning of state laws. Columbia University Law School professor Herbert Wechsler, in retrospect the most influential American criminal law scholar of his century, was the Chief Reporter for the Model Penal Code. The key drafters of the Code's sentencing and corrections provisions, and the oversight committee, included leading law professors, judges, prosecutors, psychiatrists, mental health specialists, and corrections professionals. Sanford Bates and James V. Bennett, for example, successive reformist heads of the U.S. Bureau of Prisons, and Paul W. Tappan, sometime head of the U.S. Parole Board, and comparable state officials, were active participants. Over a ten-year period, from 1953 to 1962, drafts of various proposed sections were discussed at ALI annual meetings and final approvals were given in 1961 (sentencing and corrections) and 1962 (the rest).

I describe ALI and its processes to highlight that it is about as establishmentarian as an organization can be. Its center of gravity in the elite commercial bar implies institutional conservatism. Its deliberative processes are ponderous and unwieldy and, at day's end, require that the text of a proposed model criminal law pass muster with an ALI membership composed largely of judges and business lawyers. In other words, it is not an organization predisposed to cutting-edge ideas or radical innovation in the criminal law.

Curiously, though, the provisions of its Model Penal Code are so radical by contemporary standards as nearly to be unimaginable. University of Chicago law professor Albert Alschuler (1978, p. 552) expressed this in 1978, commenting in close retrospect on the indeterminate sentencing systems the Model Penal Code proposed, "That I and many other academics adhered in large part to this reformative viewpoint only a decade or so ago seems almost incredible to most of us today."

With hindsight, it is striking how much attention the drafters gave to the perceived need to accommodate offenders' treatment needs and prospects and how little to notions of "deserved punishment," "just deserts," or public opinion. The following paragraphs set out the principal sentencing, parole release, and good time provisions (ALI 1954, 1956, 1960; ALI Proceedings 1954, 1956, 1960, 1961) and the primary justifications offered in their support. I do this with apologies to readers who are not sentencing specialists. For those who are, the reminder of the distance between the sensibilities of the Code's drafters, and those of our own era that the Code's provisions illustrate, may be enlightening. In reading the next few paragraphs, bear in mind that modern sensibilities are hostile to judicial and parole board discretion, often opposed to parole release itself, enamored of the idea that punishments should relate primarily to the crime and not the criminal, supportive of the idea that the public opinion should be taken into account, and suspicious of rehabilitation as a purpose of punishment. The generalizations in the preceding sentence apply about equally to conservatives and liberals.

Purposes of Sentencing

The first official draft, from 1962, lists eight "general purposes of the provisions governing the sentencing and treatment of the offender." The first three are "To prevent the commission of offenses; To promote the correction and rehabilitation of offenders; To safeguard offenders against excessive, disproportionate or arbitrary punishment" (ALI 1962, pp. 2–3). "Safeguarding against disproportionate punishment," please observe, is not at all the same thing as "assuring proportionate punishment." To argue that an offender should not be punished more harshly than he deserves implies neither that he should be punished as much as he deserves nor that he may not be punished less than he deserves. Norval Morris's (1974) "limiting retributivism" and Finnish "asymmetrical proportionality" (Törnudd 1997; Lappi-Seppälä 2001), for example, both allow for fixed upper limits to punishment, based on proportionality ideas, but impose few or no lower limits. Nowhere in the Model Penal Code is mention made of "imposing deserved punishment," "acknowledging the seriousness of the crime," "expressing public outrage," or anything similar.

Authorized Prison Sentences

The first proposed draft divided all felonies into three classes. Judges set minimum sentences and maximums were prescribed by statute. For first-degree felonies, the minimum was one to twenty years and the maximum was life. For second-degree felonies, the minimum was one to three years and the maximum ten. For third-degree felonies, the minimum was one to two years and the maximum five (tentative draft 2, ALI 1954). In other words, a judge could impose a one-year minimum sentence, no matter how serious the offense. This is flatly inconsistent with modern attitudes that underlay mandatory minimums, truth-in-sentencing laws, and three-strikes laws. The rationale was that, no matter how horrible the crime, particular circumstances may make a lengthy sentence unwise or unjust.

Authorized Probation Sentences

The first proposed draft authorized judges to sentence any person to probation, including those convicted of murder and other first-degree felonies potentially punishable by a life sentence, when the judge "deems that his imprisonment is unnecessary for protection of the public." To make certain no one could misunderstand, the commentary explains that the draft "is based upon the view that suspension of sentence or probation may be appropriate dispositions on conviction of *any* offense" (tentative draft 2, ALI 1954, p. 34; emphasis added) unless a mandatory sentence of death or life imprisonment is prescribed. No matter how horrible the crime, the judge may conclude that a prison sentence is unwarranted under all the circumstances, and the provision allowed for a sentence of probation in those instances.

Reconsideration of Sentences

The first proposed draft made every prison sentence "tentative" for the first year and authorized the corrections commissioner to petition for resentencing. The commentary explains that judges have limited opportunity to study the offender and that corrections officials may decide that the judge "proceeded on the basis of misapprehension as to the history, character or physical or mental condition of the defendant" (ALI 1954, p. 57). Herbert Wechsler explained during the ALI deliberations, "This is a really fundamental provision of the draft. One of the great arguments against judicial sentencing has always been that the judge must decide too much, too soon. . . . Even with a good pre-sentence report there has been a limited opportunity to study the offender" (ALI Proceedings 1954, p. 143). Even Judge Alger Fee from Oregon, one of the ALI's few skeptics about the Code's deference to the expertise of experts, was happy to authorize judges to reconsider sentences: "[A]s many times as the correctional authority desires to bring the case before the judge again it should be done" (ALI Proceedings 1954).

Mitigation of Sentences

The first proposed draft empowered judges, when they believed the offense of conviction authorized sentences that were too harsh under all the circumstances, to sentence an offender convicted of any felony as if he or she had been convicted of a lower degree felony or a misdemeanor (tentative draft 2, ALI 1954). Wechsler explained that the provision was "really a kind of introduction of equity, the basic Aristotelian idea of equity into law that every generalization—and law must be general—has unstatable qualifications that must be acknowledged when the case arises" (ALI Proceedings 1954, p. 92).

New York County Prosecutor Sarafite agreed that "one of the most important functions of their [the prosecutors'] office is to cooperate in the process of mitigating the rigor of the law in appropriate cases" (ALI Proceedings 1954, p. 92). Sarafite was firmly "in favor of anything that would mitigate an unduly harsh sentence that the judge finds he has to impose after a jury conviction" (ibid., p. 92), but not in the case of guilty pleas. Wechsler responded that "the whole reason for doing it this way was to transfer a certain amount of authority in this area from the District Attorney to the Courts" (ibid., p. 93). In our time, to the contrary, legislators have purposely transferred discretion from judges to prosecutors to reduce chances that judges will mitigate sentences. That is a primary purpose of mandatory minimum sentence and three-strikes laws.

Good Time

The first proposed draft directed that prisoners receive six days' time off for good behavior for each month satisfactorily served, and that corrections officials could award another six days per month for "especially meritorious behavior or exceptional performance of his duties" (tentative draft 5, ALI 1956, p. 81). The good time credits would apply to (and thus advance) both the minimum to be served before parole release eligibility and the maximum to be served before mandatory release. Modern truth-in-sentencing laws, with their requirement that at least 85 percent of the sentence be served, are premised on ideas that sentence reductions for good behavior are bad things.

Parole Release

The first proposed draft made prisoners eligible for parole release on completion of their minimum sentences less any applicable good time and created a presumption in favor of release when prisoners first became eligible. Prisoners were required to be released when they had served their maximum sentences (net of good time) (tentative draft 5, ALI 1956). In our time, sixteen states have abolished parole release altogether and, contrary to the presumption that release should occur at the earliest possible time, many modern sentencing laws are designed to prevent or minimize early release of any kind.

Public Sentiments

The Model Penal Code created no mandatory sentences or probation ineligibility provisions (except concerning life sentences and the death penalty [on which it took no position]). The final draft, however, almost as an afterthought that had not arisen during a decade's discussions, acknowledged that public opinion might sometimes be relevant. In a provision creating a presumption against imprisonment and for probation in every case, the final draft added a new criterion, "a lesser sentence will depreciate the seriousness of the defendant's crime," among the reasons for disregarding the presumption and ordering a term of imprisonment (ALI 1962, p. 106). A similar provision was added to a list of considerations that might justify disregarding the presumption that prisoners be released at first parole eligibility.

Wechsler explained in 1961, however, that the new language was not meant to direct a judge to respond to public sentiment about a particular crime, but instead to consider deterrent processes: "[W]hat really is of concern to the court in relation to deterrence is not the stiffness of the disposition of this particular man, but that the disposition not have a general effect on the community which tends to depreciate the gravity of the crime and thus imply a license to commit it" (ALI Proceedings 1961, p. 340).

The tone of the discussions on the relevance of public opinion was set by Corrections Commissioner (and former judge) Anna M. Kross of New York. Her concern was that public opinion might sometimes influence judges' decisions. She worried that "sentencing power [would] . . . remain in the hands of a judge who at the time is in the first place influenced by the temper of the people. He is worried about what they are going to say about him. He is worried about what the newspapers are going to print. His judgment, no matter how well adjusted and how sound and how sane and how honest he is, necessarily is affected. He is only human" (ALI Proceedings 1954, p. 75).

Only one speaker spoke of public opinion in modern (ca. 2003) terms. Judge James Alger Fee of California, after telling of his father's life as a judge in frontier Oregon, observed:

> There is one place where I do not agree at all with some of the sentiments that have been expressed here. I think that local thought on the subject of penalty is one thing you should recognize because it is to the community eventually and the local community, not some United Nations or Federal community—that you are really responsible. It is the people that make and enforce the law, and it is community sentiment that backs up a law." (ALI Proceedings 1954, p. 78)

Others acknowledged the existence and force of public opinion, but as something to be managed or evaded, not as something to be respected, and thought judges were better placed than administrators to resist popular pressures and public opinion. Judge Gerald F. Flood of Pennsylvania, for example, preferred to place powers in judges' than administrators' hands because judges were better able to withstand the force of public opinion:

> [S]omeone has to take up the shock of the community outrage and community pressure. And I think that Dr. [Thorsten] Sellin [about to go to California for ALI to study California practices] will find (it was a visit to California

that changed my mind, really) the community pressure is less able to be resisted by a Board than it is by a Judge. A Judge is elected for a long period, and he can much more easily resist pressure than can a Board which can be thrown out of office by a Governor the next morning. (ALI Proceedings 1954, p. 79)

Wechsler noted the problem, but in an oddly circumscribed way. The original proposals on minimum sentences allowed judges to set minimums as long as twenty years for first-degree felonies such as murder. Wechsler explained this as a response to public passions:

It often happens that crimes of violence are shocking crimes and are perpetrated by individuals who three or four years later do not, to the people who study them, seem to present the kind of threat for the future that the particular act that they committed suggests. But the public remembers the act. Therefore we thought that in this area where by hypothesis public indignation as to the offense in the sense of need for a general deterrent penalty would be very strong, it would be prudent to give the Judge power at the time of sentence to satisfy the community that this person would be taken out of currency for a substantial period of time. (ALI Proceedings 1954, p. 74)

And so the Code provided (though, as eventually adopted, the twenty years was reduced to ten). It strikes me as noteworthy that Wechsler described the public demand in terms of "a general need for a deterrent sentence" rather than in terms of retributive or expressive needs. It also strikes me as noteworthy that judges could (but need not) impose up to a lengthy minimum for a first-degree felony (but only up to three years for any other), but could also impose probation in the same case, and could reconsider any prison sentence at any time within a year of imposition.

This is written in a time when powerful ideas like "truth in sentencing," "do the crime, do the time," and "just deserts" have great influence. They are not new ideas. Cesare

Beccaria would have found the concepts though not the phrases familiar. Herbert Wechsler, and many of the judges, lawyers, and law professors with whom he worked, would have been familiar with the writings not only of Beccaria but also of Kant, Hegel, Stephen, and many other proponents of ideas that are only very weakly discernible in the Model Penal Code. That so talented a group of law reformers, working within so inherently conservative and establishmentarian a setting as the American Law Institute, produced and won approval of a document so uninfluenced by powerful and influential ideas, should make us wonder what similarly powerful ideas are being ignored in our time.

"Prison Works": Recidivism of First-Time Prisoners

One striking sign of the differences in penal sensibilities between our and earlier times is in the way we think, speak, and write about prisoner recidivism. Two robust recidivism findings were evident in the 1960s and today. I overstate them for effect, because inevitably methodological qualifications warrant mention—for example, results vary with the measure of recidivism (self-report, rearrest, reconviction, reimprisonment), what counts (any offense, only felonies, only particular types of offense), the follow-up period (one year, two, three), and the reliability of the data sources—but they nonetheless express an important contrast.

First, answering a question researchers often asked in the 1950s and 1960s, *of people released from a first prison sentence*, two-thirds do not return to prison. I simplify here for rhetorical purposes and do so again when I discuss recidivism rates based on all releasees. I could have said 60 percent or given a range, say 60–70 percent, or said approximately two-thirds. Prison works in the sense that most people sent there do not want to go back and organize their future lives so as not to go back. Or, alternately, prison can be said often to be unnecessary and the low return rates to demonstrate that many people are sent to prison who present little public safety risk and could safely, responsibly, and more cost-effectively be sanctioned in other ways.

Second, answering the question researchers asked in the 1980s and 1990s, *of people released from prison in a given year* or as part of a representative release sample or cohort, considerably more than half, often two-thirds, return to prison. Prison does not work in the sense that most people released from prison do not manage thereafter to conduct law-abiding lives and to refrain from the kinds of unlawful behavior that lead to apprehension, conviction, and imprisonment.

Both statements can be true because they are statements about different groups of people. The first statement refers to people in prison for the first time. Some have done things, including violent things, that are the product of unusual circumstances and out-of-character, and they would be subsequently law-abiding whether or not they were sent to prison. Some may be essentially conformist people with prosocial values who behaved criminally and are shamed or shocked by their imprisonment into law-abidingness. Some may be young offenders who committed crimes but were not too badly damaged by their prison experiences and after release found love, work, or God, or just aged out of their offending years, as most young offenders do. For some, prison may have provided a short sharp shock that captured their attention and made them resolve to obey the law. And some, a minority, are so developmentally disadvantaged, or so predisposed to deviance, or so committed to a life of crime, that they return to crime and in due course to court and prison.

The second statement refers to all people released from prison in a representative sample of releasees. This means they include a small fraction who are being released from prison for the first time, and have a one-third likelihood of returning to prison, and a much larger fraction who have been released from prison before, and have a much higher likelihood of returning to prison. The clearest example of this is found in data on return to prison for all persons released from Florida prisons between July 1, 1986 and February 1992. Of those with no prior incarcerations, only 31.6 percent returned to prison, compared with 42 percent of those with one prior incarceration and 52 percent of those with four or more (Florida Legislative Office of Program Policy Analysis and Government Accountability 1995, exhibit 9).

Because recidivism and reincarceration of first-time prisoners have not received much attention for three decades, data on the subject are not readily available, but other data support strong inferences. For example, a U.S. Bureau of Justice Statistics survey of arrest data for all prisoners released in 1983 from prisons in eleven states found that, within three years, 62.5 percent were rearrested for a felony or serious misdemeanor, 46.8 percent were reconvicted, and 41.8 percent were returned to prison or jail (Beck 1989). However, of those releasees with only one prior arrest at the time of the study (that which led to the incarceration), 38.1 percent had been rearrested within three years compared with 63.2 percent for the entire sample and in excess of 75 percent for the half of the group who had been arrested six or more times (Beck 1989, table 11). Similarly, of all adult Minnesota prisoners released in 1992, 59 percent were rearrested within three years, 45 percent were reconvicted, and 28 percent were reimprisoned for a new offense (Minnesota Legislative Auditor 1997, figure 3.2). (These numbers are comparatively low because only state prison sentences are counted.) However, of those with no criminal history (no prior adult felony convictions and not more than one minor petty misdemeanor), 39 percent were rearrested and only 24 percent were reconvicted (ibid., table 3.6).

None of this should be surprising. Research on age and crime shows that crime participation rates for property crime peak in the mid-teens and for violence in the late teens, and that most criminally active people desist by the early twenties (Farrington 1986, pp. 189–250). Research on criminal careers shows that the probability of rearrest given one arrest is not high but that the probability rises monotonically with each subsequent arrest, until it stabilizes around 80 percent by the sixth arrest. Putting the two findings together should make it apparent that most people sent to prison, and hence released, will be persistent offenders, and accordingly that on average people released from prison will present relatively high risks for recidivism.

Is it not odd though, that in our time, we have forgotten the lower risk first-timers, and do not even think in our research to ask separately about them? Social scientists who self-select to study criminals and prisoners are not especially known for their conservatism or for voting Republican and yet, in our time, they have forgotten that the question they ask—What percentage of prisoners fail?—provides an answer that supports the penal policies of our time, while a different question about first-time prisoners would not.

The Costs and Benefits of Crime

Equally blind has been the failure to take offenders into account in calculating the costs and benefits of crime control policies. There was not much writing on this subject until Chicago School economists Gary Becker (1968) and Richard Posner (1977, 1980) began to offer economic analyses of the likely effects of alternate punishment policies. Their work, however, was primarily theoretical, built on hypotheses about individuals' rational calculations of likely gains and losses, and the likely general deterrent effects of possible policies. In this, they resembled Bentham, who offered a variety of rational actor proposals:

Rule 1. The value of the punishment must not be less in any case than what is sufficient to outweigh that of the profit of the offence.

Rule 2. The greater the mischief of the offence, the greater is the expence, which it may be worthwhile to be at, in the way of punishment.

Rule 3. Where two offences come in competition, the punishment for the greater must be sufficient to induce a man to prefer the less.

Rule 4. The punishment should be adjusted in such manner to each particular offence, that for every part of the mischief there may be a motive for the offender from giving birth to it.

Rule 5. The punishment ought in no case be more than what is necessary to bring it into conformity with the rules here given.

Rule 6. That the quantity actually inflicted on each individual offender may correspond to the quantity intended for similar offenders in general, the several circumstances influencing sensibility ought always to be taken into account. (Bentham 1938–43; quoted in von Hirsch and Ashworth 1998, pp. 54–56)

Though written in prose of less than crystalline clarity, with pondering, Bentham's meaning becomes clear. The first four rules are simple deterrence. The penalty should be greater than the likely gain. Lesser crimes should receive lesser punishments than more serious crimes to encourage offenders to commit the lesser. Requiring lesser penalties for attempted than for completed crimes gives offenders an incentive to stop part way through.

The fifth and six rules, however, focus on the offender. The fifth, the parsimony rule, forbids punishments harsher than the minimum required to achieve the purpose. The sixth requires that punishments be tailored to offenders' sensibilities, the ways that punishments might affect them differently than other people. Finally, Bentham describes circumstances when punishment would not be justified, including "where it is unprofitable, or too expensive; where the mischief it would produce would be greater than what was prevented" (von Hirsch and Ashworth 1998, p. 57). In other words, punishment cannot be justified when, taking all the "mischief" (synonyms used by Bentham elsewhere include pain and unhappiness) into account, including to the offender and his family, punishment would cause more mischief than it would prevent.

Where Becker, Posner, and most others who have written about costs and benefits of punishment differed from Bentham was that their emphasis was on comparing only the financial costs of punishing offenders with benefits that might be gained through deterrence. Bentham, by contrast, was interested in measuring society's, victims', offenders', and others' happiness or unhappiness (or pain and pleasure, utility and disutility).

For Bentham, punishment was justifiable only when it served to maximize human happiness, or minimize human suffering, taking everybody, including offenders, into account. Punishment, Bentham argued "itself is an evil and should be used as sparingly as possible . . . it ought only to be admitted in as far as it promises to exclude some greater evil" (Tonry 1994, p. 63, quoting Bentham 1789).

A new cost-benefit literature began to emerge in the 1980s, focused primarily on incapacitation rather than on deterrence (Zedlewski 1987; Cohen 1988; DiIulio 1990; Kleiman and Cavanagh 1990). Much imagination was invested in calculating the costs of crime and the criminal justice system, but no one thought to take the offender and his costs and suffering into account. The principal aim was to calculate whether "prison works" in the sense that the economic value of crimes prevented through locking people up outweighed the costs of operating the criminal justice system, including the prisons.

The earliest article, by Edwin Zedlewski of the U.S. National Institute of Justice, concluded that, for one average prisoner, "a year in prison [at] total social costs of $25,000" would produce a saving of "$430,000 in [reduced] crime costs" (Zedlewski 1987, pp. 3–4).It provoked a fierce response (e.g., Zimring and Hawkins 1988). Should the costs of the police be included in the calculation, since every society has a police force? Should crime prevention costs from burglar alarms to private security firms' fees? Were the estimates of the numbers of crimes prevented per locked-up offender accurate or even remotely plausible? Should both incapacitative and deterrent effects be predicted or only incapacitative effects?

Gradually, over time, the estimation techniques improved and general agreements were reached about what should be taken into account. The most striking development, and the most influential, was the development by economist Mark Cohen of estimates of the victims' direct out-of-pocket expenses, their pain and suffering, and their risk of death (Cohen 1988, p. 546). For most crimes, the intangible costs of pain and suffering and risk of death far outweighed out-of-pocket costs. For rape, direct costs totaled $4,617, intangible costs $46,441. For personal robbery, direct costs totaled $1,114, intangible $11,480; for assault, $422 and $11,606. Cohen developed these estimates by adapting data from jury awards in tort (accident) cases, and generalizing from them to crime.

This was a cockamamie thing to do for a number of reasons. Only very serious accidents result in jury awards (most are settled) and he was thus using data on the most serious accidents to estimate the costs of average crimes. Jury awards are inflated to include attorneys' fees (a third to a half of the total). Cohen's inflated estimates, however, soon became widely used. This is probably because they were the only ones around.

Whether or not Cohen's estimates are plausible, however, is not the point. What is important is what is missing. Nowhere in this literature, including even in vigorous critiques of its quality and value (Zimring and Hawkins 1995, chap. 7), did anyone take account of offenders. A prison sentence entails pain and suffering by the offender. When he is released, he will be stigmatized and face numerous obstacles to resuming a normal life. These range from ineligibility for many professions, inability to vote, and employer resistance to employing ex-cons. He will after prison have lower life chances, life expectancy, and lifetime earnings than if he had not spent time in prison. His family also will have suffered, economically, socially, and psychologically, if it survived intact.

Clever economists can devise estimates of the economic value of almost anything. They could have calculated the costs of punishment policies generally and imprisonment in particular to prisoners and their families. Jeremy Bentham understood all this and would have taken all of these things into account. They are absent from almost all of the cost-benefit literature on punishment. A recent book by economists Philip J. Cook and Jens Ludwig (2001) on the costs of gun violence is a notable, but recent exception.

Paralleling social scientists' neglect of recidivism by first-time offenders, social scientists did little better in relation to the effects of punishment on offenders. My 1995 *Malign Neglect* was one of the first calls for attention to collateral effects of imprisonment on prisoners, their families, and their communities. When, in 1997, I commissioned an essay from John Hagan and Robin Dinovitzer (1999) on the collateral effects of punishment, they had to report that the literature was fragmentary and fugitive, though they did their best to pull it together. On many important subjects—for example, the effects of a parent's imprisonment on children's development and well-being or the effects of imprisonment on offenders' later health and life expectancy—there was no respectable social science literature. The inattention is beginning to end and work is beginning to appear on the effects of imprisonment on prisoners' communities (Clear Rose, and Ryder 2001) and on collateral costs more generally (Mauer and Chesney-Lind 2002).

Under the influence of the penal sensibilities of the final decades of the twentieth century, even politically liberal social scientists forgot something that was obvious to Jeremy Bentham two centuries earlier—punishment hurts offenders, and ethical policy makers and analysts should factor that reality into their thought. A half-century ago, the draftsmen of the Model Penal Code knew about the retributive moral arguments of Kant and Hegel, but took no account of them. They thought them antiquarian and vindictive and no longer relevant to the concerns of a more humane age. Bentham thought and wrote about the overall costs and benefits of punishment but, in our time, those who were "for victims" did not care about the costs to offenders and those who rejected the for victims/for offenders dichotomy somehow overlooked the subject altogether.

That is the last of the non-barking dogs described in this chapter. Taken together, the various forgotten and over-looked issues demonstrate a collective partial amnesia, which is odd, given the universality of the underlying issues and principles. They demonstrate the power of penal sensibilities over men's and women's minds.

8

Better Understanding, People, and Policies

The United States has adopted criminal justice policies that reflective people should abhor and that informed observers from other Western countries do abhor. An anecdote makes the point. I spoke recently in Noordwijk, the Netherlands, at a European Union meeting on crime prevention. My assignment was to survey current research findings on "what works," and in doing so I described Swedish educational programs that had successfully and substantially reduced criminal activities of immigrant children. It has been known for a century, popular beliefs to the contrary notwithstanding, that first-generation immigrants tend to have lower crime rates than the resident population, but that second-generation immigrants typically have higher rates than their parents or the resident population. Sweden had accomplished something noteworthy that furthered both crime prevention and social welfare goals.

As I headed toward my seat, the moderator, Hans Dijkstal, then the head of the Dutch Interior Ministry (popularly called, in English, the "cops agency") and a member of the Liberal Party, the most conservative party in the coalition government, thanked me and said that he found my remarks on minority groups particularly interesting. "It was good," he continued, "to hear on such a topic from a member of a U.S. minority group." My mind raced as I wondered what he could possibly mean. Few who meet me would be surprised to learn that my immediate background is middle-class white American and that my ancestors are a mix of Germans, Irish, Scots, and English. After I sat down, the minister went on, "It is good to have with us one of that minority of American crime experts who hold humane and progressive views." I had not met the minister before and no one had seen a draft of my talk. He could have had no idea I was going to mention immigrants or Sweden. His quip was impersonal and spur-of-the-moment.

Another anecdote, this one semantic, illustrates the same point. In European English, as opposed to American or British, it is common to contrast preventive and repressive policies. In that usage, "repressive" is a synonym for "law enforcement" and "preventive" encompasses a wide array of social, architectural, and community measures aimed at preventing crime. Once I urged an American friend not to be defensive about a reference in a Dutch government report to repressive U.S. drug policies, because, I explained, "repressive" merely meant law enforcement. "No, my friend," a Dutch colleague intervened, "When we refer to 'repressive U.S. drug policies,' we mean it in both senses; they rely heavily on law enforcement agencies and they are cruel." I often edit scholarly articles written by Europeans for whom English is not a first language, and for years smugly translated Europeans' repressives into words that would not be misinterpreted by Americans as polemical. Now I ask every time what is meant.

As vigorous objections should be made, however, to the processes by which American crime control policies were set as to the policies themselves. For a quarter century, American policy makers year-by-year made policies and punishments harsher. Different policy makers endorsed different policies for different reasons, but no one doubts that political self-interest and cynicism played major roles. By the late 1980s, Bill Clinton and the Democratic Leadership Council that he shaped decided never to be less tough than their Republican opponents, no matter how unjust, wasteful, or ineffective the policies under consideration.

California's overbroad three-strikes law was enacted, according to Franklin Zimring and colleagues (2001, p. 6), because Democratic legislators agreed to pass any proposal Governor Pete Wilson supported, in hopes "that he would back down from an unqualified 'get tough' stand or be politically neutralized." Wilson did not blink and the law was passed because both sides were "unwilling to concede the ground on 'getting tough' to the other side in the political campaign to come."

Similar stories can be told of the passage of most high-profile crime legislation in the 1980s and 1990s. Rising crime rates in the 1960s and 1970s influenced policy makers, as no doubt did public anxieties and fears. Those factors explain why crime control policy was on legislative and executive branch agendas, however, but not why policy makers took so little account of whether or how new policies would work, what they would cost, or what damage they would do to offenders, their families, and their communities.

NYU sociologist David Garland explains that policy makers in the 1980s and 1990s ceased being interested in evidence—of what works, of foreseeable effects—because they were not primarily interested in crime reduction per se. The state "abandon[ed] reasoned, instrumental action and retreat[ed] into an *expressive* mode that we might . . . describe as *acting out*—a mode that is concerned not so much with controlling crime as with expressing the anger and outrage that crime provokes" (2001*a*, p. 110; emphasis in original).

Garland's explanation for this is more benign than mine. He argues that American governments adopted needlessly harsh policies because politicians doubted any policies would be effective but believed they would win favor with voters by at least acting tough. I think policy makers responded unreflectively to prevailing sensibilities about crime and disorder and that cynicism and self-interest played a large role. Except for white-collar criminals, most offenders come from poor disadvantaged backgrounds and no powerful interest groups exist to promote or protect their interests. If policies promoted to win elections do unnecessary damage to offenders and their families, I suspect many conservative politicians thought, so be it. That account, however, treats recent policies as the outcome primarily of selfish politicians and clearly more than that was going on. Many harsh policies were consistent with prevailing sensibilities. Does that justify them?

That strong social and psychological forces of a moment or a year can cause many people to act intemperately and cruelly may, in some ways, be understandable. To understand is not necessarily to forgive, but it is to understand. Individuals sometimes lose control and so do collectivities. The latter demonstrates the power of mob psychology, and sometimes it takes over. We are at best only partly rational animals and, regrettable though it is and often in retrospect regretted, extreme circumstances can beget bad decisions. For nearly two decades, however, U.S. crime policy has been driven more by ideology, emotion, and opportunism than by humane analyses of options and reasoned discussion, and that is much too long for reason and compassion to have been held in abeyance.

Most people have a doppelgänger who sits invisibly on a shoulder and speaks up when we have misbehaved. Freud's super-ego and poets' inner voices perform similar functions. For the past twenty years those quiet reminders have seldom been heard or acted upon in relation to crime policy. The cyclical effects of steeply rising and then sharply falling crime rates on prevailing sensibilities, and through them on American penal culture and policies, produced the criminal justice system Americans now have. That combination of factors created conditions resembling a continuous moral panic, and many American policy makers acted as panicked people do.

How harshly should policy makers of the past quarter century be judged? I have no doubt our successors will be condemnatory of the severity of American crime and drug policies, of the lives they damaged and ruined, and of the foreseeable and disproportionate burdens they placed on black Americans. And I believe many contemporary politicians will be condemned for the cynical ways they manipulated public anxieties and racial tensions to achieve short-term political goals. Beyond that it gets blurrier.

Prevailing sensibilities do shape what people think and believe. No doubt some in public life believed one must be for criminals or for victims, that harsh policies can reduce crime, and that harsh policies did reduce crime. In their simplest forms all those claims are wrong. In complex forms the first is nonsense and the latter two are partly true, but the full truth is vastly more complicated. What moral judgments should be made of policy makers who should have known better but did not? Of policy makers who suspended their critical judgments for longer than they should have? Of policy makers who came to realize their policies were not working, or were doing harm, but continued to support them for other reasons?

Those are questions for posterity to answer. What needs to be done now is to figure out how to undo unnecessary damage and lessen the chances that similar excesses will recur. It helps me think about this to liken it to the ways individuals try to remake themselves. Imagine an occasionally violent alcoholic who desperately wants to remake his or her life, reduce chances of relapse, and make up for damage that was done. Remaking a life requires self-understanding. It is an ethical enterprise. For an alcoholic man, it includes recognizing what alcohol does to him, what he does under its influence, and why that behavior is wrongful and destructive. Reducing chances of relapse requires self-aware efforts to understand the dangers posed by various situations and people and to devise ways to lessen those dangers. Making up for damage requires working to understand what damage has been done, devising a plan to undo it or make amends, and then carrying it out.

The corresponding three tasks at a collective level are ethical introspection, institutional change, and remediation. Breaking loose from contemporary American crime control politics will require us, like the metaphorical drunkard, to address all three tasks. We need to learn to restrain our collective emotions in public life, to change governmental institutions to provide greater insulation from the passions of the moment, and to devise structural arrangements that will force greater reflectiveness on policy makers. Changing collective emotions and governmental arrangements are daunting ambitions, so though I address them and suggest what needs to be done, closer and more detailed attention is given to more modest policy proposals that can undo damage and lessen its future likelihood.

Ethical Introspection

U.S. crime policy is at a place where no one would have wanted it to be for a combination of historical and structural reasons. Because of an interaction between changes in sensibilities about crime and criminals, and a series of moral panics about crime and drugs, harsh and simplistic policies were proposed at a time when they found uncritical support. Because American institutions of government do not buffer policy from the effects of short-term emotionalism, as do institutions in other Western countries, harsh and simplistic policies were adopted. Politicians' risk aversion makes change difficult. The first step is to admit what has happened and why and then to set about the task of learning to restrain our collective emotions.

By that pompous-sounding phrase, "learning to restrain our collective emotions," I mean trying to incorporate into public life some of the ethical folk wisdom of private life: "Don't take it out on your child." "Sit down and count to ten." "Never strike in anger." "Write the angry letter today but don't send it until tomorrow." Aphorisms like these are commonly part of our personal ethics because we know that things that make us angry or depressed often make us irritable and at danger of overreacting or taking out our upset on whoever is close at hand.

The ways we react privately to people who unfairly or unreasonably take out their anger or frustration on others provide a useful analogy for thinking about crime control policy. We become progressively less empathetic as the harm caused increases. Some expressions or displacements of anger are understandable and tolerable, some are less so, and some are not at all.

We understand and sympathize when someone swears or pounds a fist on the desk or throws something to the floor in the face of great unfairness or disappointment. It has happened to everyone. We know how they feel. They are letting off steam, and not hurting anyone else, so why not? If it helps, more power to them.

We understand but sympathize less when the upset produces unkind or hurtful words directed at a serendipitous object whose misfortune is to be in the wrong place at the wrong time. This might be thought the level at which "sit down and count to ten" or "write the angry letter but . . ." are apposite. Yes, we understand how you feel but that is no justification for acting unfairly or hurtfully toward someone else. If we had done what you did, we would feel guilty, and should feel guilty. Pounding a fist on a table is an expressive action that communicates unhappiness. Screaming at someone also expresses unhappiness, but it hurts the recipient or makes him uncomfortable. That is not fair. Expression of the unhappiness can be justified. Hurting the bystander cannot. A good person would be sufficiently self-aware to recognize his or her emotional state and find a way to avoid hurting someone else because of it. If not, a good person would soon realize they had behaved badly, feel guilty, apologize, and try to make up for it.

Sympathy disappears altogether when the upset produces physical violence toward a serendipitous victim, or emotional abuse of a child, spouse, or employee or someone who is handicapped or otherwise vulnerable. This is the "never strike in anger" or "don't take it out on your child" level. There can be no justification. Hurting someone for no reason that relates to them is wrong, and that is that.

These are simple but timeless ideas. Anger is the emotion that underlies the populist punitivist impulse to hurt wrongdoers, and that gives rise in turbulent times to calls for more executions and harsher punishments. The style and content of recent policies, David Garland wrote, are shaped by "the sense of a fearful, angry public" (2001a, p. 10).

And yet, most people understand, as Pietro Aretino, the Renaissance poet and critic, wrote, "Angry men are blind and foolish, for reason at such times takes flight, and in her absence anger plunders all the riches of the intellect" (Grayling 2001). Seneca, the Stoic philosopher, called anger "the most hideous and frenzied of all the emotions," and urged resistance to its demands. Failing that, he continued, "There are two rules: avoid anger if you can, and if you cannot, in your anger do no wrong" (Grayling 2001).

Anger is humanly understandable, the ancients acknowledged, but not if it leads to behaviors that are inappropriate or disproportionate. "It is not easy," Aristotle wrote, "to define how, with whom, at what, and for how long one should be angry, and at what point right action ceases and wrong begins. . . . But so much is plain, that the middle state is praiseworthy—that in virtue of which we are angry with the right people, at the right things, in the right way, and so on, while the excesses and defects are blameworthy" (Barnes 1984, p. 1777).

"In your anger, do no wrong." That does not mean that we should not be angry with people who commit crimes or that they should not be punished. It does mean that their interests should be fairly considered and that they should not be punished more severely than can in principle and humanity be justified.

Precisely how severely criminals may justly be punished depends on why punishments are imposed, and reasonable people differ in their views about this. Retributivists believe that punishment should be tied closely to offenders' blameworthiness, and that the amount of punishment should be scaled to the relative seriousness of their crimes. The more serious the crime, the severer the deserved punishment, and vice versa.

Consequentialists believe that punishment can be justified only in terms of its good effects. Consequentialists also believe that pain and unhappiness, including those of offenders, are undesirable. Punishments accordingly may be imposed only to such an extent as can be justified on the basis of evidence or plausible hypotheses that their crime prevention effects will prevent more pain and unhappiness than they cause.

The ethical frameworks that retributivists and consequentialists consider relevant are different, but they agree that a punishment that cannot be justified in principle is unjust. Consider, for example, the notorious case of Jerry Dewayne Williams, the man who was sentenced to twenty-five years' imprisonment under California's three-strikes law for taking several slices of pizza. Retributivists would consider that penalty unjustly severe on proportionality grounds, since people convicted of much more serious, violent crimes receive much less severe sentences. If a rape or a robbery results in a prison sentence of a few years, how can twenty-five years possibly be justified for such a minor offense? That violates the principle that just punishments should be scaled to offenders' moral culpability and accordingly that more serious crimes should receive severer punishments than less serious crimes. Consequentialists would consider that penalty unjustly severe because no plausible case can be made that its crime prevention effects could be sufficiently large to justify depriving the offender of most of his life. The current state of knowledge concerning rehabilitative, deterrent, and incapacitative effects of punishment cannot justify twenty-five-year sentences for people who take property of nominal value.

The pizza slice case is extreme, but the analysis would apply to, and condemn, many contemporary American sentencing laws as unjustifiably severe and insufficiently respectful of offenders' interests. Ten- and twenty-year sentences for routine drug offenses cannot, for example, be squared with substantially shorter sentences for most assaults, rapes, robberies, manslaughters, and some murders. The laws requiring such harsh penalties for drug offenses reflected the sensibilities of the moment of their adoption and expressed understandable anger at criminals and crimes, but that does not justify them. They are in this respect the collective equivalent of the understandably upset woman who in her unhappiness inexcusably strikes her child. The drug law penalties are wrong. They violate the injunction never to strike in anger and they do great and unnecessary damage to peoples' lives.

What is unjustifiable in private lives is unjustifiable in public life. Moral panics, cyclical patterns of moral intolerance, and anxieties associated with fundamental social changes all increase pressures for adoption of harsh, inhumane, and ill-considered crime control policies. Knowing that, policy makers should try all the harder to separate the ephemeral and emotional from the lasting and reflective, and to resist those pressures. Most elected officials in their private lives no doubt do try to manage their outbursts of emotion and their displacements of anger. If they did so in their public lives, contemporary American crime policies would look very different.

Institutional Change

Exhortations to resist anger and excess and to embrace moderation and principle are unlikely to provide strong protections against the surging passions of a moment. Members of the Congressional Black Caucus generally favor preventive programs over punitive policies, and generally oppose mandatory penalty laws because of their disproportionate effects on black defendants. Under the influence, however, of the moral panic associated with the appearance of crack cocaine in inner cities and the crack overdose death of Len Bias, a University of Maryland basketball star who was expected to become an NBA superstar, eleven of twenty-one black congressmen voted for the 1986 law creating the federal crack/powder 100-to-1 sentencing policy (R. Kennedy 1997, p. 370). Nearly all later changed their minds. The Caucus has been an outspoken opponent of the 100-to-1 rule and repeatedly sought its repeal, but at the time, for a while, some of its members got carried away and supported a law that, on cooler reflection, they realized is unwise and unjust.

A parallel story, this time of personal tragedy and horror, is part of the backdrop to passage of California's three-strikes law. Shortly after the murder of 12-year-old Polly Klaas, kidnapped from a slumber party in her bedroom by Richard Allen Davis, a sex offender recently released from California's prisons, her father, Marc Klaas, was asked to endorse the proposals for a California three-strikes law. "I was very distraught," he later recalled, and endorsed it without much thought, according to former *U.S. News & World Report* reporter Ted Gest (2001, p. 194). After a while,

> Marc Klaas was having second thoughts. He had endorsed three strikes in a moment of anguish. Now he and his family decided that Reynolds's plan was too broad. In some ways, it made little sense. It was fine to treat repeat criminals harshly, but the possibility that just about any felony could count as the third offense meant that a third-time bicycle thief could get a prison sentence five times as long as a first-time murderer. Klaas and his allies . . . withdrew their support. (Gest 2001, p. 195)

It was too late. Too much momentum had built up. The proposed law was enacted by the legislature and later approved by voters in a referendum.

Why is it that only the United States among Western countries experienced skyrocketing prison populations or adopted policies such as three strikes, life sentences without possibility of parole, or increased use of capital punishment? Horrifying crimes occasionally happen in all countries, and crime rates rose sharply in all Western countries from mid-century through the early or mid-1990s. One reason the United States adopts extreme policies, as other chapters show, is that the beliefs and opinions shaped by long-term sensibility cycles interacted with the passions generated by moral panics to foster willingness in the United States to take too extreme measures. Those provoked by the deaths of Polly Klaas and Len Bias are but two of many. But why do overreactions like those occur often in the United States and seldom elsewhere?

Judges and Prosecutors
as Career Civil Servants

The answer relates to differences in legal culture and the structure of government between the United States and other countries with which it is ordinarily compared. The institutional organization of the American criminal justice system and its close connection to electoral politics conduce to punitive excess. In every other Western country I know, the prevalent view among public officials and criminal justice practitioners is that sentencing and punishment should be insulated from short-term emotionalism and swings in public opinion. This means that discretion over individual cases should be left in the hands of judges and corrections officials who are close enough to the facts of the individual crime and the circumstances of the individual criminal to deal with them sensibly and justly. That is why three-strikes, lengthy mandatory minimum, and life-without-possibility-of-parole laws are rarely adopted in other English-speaking countries and never in continental Europe. Other countries' legislatures have the power to enact such laws. They just do not use it because they do not think such laws are a good idea.

Consistent with the idea that just disposition of individual cases should be insulated from political influence and short-term public opinion is the practice in other Western countries that judicial system officials are appointed, not elected. In much of continental Europe, people who wish to become judges or prosecutors receive specialized training from law school onwards and become career civil servants. In England, Canada, and Australia, they are appointed on the basis of merit after professional screening. They are substantially removed from partisan political influence and the temptation to do things solely because they are politically popular. Most senior Justice and Interior Ministry officials are career civil servants. And crime policy is commonly seen, including by elected officials, as something that should be insulated from short-term political pressures and that should be based to a large extent on systematic evidence and accumulated experience. American political values and institutional arrangements provide few buffers.

Achievement of moderate, humane practices and policies is easier in countries where judges and prosecutors are non-political, career civil servants, or where they are appointed under circumstances in which partisan considerations are generally regarded as inappropriate. Career officials are more likely than politically selected officials to decide individual cases on the merits of their distinctive circumstances and to consider policy proposals from long-term perspectives of whether they will improve the quality of justice or the effectiveness of administration. Commitment to abstract principles of justice is part of the professionalism and professional self-esteem of career officials, and buffers individual decisions and policy choices from raw emotions and officials' self-interest.

Politically selected officials, by contrast, are more likely than career officials to be influenced by short-term or self-interested considerations. At the extreme, many American prosecuting attorneys are continuously campaigning and formulate their law reform proposals, their general policies, and their tactics in individual cases on the basis of how they will be reported on the evening news programs, and how the reports will be received by the general public. Elected judges are not immune from influence by consideration of the effects of their decisions on their re-election prospects. Honest, honorable judges I have known have privately admitted to me that an impending election makes them less likely than at other times to impose a sentence others might see as unduly lenient.

American officials, conversely, are less likely to be influenced by long-term considerations, institutional history, and abstract principles of justice. Many judges come from civil law practice backgrounds that give them little knowledge of criminal law, criminal courts, or criminal justice policy. American judges receive no special training in law school, often take up those roles in middle age, and typically have shorter careers than their counterparts in other Western countries. This means that they often lack awareness of the past experiences of their offices or of their profession, and lack a personal or professional interest in long-term effects of changed policies on the justice system.

Where turnover is high, institutional memories are short and commitment to professional values is weak. Many elected state prosecutors and appointed U.S. attorneys serve only for a few years and aspire to be appointed to a judgeship, to be elected to higher office, or to enter a lucrative private law practice. Assistant state and federal prosecutors typically start immediately after law school and plan to stay only for a few years while they get litigation experience. Many then enter private law practice and earn much more money.

Changing institutional arrangements so that judges and prosecutors are less likely to act out of anger, cupidity, ignorance, or self-interest will not prevent bad decisions and adoption of bad policies, but it will help. The goal should be to shift from the current American model of criminal justice as an instrument of politics, in which prosecutors and judges are elected, to a professional model of criminal law as an instrument of justice, in which they are career civil servants. Replacing elected judges and prosecutors with career civil servants would, over time, change the legal culture and revive support for the once self-evident idea that judicial and other proceedings affecting individuals' liberties should be insulated as much as possible from political influence and public emotion. As chapter 7 shows, as recently as the 1950s those were uncontroversial mainstream ideas in the United States.

A legal system in which judges and prosecutors are career civil servants would improve penal policies and practices indirectly and directly. The more powerful but indirect effects would derive from recognition that penal policies that fundamentally affect and diminish offenders' lives should not be the subject of partisan and self-interested politics. Moving toward a civil service model would signal that recognition. In addition, once a professional judiciary and prosecution system was in place, judges and prosecutors would become sources of professional advice and informed experience rather than active politicians with personal agendas to pursue. They would also likely act as points of resistance to penal policy proposals that were ill-considered or motivated primarily by elected officials' pursuit of partisan or ideological advantage.

Their direct influence would come from their day-to-day work. They would be less likely than elected officials in dealing with individual cases to be influenced by political considerations, media attention, or public clamor. Personal promotion would be influenced by talent, hard work, and demonstrated observance of professional ethics and norms, rather than by editorial pages, public opinion polls, and focus groups.

Professionalizing the judiciary and prosecution, and removing them from direct partisan political pressures, would not, however, mean that public attitudes and beliefs would not influence the courts and sentencing. A sizable political science literature shows that courts have distinctive, broadly shared, legal cultures that shape perceptions of justice, that change over time, and that reflect community values. The ways lawyers behave and interact, and the decisions judges and prosecutors make, are constrained by the local legal culture. Most courts have "going rates" for sentencing. Few people like to be accused of behaving unreasonably or unjustly and the going rates provide the criteria by which assessments of injustice are made. That is one reason why practitioners circumvent mandatory minimum and three-strikes laws. Harsh contemporary laws often prescribe penalties that are just too severe according to local standards. Circumvention is a way to avoid imposing sentences that everyone involved considers unjust.

Judges and prosecutors are parts of the communities in which they live and work, however, and are not immune from influence of changes in community norms and values. In the United States in the 1970s and 1980s, for example, the day-to-day decisions of judges and prosecutors toughened in parallel to toughening of public attitudes about crime. Alfred

Blumstein and Allen Beck (1999) showed that the principal driver of the rising prison population in the 1970s and 1980s was increases in the percentages of convicted offenders being sent to prison. It is often the case that changes in sentencing patterns spelled out in new legislation begin before the legislation was enacted. That is why, as chapter 5 shows, the apparent effects of many legal changes are often better understood as the effects of changes in sensibilities. As public attitudes toward the seriousness of family violence have changed, for example, so have the attitudes and decisions of judges and prosecutors. That happens as a result of organic changes in community values.

There is no good reason why such changes should not affect how the justice system operates, and they will occur whether judges and prosecutors are politically selected or are career civil servants. Organic changes in community values, however, are different from raw, short-term emotions and partisan and self-interested politics. The former are an inevitable and desirable influence on the legal system. The latter are the reason why American penal policies are as they regrettably are.

Delegated Policy Making

If making judges and prosecutors into career civil servants seems too radical or large a step to take, another way to depoliticize and de-emotionalize penal policy is to delegate rule-making authority to specialized administrative agencies. Experience with existing sentencing commissions shows that delegation can work. That experience could be extended to parole and pardons.

Judge Marvin Frankel's initial proposals for creation of sentencing commissions and guidelines had two premises. First, administrative agencies would accumulate specialized expertise that would enable them to do a better job at formulating and overseeing sentencing policy than could legislatures. Second, sentencing policy needs to be insulated from partisan politics and short-term expediencies. Delegation of rule-making authority to an administrative agency is a good way to do that (Frankel 1972). The irony is that, while some commissions' guidelines showed they could achieve their functional goals more effectively and justly than legislatures had, some commissions abandoned the effort to insulate policy from politics (Tonry 1996, chap. 3).

Several states' commissions had notable successes at achieving the goals set for them. Sentencing disparities were reduced generally and in relation to ethnicity and gender. Greater consistency made sentencing fairer by increasing the chances like-situated offenders would receive comparable sentences. Greater consistency made sentencing more predictable and thereby enabled states to improve their corrections planning and budgeting. Publication and use of guidelines and adoption of requirements that judges explain their decisions brought greater transparency to sentencing. That enabled offenders, victims, the media, and the general public to know what was happening and why. Guidelines and reasons requirements made appellate sentence review possible and made judges more accountable for their decisions.

In some states that created sentencing commissions, including Minnesota, Washington, Oregon, and North Carolina, the commissions for a time did significantly insulate sentencing policy from political partisanship and self-interest. The citizens of those states were spared some of the excesses that swept the country. All of those states had less steep increases in prison populations and budgets than the national average and all managed to tie their sentencing policies to their correctional resources. In other jurisdictions that established sentencing commissions, including the federal government, Virginia, and Florida, sentencing commissions abandoned their insulating functions and competed with elected officials to show who was tougher. In Oregon and Washington, sentencing policy changes enacted by legislation and referendums eventually overrode the commissions' more moderate and rationalistic policies.

It is not too late to revive the idea of the sentencing commission as an administrative body with specialized knowledge, an institutional memory, and some distance from electoral and legislative politics. Franklin Zimring and colleagues (2001) show how criminal justice policy in California in the 1990s was distorted by its centrality in partisan and personal politics, and argue that something like a sentencing commission is needed to lessen the odds of that happening again. The Federal Reserve Board is an example they give of a successful administrative body that has been partially removed from partisan politics because of the importance of its function, the need for specialized expertise to carry it out, and the need for insulation from short-term political pressures. Policies concerning deprivation of citizens' liberty, they argue, deserve similar protection.

The considerations that support creation of sentencing commissions also apply to parole and pardon. More than half of American states retain parole boards with authority to decide when prisoners are released. And if recommendations offered below for establishing systems for reviewing long sentences imposed in recent years are adopted, more states will establish parole-like agencies or processes. Most of the aims of sentencing guidelines—consistency, fairness, predictability, transparency, accountability—also apply to parole. Parole commissions, like sentencing commissions, set general policies, and those policies guide decisions in individual cases. The public interest in having decisions to release people from prison made consistently, fairly, predictably, openly, and accountably is no less than or different from the public interest in having decisions to lock people up satisfy those criteria.

The notoriety surrounding President Clinton's late-night pardons his last day in office in January 2001 demonstrate why such decisions should also satisfy those criteria. Different people for different reasons objected to various of the Clinton pardons. The controversy resulted mostly from appearances that pardons went to personal cronies, campaign contributors, and people whose causes were promoted by Clinton family members and politically connected lawyers, some of whom were paid large sums to exercise their personal influence.

A pardon is an act of executive grace, but to be seen as legitimate it needs to be handled openly and fairly. The traditional reasons for pardons, such as the belief that a miscarriage of justice has occurred or that a prisoner's ill-health, age, or other special circumstances justify early release or exoneration, are different from those for why sentences are imposed or why routine parole release is granted. There is no reason, though, why pardon decisions should not be made fairly, openly, and accountably. That is why many states have pardon boards and why the U.S. Department of Justice includes the Office of the Pardon Attorney.

The sentencing, parole, and pardon commission proposals in the preceding few paragraphs can be adopted through ordinary legislation. Those in the preceding section calling for radical changes in the selection of judges and prosecutors and in the organization of public prosecution and the judiciary can be accomplished in most states and the federal system only by means of constitutional amendments. That would be difficult and time-consuming even were there widespread support for depoliticizing American crime control and sentencing policy. That support does not now exist everywhere, though it may in some states.

Remediation

Calling for moderation in the national tendency toward emotional excess and for fundamental changes in political culture, constitutional arrangements, and governmental structure is to call for a lot. The call should be made nonetheless and efforts should be made to act on it. Less heroic steps, however, can move the United States from its current policies and undo some of the damage they have caused. The two overriding goals for crime policy change should be to refashion policies to make them less severe, costly, and destructive, and to diminish the disproportionate burdens they impose on minority communities and people.

The emphasis on minority groups warrants explanation. Current crime control policies cause avoidable collateral damage to offenders, their families, and their communities. Prisoners lose years, sometimes decades, of their lives and are exposed to destructive influences in prison, but they also often lose their families and their livelihoods. They exit prison with the likelihood of reduced employment prospects, average earnings, lifetime earnings, and life expectancies. Their partners lose loved ones and income support. Their children lose parents and the experience of family life and suffer from reduced living standards. Their communities often become places characterized by single-parent families, welfare dependence, abnormal age composition, and too few young men to work or become partners to young women.

That damage is disproportionately done to minority groups and communities and interferes with achievement of policy goals relating to civil rights and social inclusion. The as-yet-incomplete accomplishment of the goals of the Civil Rights Movement is one of the great successes of modern America, but the time when race and ethnicity do not limit individuals' life chances is yet to come. Educational, housing, public health, and other policies aim to further the goals of the Civil Rights Movement. Contemporary penal policies undermine those efforts.

The disproportionate burden of contemporary crime control policies on members of some minority groups results from several things. Black and Hispanic Americans are more extensively involved than whites in the kinds of drug and violent crimes that provoke lengthy prison sentences. The extreme example is the federal 100-to-1 crack/powder cocaine sentencing differential: More than 90 percent of those sentenced in federal courts for crack offenses are black. Blacks and Hispanics are also more extensively involved than whites in violent crimes, particularly murder, rape, and robbery. To a real but unmeasured extent, members of minority groups are adversely affected by officials' conscious bias and unconscious stereotyping.

Members of some minority groups are affected by unequal distributions of social capital and life chances, which explains why they become disproportionately involved in inner-city drug crimes and violent crimes. Relative to other available opportunities, dealing in drugs and participating in gangs often seem sensible things to do. People barred from achieving self-esteem from conventional school and work sources seek it from deviant peers, gangs, and the satisfactions of illegal incomes. People with little to lose take risks that others do not.

Finally, minority defendants are adversely affected by the implementation of policies and practices that are not meant to treat minority citizens especially harshly but work out that way in practice. These are usually referred to as problems of "disparate impact." An example is decisions about pretrial release on bail or "personal recognizance," which are usually based on whether criminal defendants have a job, a good education, a permanent home, and a stable home life. Poor people are less likely to have these things, and disproportionate numbers of blacks and Hispanics are poor. Standard bail release policies thus result in relatively fewer black and Hispanic defendants being released before trial and thus produce a "disparate impact."

Changes in crime control policy can not address all those problems but can address some and lessen their adverse effects. Only a few of the following proposals expressly address minorities' issues per se. If policies are too harsh, simplistic, costly, and destructive, they are those things for everyone they affect. Changing them, however, will disproportionately benefit people they now disproportionately damage.

First, enact "safety valve" laws authorizing corrections officials or specialized administrative agencies to award early release, according to established criteria, to anyone sentenced to more than ten years' imprisonment who has served the lesser of one-third of the sentence or five years. Those not released then should be reconsidered for release not less than every two years afterwards. In most Western countries, fewer than 1 percent of prisoners serve sentences of five years or longer, so five years seems a reasonable maximum time before release consideration. Being eligible for release after serving five years does not mean prisoners will be released. Some crimes are so serious or notorious that imprisonment for longer than five years is justifiable. Many offenders who committed very serious crimes would no doubt continue to be confined. Guidelines could be established for such decisions. The details and the criteria would vary from state to state.

U.S. prisons contain huge numbers of people serving decades-long sentences for non-violent drug and property crimes and of otherwise law-abiding people serving long sentences for violent crimes committed under circumstances of great emotion or stress. Many of these people should be released long before their current sentences expire. Individualized consideration, case-by-case, of whether their sentences are simply too long is the only way to assure that happens.

Second, repeal all three-strikes laws and any laws requiring judges to impose mandatory minimum sentences. Nearly every nonpartisan examination in the last fifty years of the desirability of mandatory minimum and similar sentencing laws has concluded that they are unwise, and for nearly always the same reasons. They are unnecessary for really serious cases that would command long sentences anyway. They have either no discernible deterrent effects or short-term effects that soon waste away. They result in unjustly harsh punishments for some offenders. They foster cynical circumvention by judges and lawyers. The unpredictable interactions of the previous two deficiencies produce stark disparities in sentencing of like-situated offenders. Because they typically apply to drug and violent crimes, for which comparatively more blacks and Hispanics are arrested than whites, they worsen racial disparities in prison.

Repealing three-strikes and mandatory minimum sentence laws does not mean that people who commit serious crimes will not receive appropriately severe sentences. That can be assured by adoption of systems of sentencing guidelines that direct judges to impose particular sentences unless they give good reasons for ordering some other sentence. If prosecutors disagree with the judge's reasons, appeals can be filed and appellate courts can decide whether the trial judge's reasons, and the sentence imposed, are sound. A dozen or more states now operate systems of sentencing guidelines that operate in the way I just described. In their current forms, mandatory minimums prescribe sentences of ten, twenty, and thirty years, and in some cases life, for serious crimes.

Third, if three-strikes and other mandatory minimum sentence laws are not repealed, they should be amended to authorize judges to impose a lesser sentence if in their judgment the prescribed sentence would be unjustly severe. The principal reason why mandatory penalty laws are typically applied inconsistently, and why judges and lawyers often devise ways to circumvent their application, is that they mandate harsher sentences than local practitioners consider just. England and Australia, the only two Western countries to adopt mandatory sentence laws based on U.S. models, almost always included provided-however clauses that authorize judges to pull the laws' punches in cases in which they believed that to be appropriate. The United States should do likewise.

Fourth, reconsider sentencing guidelines and laws with a view to establishing whether less severe penalties could achieve the same or comparable crime prevention effects without unduly depreciating the seriousness of the crimes to which they apply. This is happening to a limited extent in some states already, usually indirectly by creating diversionary policies that exempt classes of offenders from general rules, rather than by explicitly reducing the severity of punishments. Washington State, for example, introduced drug treatment and boot camp options into its sentencing guidelines as a way to substitute shorter and more constructive sentences for offenders otherwise subject to lengthy mandatory minimums. Even the U.S. Congress in 1994 enacted a "safety valve" exception to the mandatory minimums for some first-time drug offenders. In addition, led by a California policy adopted as a result of a citizen referendum, some states' policies now prescribe diversion into drug treatment of first- and second-time offenders charged with nonviolent crimes. Drug courts, established in hundreds of American counties, can also be seen as diversion programs, since many receive their clientele as the result of prosecutorial decisions to redirect cases from regular processing or judicial decisions to sentence to the drug court rather than to some other penalty.

However, there is no good reason not to decrease the severity of sentences across-the-board. No credible evidence supports the belief that a five-year prison sentence is a better deterrent than three years, that three years are better than two, or that incremental changes in punishments have any deterrent effect. Certainty of punishment is what matters, not severity. Nor does existing evidence on the incapacitative or rehabilitative effects of prison sentence support current sentence lengths.

Fifth, amend all existing sentencing laws to add sunset clauses that provide for automatic expiration after ten years and require inclusion of such clauses in all new sentencing laws. If the "don't-take-it-out on your . . ." adjuration were extended to legislation, sunset laws would be ubiquitous. Sunset provisions force legislators to reconsider whether punishment policies that once seemed to make sense still do. The English government, for example, acknowledging civil liberties concerns, included a five-year sunset clause in recent legislation that strengthened law enforcement powers concerning terrorism. The U.S. Congress likewise included sunset clauses in antiterrorist legislation enacted in 2001.

The risk aversion of U.S. politicians in relation to crime control policies makes the case for sunset clauses especially strong. Very few people off-camera any longer defend the federal 100-to-1 crack/powder sentencing differential. Crack and powder are, after all, pharmacologically indistinguishable. Overwhelming and uncontested evidence shows that the 100-to-1 rule is a major cause of racial disparities among federal prisoners, but it remained on the books seventeen years after it was enacted and few elected officials dared openly oppose it.

In 1993 the U.S. Sentencing Commission recommended that the differential be eliminated altogether, a conclusion that Attorney General Janet Reno initially endorsed. Ted Gest (2001, p. 126) reports, however, that "it seemed that hardly any legislator ever wanted to be associated with lowering a crime penalty," and President Clinton and the Congress did no more than agree on a bill to override the commission's proposal. In 1997, the commission tried again and proposed retaining some but a lesser differential. Attorney General Reno and "drug czar" Barry McCaffrey proposed a 10-to-1 differential. Nothing happened. In 2002 the U.S. Sentencing Commission issued a major report on the racial disparities caused by the rule. This time they did not propose eliminating a crack–powder distinction but did propose narrowing it. In March 2002 Bush administration spokesmen unequivocally expressed their support for maintaining the 100-to-1 differential. Had the 1986 legislation contained a sunset clause, however, the 100-to-1 rule that few people endorse on the merits would almost undoubtedly have lapsed.

Sixth, require all proposals for sentencing legislation to be accompanied by or subjected to impact projections that make their resource implications clear. This should not be controversial. Some states with competent sentencing commissions do it as a matter of routine. The first sentencing guidelines commission, in Minnesota, was the pioneer (Knapp 1984; Parent 1988). Its enabling legislation contained broad language directing the commission to take available resources into account in developing guidelines. The commission interpreted the language as a legislative mandate that any guidelines developed must satisfy a resource constraint policy. The Minnesota commission interpreted this to mean that the projected implementation of the guidelines should not produce a prison population in excess of 95 percent of the rated capacity of the state's prisons. If impact projections showed the limit would be exceeded, the commission would have to, and several times did, change the guidelines to meet the target. Or, if proposed penalty increases for a particular crime would cause the prison population to exceed the limit, either the proposal had to be changed or penalties for some other crimes be reduced to offset the forecast increase. Oregon, Washington, North Carolina, and other state commissions followed suit and adopted similar population constraint policies. Not all commissions did. Pennsylvania, for example, expressly chose not to be guided by resource considerations and the U.S. Sentencing Commission simply ignored a statutory directive to take account of available resources.

Experience, however, makes clear that states that want to manage their prison populations and corrections resources can. Policy histories of the North Carolina (Wright 2002), Minnesota (Frase and Dailey 2004), and Washington (Boerner and Lieb 2001) sentencing commissions all tell of proposed legislation that was abandoned or substantially altered when its resource and financial implications became clear. Other states also, generally in less sophisticated and effective ways, require fiscal notes or correctional impact projections.

Seventh, require all proposals for sentencing legislation that is projected to require new resources to contain provisions authorizing whatever additional resources are needed and appropriating funds to pay for them. In the 1970s, state legislatures routinely passed laws requiring more and longer prison sentences while treating corrections resources as if they cost nothing and somehow would become available when need arose. Severe overcrowding resulted with prisons in some states operating at 150–200 percent of capacity. At various times during the 1980s, individual prisons and sometimes entire prison systems in as many as forty states were subject to federal court orders based on findings of overcrowding and other unconstitutional conditions. Some states, including Florida, North Carolina, and Texas, operated under federal court orders or consent decrees establishing population caps that required that prisoners be released whenever the cap was exceeded.

The federal courts' intervention and prison riots eventually captured policy makers' attention. A few states, including North Carolina and Kansas, adopted sentencing guidelines and brought prison numbers under control that way. A sizable number of other states established sentencing commissions and directed them to develop guidelines that would take account of available prison resources. Some states—Texas, Oklahoma, and Florida are the extreme cases—undertook massive programs of prison building. Future programs of prison and criminal justice system expansion should, in fairness to taxpayers and to offenders, be pay as you go.

Eighth, require all proposals for sentencing legislation to be accompanied by or subjected to impact analyses that project their differential effects for women and for nationality and ethnic groups. This does not feel like a radical proposal, but no state or country does it. Some disadvantaged ethnic or national minority in every country is heavily overrepresented among crime victims, offenders, and prisoners (Tonry 1997). Generally, this is widely seen as regrettable and by some it is seen as the result primarily of either intentional or "institutional" racism.

The causes of racial and ethnic disparities invariably include policies that in principle apply to everybody but in practice disproportionately affect particular groups. The federal 100-to-1 rule that punishes sale of five grams of crack cocaine as harshly as the sale of 500 grams of powder cocaine is facially neutral. Because, however, poor blacks typically sell small amounts of crack and whites typically sell powder in varying quantities, in practice the distinction produces longer sentences for black than for white drug dealers and worsens racial disparities in imprisonment. The disparate effects were foreseeable in 1986 when the 100-to-1 rule was enacted.

If disparate impact projections and analyses were an obligatory part of the legislative process, policy makers would have had explicitly to weigh wanted crime prevention effects against presumably unwanted but foreseeable disparate impacts on white and black defendants. This would have had the salutary effect of forcing realistic assessments of what preventive effects were likely and how confidently they could be expected to occur. Perhaps after such deliberations, Congress might still have enacted the 100-to-1 rule, but then the decision would have been explicitly made that the likely gains outweighed the undesirable side effect of punishing blacks more severely. Or, the likely drug-abuse reduction gains might have been deemed so speculative that they did not justify the disparate effects at all or that the differential should have been less. Or even, possibly, the decision might have been made that, given a choice between higher drug abuse or crime rates and worsened racial disparities, the latter was the greater evil and the rule should not be adopted. In any case, such analyses would force explicit choices to be made between crime control policy goals, whether expressive or substantive, and race relations goals.

Policy makers shy away from directly addressing racial issues in the criminal justice system. One reason for this is a combination of bad motive and hypocrisy. Some people argue that many features of the federal war on drugs that disproportionately affect blacks are best explained this way (Tonry 1995; Wacquant 2001).

Two other reasons for avoiding disparate impact analyses are that the issues they raise are difficult and sensitive. The difficulty is illustrated by the U.S. Supreme Court's decision in *McCleskey v. Kemp*, 481 U.S. 279 (1997), in which the Court accepted the validity of empirical evidence that, all else equal, capital punishment in Georgia was much more often ordered for blacks who killed whites than for black-on-black, white-on-white, or white-on-black killings. The issue was devilishly difficult. The Court had to decide whether to allow McCleskey to be executed in the face of evidence that people like him are more likely to be executed because of their and their victim's race, or to accept the inferences raised by the statistical evidence and effectively end capital punishment in Georgia (and by implication, the rest of the country). In the face of evidence that race matters, the Court nonetheless held that the statistical evidence was immaterial and that only proof of racial bias in the individual case was relevant. McCleskey's lawyers could not show this—few biased judges or lawyers openly admit that they are acting discriminatorily, and much discrimination in any event is unconscious and based on insensitivity and stereotypes. McCleskey in due course was killed by the State of Georgia.

In explaining the Court's decision, an obviously troubled Justice Lewis Powell pointed out that the logic of Mc-Cleskey's claim, that statistical evidence of inexplicable racial disparities should raise a presumption of bias that the state must refute, might apply throughout the criminal justice system. The Court could have avoided that result by asserting that "death is different," but in principle Powell was right. Some would argue that statistical evidence of unaccountable disparities *should* raise presumptions of bias, and if that benefits minority defendants, so be it.

Reasonable people differ about the question whether courts should create such presumptions, but no one doubts that legislatures can (and in some contexts such as employment opportunity and college athletics, have). A Martian might find it a bit ironic that an employer who hires a lower percentage of blacks than reside in the local community, according to statistical evidence, is legally presumed to have acted discriminatorily and must justify its hiring practices or be adjudged guilty of employment discrimination, while equivalent but much stronger evidence about capital punishment raises no legal presumptions at all. The seeming inference is that the law cares more about peoples' jobs than their lives.

That was a difficult issue. Here is a sensitive one: Should the race of offenders be taken into account in deciding whether to increase penalties for homicide? The analysis would apply also to three-strikes laws and to mandatory minimum and truth-in-sentencing laws covering violent crimes. The threshold problem is that blacks are arrested for violent crimes much more often relative to population than are whites. Thirteen percent of the U.S. population in 2000 was black. Of people arrested in that year for homicide, rape, and robbery, 27.9

percent, 34.1 percent, and 53.9 percent, respectively, were black.

Assume for purposes of argument that arrest percentages are an accurate indicator of racial patterns of serious violent crime (the best evidence is that for serious violent crime, arrest proportions are reasonably valid indicators). A proposed law increasing the minimum prison sentence for homicide from ten to thirty years would, because of the racial offending pattern, disproportionately affect blacks. Over time, racial disparities in U.S. prisons would worsen. Is that a good thing or a bad thing?

Preventing crime is a good thing, but so is preventing racial disparities. If we knew that the increased lengths of sentence would through deterrent and incapacitative effects decrease the homicide rate by x percent or save the lives of y plus or minus ten people, the trade-off could be discussed. Does an estimated crime reduction effect of a particular amount justify an increase from, say, 46 to 50 percent of the prison population who are black? What if no crime reduction effect could credibly be estimated? Could any increase in racial disproportions be justified, or any increase in penalties that would disproportionately affect blacks? Whatever the crime reduction estimate, does it matter that violent crimes, especially homicide and rape, are heavily intraracial, and thus that violent black offenders mostly have black victims? Punishing violent offenders more harshly will, if that has crime prevention effects, reduce victimization rates and disproportionately benefit potential black victims.

Comparable analyses of projected effects of alternative public policy choices are commonplace (Cook and Ludwig 2001). Planners explicitly weigh estimates of lost life against cost in building roads or designing aircraft. No action can be made perfectly safe and cost inevitably is a consideration. If all automobiles were design-limited to ten miles an hour and built with heavy steel bodies, we would have many fewer traffic fatalities and injuries. Decisions to make cars faster, lighter, and cheaper produce higher projected rates of injury and death and higher medical-care costs. The trade-offs are explicitly discussed. Similar trade-offs should be discussed, and explicit choices made, in relation to race and sentencing.

Ninth, conduct disparity audits of all criminal justice system practices to establish whether and to what extent they exacerbate or ameliorate disparities in outcomes affecting women and members of minority groups. This is a variation on the last point and the argument is much the same. Many facially neutral practices have racially disparate effects. Here are two examples.

First, as mentioned earlier, guidelines for decisions about pretrial release often give weight to social factors such as the defendant's educational background, vocational skills, or family status. These are not nonsensical factors. The key issue is whether the defendant will appear for trial or run away, and indicators of social stability or connections are plausible criteria for predicting the defendant will not disappear. Unfortunately, relatively more blacks and Hispanics than whites are poor and socially disadvantaged. They will be less likely to benefit from the social factors and more likely to be held in jail pending trial. In addition, a large body of research shows that defendants held in jail before trial, all else equal, are more likely to receive prison sentences and to receive longer prison sentences (even after pretrial time in jail is factored in) than offenders who were released before trial (Tonry 1995). This means that pretrial detention practices create another disparate impact for minority defendants. Happily, these disparate impacts can easily be reduced, once the problem is recognized. Other factors related solely to current or past criminality provide as good predictions of appearance at trial.

The second example is harder. In most countries, defendants from some disadvantaged minority groups are less likely than majority group members to plead guilty, and when they do plead guilty to do it later in the process (Tonry 1997). Most systems provide sentence reductions, openly or otherwise, to defendants who plead guilty. In England, to give a concrete example, the so-called progressive-loss-of-mitigation doctrine explicitly provides a one-third reduction of sentence to defendants who plead guilty at the outset, with successively lesser reductions for later pleas (hence, "progressive loss"). Afro-Caribbeans lose on both counts. They plead guilty less often than whites, and typically later (Hood 1992). Disparate impact audits would force policy makers explicitly to decide and declare whether the discount's presumed cost-reduction goals outweigh the disparities that foreseeably are caused. This is a particularly difficult choice to make, since the noncooperation surely results in part from minority defendants' sometimes justified alienation from a criminal justice system in which they believe they are unfairly treated, especially by the police.

Implementing the last two proposals will not be easy, but they are necessary if American jurisdictions are to reduce the overrepresentation of minority group members in prisons and jails. The necessary research and statistical analyses will not be difficult, but the policy decisions often will be. The illustration of bail-or-jail criteria given above is easy. Once the problem is recognized, criteria that do not treat groups of offenders differently, or that reduce the extent of differential treatment, can be substituted. More difficult are instances like the 100-to-1 rule where the goal (try to reduce the direct and indirect effects of drug trafficking) seems desirable but the effect (treat black defendants much more harshly than whites) does not. Among the choices are to accept the unwanted racial disparity, to abandon the drug policy goal, or to compromise. My guess is that compromise is what would have happened had the choices been starkly presented. Black crack defendants would still have been sentenced more harshly than white powder defendants, but the differential, and the resulting racial disparities, would have been less. That would have been a small victory, but a victory all the same.

It could be that forcing policy makers openly to discuss difficult and sensitive racial issues relating to the criminal justice system would change the outcomes of policy processes. Bad or bigoted motives might be imputed to people who vigorously promote policies that will treat blacks or

Hispanics or members of other minorities more harshly than whites or that will worsen disparities. No one wants to be called a racist or a bigot and that risk might make policy makers less likely to promote such policies. In lawyers' language, open discussion of racial dimensions of policy might have a chilling effect. Some good-faith proposals might not be offered from fear that motives will be misinterpreted or that epithets will unfairly be brandished. In an ideal world, of course, that would be a pity. Policies should be based on evidence and values, openly discussed and critically examined, and decisions should result from reconciliation of different interests and perspectives. In our somewhat less than ideal world, the trade-offs are not so clear. It would not be a bad thing if chilling effects associated with open discussion of racial issues in sentencing policy prevented promotion or adoption of policies that would worsen racial disparities.

The proposals set out in this chapter would, if taken seriously, move American policies and practices closer to the mainstream of contemporary Western values and practices. They will not be easy to adopt or implement, and they might not work as well as I hope they might. I suspect though, that if we try, we will stand higher in the esteem of our descendants, and of our current and future friends in other lands, than if we continue our current practices or merely tinker at the edges.

References

Albrecht, Hans-Jörg. 2001. "Post-Adjudication Dispositions in Comparative Perspective." In *Sentencing and Sanctions in Western Countries*, ed. Michael Tonry and Richard S. Frase. New York: Oxford University Press.

ALI, *see* American Law Institute

Alschuler, Albert W. 1978. "Sentencing Reform and Prosecutorial Power." *University of Pennsylvania Law Review* 126: 550–77.

American Law Institute. 1954. *Model Penal Code: Tentative Draft No. 2*. Philadelphia: American Law Institute.

———. 1956. *Model Penal Code: Tentative Draft No. 5*. Philadelphia: American Law Institute.

———. 1960. *Model Penal Code: Tentative Draft No. 12*. Philadelphia: American Law Institute.

———. 1962. *Model Penal Code (Proposed Official Draft)*. Philadelphia: American Law Institute.

———. 1998. *The American Law Institute Seventy-Fifth Anniversary 1923–1998*. Philadelphia: American Law Institute.

American Law Institute Proceedings. 1954. *31st Annual Meeting. The American Law Institute. Proceedings*. Philadelphia: American Law Institute.

———. 1956. *33rd Annual Meeting. The American Law Institute. Proceedings*. Philadelphia: American Law Institute.

———. 1960. *37th Annual Meeting. The American Law Institute. Proceedings*. Philadelphia: American Law Institute.

―――. 1961. *38th Annual Meeting. The American Law Institute. Proceedings.* Philadelphia: American Law Institute.

Andenaes, Johannes. 1974. *Punishment and Deterrence.* Ann Arbor: University of Michigan Press.

Applebome, Peter. 1996. *Dixie Rising: How the South is Shaping American Values, Politics and Culture.* New York: Times Books.

Barclay, Gordon, and Cynthia Tavares. 2002. *International Comparisons of Criminal Justice Statistics 2000.* London: Home Office, Research, Development, and Statistics Directorate.

Barnes, Jonathan, ed. 1984. *The Complete Works of Aristotle: The Revised Oxford Edition.* 2 vols. Princeton, N.J.: Princeton University Press.

Bauman, Zygmunt. 1991. *Modernity and Ambivalence.* Cambridge: Polity Press.

Beck, Allen J. 1989. *Recidivism of Prisoners Released in 1983.* Washington, D.C.: U.S. Department of Justice, Bureau of Justice Statistics.

Beck, Ulrich. 1992. *Risk Society: Towards a New Modernity.* Trans. Mark Ritter. London: Sage.

―――. 1996. "Risk Society and the Provident State." In *Risk, Environment and Modernity: Towards a New Ecology,* ed. Scott Lash, Bronislaw Szerszynski, and Brian Wynne. London: Sage.

―――, and Elisabeth Beck-Gershheim. 1995. *The Normal Chaos of Love.* Cambridge: Polity Press.

Becker, Gary S. 1968. "Crime and Punishment: An Economic Analysis." *Journal of Political Economy* 76: 169–217.

Beckett, Katherine. 1997. *Making Crime Pay: Law and Order in Contemporary American Politics.* New York: Oxford University Press.

Begasse, Jen Kiko. 1997. "Oregonians Support Alternatives for Nonviolent Offenders." In *Sentencing Reform in Overcrowded Times,* ed. Michael Tonry and Kathleen Hatlestad. New York: Oxford University Press.

Ben-Yehuda, Nachman. 1990. *The Politics and Morality of Deviance: Moral Panics, Drug Abuse, Deviant Science, and Reversed Stigmatization.* Albany, N.Y.: State University of New York Press.

Bennett, William J., John J. DiIulio, and John P. Walters. 1996.

Body Count: Moral Poverty—and How to Win America's War against Crime and Drugs. New York: Simon and Schuster.

Bentham, Jeremy. 1789 [1948]. *Introduction to the Principles of Morals and Legislation,* ed. Wilfred Harrison. Oxford: Oxford University Press.

———. 1843. *The Works of Jeremy Bentham,* vol. 4, ed. John Bowring. London: Simpkin, Marshall.

Bettelheim, Bruno. 1977. *The Uses of Enchantment: The Meaning and Importance of Fairy Tales.* London: Thames and Hudson.

Bishop, Donna M. 2000. "Juvenile Offenders in the Adult Criminal Justice System." In *Crime and Justice: A Review of Research,* vol. 27, ed. Michael Tonry. Chicago: University of Chicago Press.

Blackstone, William. 1766–69. *Commentaries on the Laws of England.* 2d ed. Oxford: Clarendon Press.

Blumstein, Alfred. 1993. "Making Rationality Relevant—The American Society of Criminology 1992 Presidential Address." *Criminology* 31: 1–16.

———, and Allen J. Beck. 1999. "Population Growth in U.S. Prisons, 1980–1996." In *Prisons,* ed. Michael Tonry and Joan Petersilia. Vol. 26 of *Crime and Justice: A Review of Research,* ed. Michael Tonry. Chicago: University of Chicago Press.

———, and Jacqueline Cohen. 1973. "A Theory of Stability of Punishment." *Journal of Criminal Law and Criminology* 64: 198–201.

———, Jacqueline Cohen, Jeffrey Roth, and Christy Visher, eds. 1986. *Criminal Careers and "Career Criminals."* Washington, D.C.: National Academy Press.

Boerner, David, and Roxanne Lieb. 2001. "Sentencing Reform in the Other Washington." In *Crime and Justice: A Review of Research,* vol. 28, ed. Michael Tonry. Chicago: University of Chicago Press.

Boswell, John. 1980. *Christianity, Social Tolerance, and Homosexuality.* Chicago: University of Chicago Press.

Bottomley, Keith. 1990. "Parole in Transition: A Comparative Study of Origins, Developments, and Prospects for the 1990s." In *Crime and Justice: A Review of Research,* vol. 12, ed. Michael Tonry. Chicago: University of Chicago Press.

Bottoms, Anthony E. 1995. "The Philosophy and Politics of Punishment and Sentencing." In *The Politics of Sentencing Reform*, ed. C. M. V. Clarkson and R. Morgan. Oxford: Clarendon.

———, and James Dignan. 2004. "Youth Justice in England and Scotland." In *Youth Crime and Youth Justice: Comparative and Cross-national Perspectives*, ed. Michael Tonry and Anthony Doob. Chicago: University of Chicago Press.

Boutellier, Hans J. 2000. *Crime and Morality: The Significance of Criminal Justice in Post-Modern Culture*. London: Kluwer Academic.

Bowling, Benjamin. 1999. "The Rise and Fall of New York Murder: Zero Tolerance or Crack's Decline?" *British Journal of Criminology* 39: 531–54.

Braithwaite, John. 1989. *Crime, Shame and Reintegration*. Cambridge: Cambridge University Press.

———. 1999. "Restorative Justice: Assessing Optimistic and Pessimistic Accounts." In *Crime and Justice: A Review of Research*, vol. 25, ed. Michael Tonry. Chicago: University of Chicago Press.

———. 2001. *Restorative Justice and Responsive Regulation*. New York: Oxford University Press.

Bureau of Justice Statistics. 1998. *State Court Sentencing of Convicted Felons, 1994*. Washington, D.C.: U.S. Department of Justice, Bureau of Justice Statistics.

———. 2000. *Correctional Populations in the United States, 1997*. Washington, D.C.: U.S. Department of Justice, Bureau of Justice Statistics.

———. 2001. *Prisoners in 2000*. Washington, D.C.: U.S. Department of Justice, Bureau of Justice Statistics.

———. 2003. *Prisoners in 2002*. Washington, D.C.: U.S. Bureau of Justice Statistics.

Burgess, Ernest W. 1928. "Factors Determining Successes or Failure on Parole." Part 4 of *The Workings of the Indeterminate-Sentence Law and the Parole System in Illinois*, by Andrew W. Bruce, Ernest W. Burgess, and Albert J. Harno. Springfield: Illinois Board of Parole.

Camus, Albert. 1960 (c. 1959). *Reflections on the Guillotine: An*

Essay on Capital Punishment. Trans. Richard Howard. Michigan City, Ind.: Fridtjof-Karla Publications.

Caplow, Theodore, and Jonathan Simon. 1999. "Understanding Prison Policy and Population Trends." In *Prisons*, ed. Michael Tonry and Joan Petersilia. Vol. 26 of *Crime and Justice: A Review of Research*, ed. Michael Tonry. Chicago: University of Chicago Press.

Casper, Jonathan D., David Brereton, and David Neal. 1983. *The Implementation of the California Determinate Sentencing Law.* Washington, D.C.: U.S. Department of Justice.

Christie, Nils. 2000. *Crime Control as Industry: Towards Gulags Western Style.* 3d ed. London: Routledge.

Clarke, Stevens H. 1987. *Felony Sentencing in North Carolina 1976–1986: Effects of Presumptive Sentencing Legislation.* Chapel Hill: Institute of Government, University of North Carolina at Chapel Hill.

Clear, Todd R., and Eric Cadora. 2001. "Risk and Correctional Practice." In *Crime, Risk, and Justice: The Politics of Crime Control in Liberal Democracies*, ed. Kevin Stenson and Robin R. Sullivan. Derby, U.K.: Willan Publishing.

————, Dina R. Rose, and Judith A. Ryder. 2001. "Incarceration and the Community: The Problem of Removing and Returning Prisoners." *Crime and Delinquency* 47: 335–51.

Cohen, Mark A. 1988. "Pain, Suffering, and Jury Awards: A Study of the Cost of Crime to Victims." *Law and Society Review* 2(3): 537–55.

Cohen, Stanley. 1972. *Folk Devils and Moral Panics.* New York: St. Martin's Press.

Cook, Philip, and Jens Ludwig. 2001. *Gun Violence: The Real Cost.* New York: Oxford University Press.

Cullen, Frank, Bonnie S. Fisher, and Brandon K. Applegate. 2000. "Public Opinion about Punishment and Corrections." In *Crime and Justice: A Review of Research*, vol. 27, ed. Michael Tonry. Chicago: University of Chicago Press.

Death Penalty Information Center. 2002. Available online at www.deathpenaltyinfo.org/index.html.

DiIulio, John J. 1990. "Crime and Punishment in Wisconsin." *Wisconsin Policy Research Institute Report* 3(7): 1–56.

Doble, John. 1997. "Survey Shows Alabamians Support Alternatives." In *Sentencing Reform in Overcrowded Times*, ed. Michael Tonry and Kathleen Hatlestad. New York: Oxford University Press.

———, and Stephen Immerwahr. 1997. "Delawareans Favor Prison Alternatives." In *Sentencing Reform in Overcrowded Times*, ed. Michael Tonry and Kathleen Hatlestad. New York: Oxford University Press.

Doob, Anthony N., and Voula Marinos. 1995. "Reconceptualizing Punishment: Understanding the Limitations on the Use of Intermediate Punishments." *University of Chicago Law School Roundtable* 2: 413–33.

Douglas, Mary. 1985. *Risk Acceptability According to the Social Sciences*. New York: Russell Sage Foundation.

———. 1992. *Risk and Blame: Essays in Cultural Theory*. London: Routledge.

Duff, R. A. 2000. *Punishment, Communication, and Community*. New York: Oxford University Press.

Durkheim, Émile. 1933. *The Division of Labour in Society*. Trans. George Simpson. (Originally pub. 1893.) New York: Free Press.

Dworkin, Ronald. 1977. *Taking Rights Seriously*. London: Duckworth.

———. 1986. *Law's Empire*. Cambridge, Mass.: Belknap Press.

Eck, John E., and Edward R. Maguire. 2000. "Have Changes in Policing Reduced Violent Crime? An Assessment of the Evidence." In *The Crime Drop in America*, ed. Alfred Blumstein and Joel Wallman. Cambridge: Cambridge University Press.

Edsall, Thomas, and Mary Edsall. 1991. *Chain Reaction: The Impact of Race, Rights, and Taxes on American Politics*. New York: Norton.

Eisner, Manuel. 2001. "Modernization, Self-Control and Lethal Violence: The Long-Term Dynamics of European Homicide Rates in Theoretical Perspective." *British Journal of Criminology* 41: 618–38.

———. 2003. "Secular Trends of Violent Crime: Evidence and Theoretical Interpretations." In *Crime and Justice: A Review of Research*, vol. 30, ed. Michael Tonry. Chicago: University of Chicago Press.

Elias, Norbert. 1978. *The History of Manners: The Civilising Process*, vol. 1. Oxford: Basil Blackwell. (Originally published 1939, Basel: Hans Zum Falken.)

———. 1982. *State Formation and Civilization: The Civilizing Process*, vol. 2. Oxford: Basil Blackwell. (Originally published 1939, Basel: Hans Zum Falken.)

Ellis, Joseph J. 2002. *Founding Brothers: The Revolutionary Generation*. New York: Vintage.

Elson, Alex. 1998. "The Case for an In-depth Study of the American Law Institute." *Law and Social Enquiry* 23: 625–40.

Erikson, Kai T. 1966. *Wayward Puritans: A Study in the Sociology of Deviance*. New York: John Wiley.

Evans, Malcolm, and Rod Morgan. 1998. *Preventing Torture: A Study of the European Convention for the Prevention of Torture and Inhuman or Degrading Treatment or Punishment*. New York: Oxford University Press.

Fagan, Jeffrey, Franklin Zimring, and June Kim. 1998. "Declining Homicide in New York City: A Tale of Two Trends." *Journal of Criminal Law and Criminology* 88: 1277–1323.

Farkas, Steve. 1997. "Pennsylvanians Prefer Alternatives to Prison." In *Sentencing Reform in Overcrowded Times*, ed. Michael Tonry and Kathleen Hatlestad. New York: Oxford University Press.

Farrington, David P. 1986. "Age and Crime." In *Crime and Justice: An Annual Review of Research*, vol. 7, ed. Michael Tonry and Norval Morris. Chicago: University of Chicago Press.

Federal Courts Study Committee. 1990. *Report*. Washington, D.C.: Administrative Office of the U.S. Courts.

Feeley, Malcolm M., and Jonathan Simon. 1992. "The New Penology: Notes on the Emerging Strategy of Corrections and Its Implications." *Criminology* 30: 449–74.

Feinberg, Joel. 1970. *Doing & Deserving: Essays in the Theory of Responsibility*. Princeton, N.J.: Princeton University Press.

Feld, Barry C. 1999. *Bad Kids: Race and the Transformation of the Juvenile Court*. New York: Oxford University Press.

Florida Legislative Office of Program Policy Analysis and Government Accountability. 1995. *Policy Review of Reincarcera-*

tion in Florida's Prisons Administered by the Department of Corrections. Tallahassee: Florida Legislature.

Fogelson, Robert M. 1977. *Big-City Police.* Cambridge, Mass.: Harvard University Press.

Foucault, Michel. 1977. *Discipline and Punish: The Birth of the Prison.* Trans. Robert Hurley. New York: Pantheon.

Frankel, Marvin E. 1972. *Criminal Sentences: Law without Order.* New York: Hill and Wang.

Frase, Richard, and Debra Dailey. 2004. "Sentencing Policy in Minnesota, 1975–2000." In *Crime and Justice: A Review of Research,* vol. 3, ed. Michael Tonry. Chicago: University of Chicago Press.

Freiberg, Arie. 2001. "Three Strikes and You're Out—It's Not Cricket: Colonization and Resistance in Australian Sentencing." In *Sentencing and Sanctions in Western Countries,* ed. Michael Tonry and Richard S. Frase. New York: Oxford University Press.

Friedman, Lawrence. 1993. *Crime and Punishment in American History.* New York: Basic Books.

Gannon, Marie. 2001. *Crime Comparisons between Canada and the United States.* Ottawa: Statistics Canada.

Garland, David. 1990. *Punishment and Modern Society: A Study in Social Theory.* Chicago: University of Chicago Press.

———. 1991. "Sociological Perspectives on Punishment." In *Crime and Justice: A Review of Research,* vol. 14, ed. Michael Tonry. Chicago: University of Chicago Press.

———. 1996. "The Limits of the Sovereign State: Strategies of Crime Control in Contemporary Society." *British Journal of Criminology* 36(4): 445–71.

———. 2001a. *The Culture of Control: Crime and Social Order in Contemporary Society.* Chicago: University of Chicago Press.

———, ed. 2001b. *Mass Imprisonment in the United States: Social Causes and Consequences.* London: Sage.

Gest, Ted. 2001. *Crime & Politics: Big Government's Erratic Campaign for Law and Order.* New York: Oxford University Press.

Giddens, Anthony. 1990. *The Consequences of Modernity.* Cambridge: Polity Press.

————. 1991. *Modernity and Self-Identity*. Cambridge: Polity Press.

————. 1998. "Risk Society: The Context of British Politics." In *The Politics of Risk Society*, ed. Jane Franklin. Malden, Mass.: Polity Press.

Gilmore, Grant. 1974. *The Death of Contract*. Columbus: Ohio State University Press.

Goode, Erich, and Nachman Ben-Yehuda. 1994. *Moral Panics: The Social Construction of Deviance*. Cambridge, Mass.: Blackwell.

Goodrich, Herbert F., and Paul A. Wolkin. 1961. *The Story of the American Law Institute 1923–1961*. St. Paul, Minn.: American Law Institute.

Gottfredson, Don M., Leslie T. Wilkins, and Peter B. Hoffman. 1978. *Guidelines for Parole and Sentencing*. Lexington, Mass.: Lexington Books.

Grayling, Anthony C. 2001. "The Last Word on Anger." *The Guardian*, December 8, 2001.

Greenberg, David F. 1988. *The Construction of Homosexuality*. Chicago: University of Chicago Press.

Greene, Judith A. 1999. "Zero Tolerance: A Case Study of Police Policies and Practices in New York City." *Crime and Delinquency* 45: 171–87.

Greenwood, Peter W., and Allan Abrahamse. 1982. *Selective Incapacitation*. Prepared for the National Institute of Justice. Santa Monica, Calif.: Rand Corp.

Gurr, Ted Robert. 1981. "Historical Trends in Violent Crimes: A Critical Review of the Evidence." In *Crime and Justice: An Annual Review of Research*, vol. 3, ed. Michael Tonry and Norval Morris. Chicago: University of Chicago Press.

————. 1989. "Historical Trends of Violent Crime: England, Western Europe, and the United States." In *Violence in America: The History of Crime*, vol. 1, ed. Ted Robert Gurr. Newbury Park, Calif.: Sage.

Gusfield, Joseph R. 1963. *Symbolic Crusade: Status Politics and the American Temperance Movement*. Urbana: University of Illinois Press.

Hagan, John, and Ronit Dinovitzer. 1999. "Collateral Consequences of Imprisonment for Children, Communities, and Prisoners." In *Prisons*, ed. Michael Tonry and Joan Petersilia. Vol. 26 of *Crime and Justice: A Review of Research*, ed. Michael Tonry. Chicago: University of Chicago Press.

Hall, Stuart, Chas Critcher, Tony Jefferson, John Clarke, and Brian Roberts. 1978. *Policing the Crisis: Mugging, the State, and Law and Order*. London: Macmillan.

Hallsworth, Simon. 2000. "Rethinking the Punitive Turn: Economies of Excess and the Criminology of the Other." *Punishment and Society* 2(2): 145–60.

Hampton, Jean. 1984. "The Moral Education Theory of Punishment." *Philosophy and Public Affairs* 13(3): 208–38.

Harcourt, Bernard E. 2001. *Illusion of Order: The False Promise of Broken Windows Policing*. Cambridge, Mass.: Harvard University Press.

Hart, H. L. A. 1968. *Punishment and Responsibility*. Oxford: Oxford University Press.

Heaney, Gerald W. 1991. "The Reality of Guidelines Sentencing: No End to Disparity." *American Criminal Law Review* 28: 161–233.

Hood, Roger. 1992. *Race and Sentencing*. Oxford: Clarendon.
———. 2002. "Criminology and Penal Policy: The Vital Role of Empirical Research." In *Ideology, Crime and Criminal Justice: A Symposium in Honour of Sir Leon Radzinowicz*, ed. Anthony Bottoms and Michael Tonry. Cullompton, Devon: Willan.

Hope, Tim, and Richard Sparks, eds. 2000. *Crime, Risk and Insecurity: Law and Order in Everyday Life and Political Discourse*. London: Routledge.

Hough, Mike, and Julian V. Roberts. 1997. *Attitudes to Punishment: Findings from the British Crime Survey*. Home Office Research Study no. 179. London: Home Office.

Howell, James C., and J. David Hawkins. 1998. "Prevention of Youth Violence." In *Youth Violence*, ed. Michael Tonry and Mark H. Moore. Vol. 24 of *Crime and Justice: A Review of Research*, ed. Michael Tonry. Chicago: University of Chicago Press.

Hull, Natalie E. H. 1990. "Restatement and Reform: A New Perspective on the Origins of the American Law Institute." *Law and History Review* 8: 55–96.

Janson, Carl-Gunnar. 2004. "Youth Justice in Sweden." In *Youth Crime and Youth Justice: Comparative and Cross-national Perspectives*, ed. Michael Tonry and Anthony Doob. Chicago: University of Chicago Press.

Jareborg, Nils. 2001. "Sentencing Law, Patterns, and Policies in Sweden." In *Penal Reform in Overcrowded Times*, ed. Michael Tonry. New York: Oxford University Press.

Jefferson, Tony, and Wendy Hollway. 2000. "The Role of Anxiety in Fear of Crime." In *Crime, Risk and Insecurity: Law and Order in Everyday Life and Political Discourse*, ed. Tim Hope and Richard Sparks. London: Routledge.

Jenkins, Philip. 1998. *Moral Panic: Changing Concepts of the Child Molester in Modern America*. New Haven, Conn.: Yale University Press.

Johnson, Paul. 1976. *A History of Christianity*. New York: Atheneum.

Kagan, David. 1989. "How America Lost Its First Drug War." *Insight* 8–17 (Nov. 20, 1989).

Kahan, Dan M. 1997. "Some Realism about Retroactive Criminal Lawmaking." *Roger Williams University Law Review* 3(1): 95–117.

———. 1998a. "The Anatomy of Disgust in Criminal Law." *Michigan Law Review* 96: 1621–57.

———. 1998b. "Punishment Incommensurability." *Buffalo Criminal Law Review* 1: 691–708.

———, and Tracey L. Meares. 1998. "The Wages of Antiquated Criminal Procedure." *University of Chicago Law Forum* 1998: 197–214.

———. 1998. "The Coming Crisis of Criminal Procedure." *Georgetown Law Journal* 86: 1153–84.

Kennedy, Joseph E. 2000. "Monstrous Offenders and the Search for Solidarity through Modern Punishment." *Hastings Law Journal* 51: 829–908.

Kennedy, Randall. 1997. *Race, Crime, and the Law*. New York: Pantheon Books.

Kensey, Annie, and Pierre Tournier. 2001. "French Prison Numbers Stable since 1988, but Populations Changing." In *Penal Reform in Overcrowded Times,* ed. Michael Tonry. New York: Oxford University Press.

Kesteren, John van, Pat Mayhew, and Paul Nieuwbeerta. 2000. *Criminal Victimization in Seventeen Industrialised Countries: Key Findings from the 2000 International Crime Victims Survey.* The Hague: WODC.

King, Ryan S., and Marc Mauer. 2001. *Aging behind Bars: Three Strikes Seven Years Later.* Washington, D.C.: The Sentencing Project.

Kleiman, Mark A. R., and David Cavanagh. 1990. "A Cost-Benefit Analysis of Prison Cell Construction and Alternative Sanctions." Unpublished manuscript. Cambridge, Mass.: Kennedy School of Government, Guggenheim Program in Criminal Justice Policy and Management.

Knapp, Kay. 1984. *The Impact of the Minnesota Sentencing Guidelines: Three-Year Evaluation.* St. Paul, Minn.: Minnesota Sentencing Guidelines Commission.

Kommer, Max. 1994. "Punitiveness in Europe." *European Journal of Criminal Policy and Research* 2(1): 29–43.

Kuhn, André. 1998. "Sanctions and Their Severity." In *Crime and Criminal Justice Systems in Europe and North America 1990–1994,* ed. K. Kangasunta, M. Joutsen, and N. Ollus. Helsinki: European Institute for Crime Prevention and Control (HEUNI).

————. 2001. "Incarceration Rates across the World." In *Penal Reform in Overcrowded Times,* ed. Michael Tonry. New York: Oxford University Press.

Kuhn, Thomas. 1996. *The Structure of Scientific Revolutions.* 3d ed. Chicago: University of Chicago Press.

Kurki, Leena. 2001. "International Standards for Sentencing and Punishment." In *Sentencing and Sanctions in Western Countries,* ed. Michael Tonry and Richard S. Frase. New York: Oxford University Press.

Kyvsgaard, Britta. 2004. "Youth Justice in Denmark." In *Youth Crime and Youth Justice: Comparative and Cross-national Perspectives,* ed. Michael Tonry and Anthony Doob. Chicago: University of Chicago Press.

Lane, Roger. 1980. "Urban Police and Crime in Nineteenth-Century America." In *Crime and Justice: An Annual Review of Research*, vol. 2, ed. Norval Morris and Michael Tonry. Chicago: University of Chicago Press.

———. 1992. "Urban Police and Crime in Nineteenth-Century America." In *Modern Policing*, ed. Michael Tonry and Norval Morris. Vol. 15 of *Crime and Justice: A Review of Research*, ed. Michael Tonry. Chicago: University of Chicago Press.

———. 1999. "Murder in America: A Historian's Perspective." In *Crime and Justice: A Review of Research*, vol. 25, ed. Michael Tonry. Chicago: University of Chicago Press.

Lappi-Seppälä, Tapio. 2001. "Sentencing and Punishment in Finland: The Decline of the Repressive Ideal." In *Sentencing and Sanctions in Western Countries*, edited by Michael Tonry and Richard S. Frase. New York: Oxford University Press.

Lieb, Roxanne, Vernon Quinsey, and Lucy Berliner. 1998. "Sexual Predators and Social Policy." In *Crime and Justice: A Review of Research*, vol. 23, ed. Michael Tonry. Chicago: University of Chicago Press.

Lindblom, Charles E., and D. K. Cohen. 1979. *Usable Knowledge*. London: Yale University Press.

Lipson, Albert J., and Mark A. Peterson. 1980. *California Justice under Determinate Sentencing: A Review and Agenda for Research*. Santa Monica, Calif.: Rand Corp.

Lupton, Deborah. 1999. *Risk*. London: Routledge.

Males, M., and D. Macallair. 1999. "Striking Out: The Failure of California's 'Three-Strikes-and-You're-Out Law.'" *Stanford Law and Policy Review* 11: 65–74.

Mauer, Marc. 1999. *The Race to Incarcerate*. New York: New Press.

———, and Meda Chesney-Lind, eds. 2002. *Invisible Punishment: The Collateral Consequences of Mass Imprisonment*. New York: New Press.

Mayhew, Pat, and Jan van Dijk. 1997. *Criminal Victimisation in Eleven Industrialized Countries: Key Findings from the 1996 International Crime Victims Survey*. The Hague: Dutch Ministry of Justice.

McIvor, Gill. 1995. "CSOs Succeed in Scotland." In *Intermediate*

Sanctions in Overcrowded Times, ed. Michael Tonry and Kate Hamilton. Boston: Northeastern University Press.

Meares, Tracey L., and Dan M. Kahan. 1998. "Law and (Norms of) Order in the Inner City." *Law and Society Review* 32: 805–38.

Messinger, Sheldon, and Phillip Johnson. 1978. "California's Determinate Sentence Laws." In *Determinate Sentencing: Reform or Regression*. Washington, D.C.: U.S. Government Printing Office.

Minnesota Legislative Auditor. 1997. *Recidivism of Adult Felons*. St. Paul: State of Minnesota, Office of the Legislative Auditor.

Moffitt, Terrie E. 1993. "Adolescence-Limited and Life-Course-Persistent Antisocial Behavior: A Developmental Taxonomy." *Psychological Review* 100: 674–701.

Moore, Mark H. 1995. "Learning by Doing: Linking Knowledge to Policy in the Development of Community Policing and Violence Prevention in the United States." In *Integrating Crime Prevention Strategies: Propensity and Opportunity*, ed. P. O. Wikström, R. V. Clarke, and J. McCord. Stockholm: National Council for Crime Prevention.

Morgan, Rod. 2001. "International Controls on Sentencing and Punishment." In *Sentencing and Sanctions in Western Countries*, ed. Michael Tonry and Richard S. Frase. New York: Oxford University Press.

Morris, Allison. 2004. "Youth Justice in New Zealand." In *Youth Crime and Youth Justice: Comparative and Cross-national Perspectives*, ed. Michael Tonry and Anthony Doob. Chicago: University of Chicago Press.

Morris, Norval. 1974. *The Future of Imprisonment*. Chicago: University of Chicago Press.

Murphy, Jeffrie G. 1985. "Retributivism, Moral Education, and the Liberal State." *Criminal Justice Ethics* 4: 3–11.

Musto, David. 1973. *The American Disease: Origins of Narcotic Control*. New Haven, Conn.: Yale University Press.

———. 1987a. *The American Disease: Origins of Narcotic Control*. Expanded edition. (Originally published 1973.) New York: Oxford University Press.

———. 1987b. "Changing Attitudes toward Drugs and Alcohol

in the United States." In *Drugs and Crime: Workshop Proceedings*, ed. Jeffrey A. Roth, Michael Tonry, and Norval Morris. A Report of the 1986 National Academy of Sciences Conference on Drugs and Crime Research. Washington, D.C.: National Academy of Sciences.

Nagel, Ilene H., and Stephen J. Schulhofer. 1992. "A Tale of Three Cities: An Empirical Study of Charging and Bargaining Practices under the Federal Sentencing Guidelines." *Southern California Law Review* 66: 501–66.

Ohlin, Lloyd E. 1951. *Selection for Parole: A Manual of Parole Prediction*. New York: Russell Sage Foundation.

Parent, Dale. 1988. *Structuring Sentencing Discretion: The Evolution of Minnesota's Sentencing Guidelines*. Stoneham, Mass.: Butterworth.

Pease, Ken. 1985. "Community Service Orders." In *Crime and Justice: An Annual Review of Research*, vol. 6, ed. Michael Tonry and Norval Morris. Chicago: University of Chicago Press.

Pelikan, Jaroslav. 1985. *Jesus through the Centuries: His Place in the History of Culture*. New Haven, Conn.: Yale University Press.

Peter D. Hart Research Associates, Inc. 2002. *The New Politics of Criminal Justice: Summary of Findings*. Washington, D.C.: Hart Associates.

Posner, Richard. 1977. *Economic Analyses of Law*, 2d ed. Boston: Little, Brown.

————. 1980. "Optimal Sentences for White-Collar Offenders." *American Criminal Law Review* 17: 409–18.

Roberts, Julian V. 1992. "Public Opinion, Crime, and Criminal Justice." In *Crime and Justice: A Review of Research*, vol. 16, ed. Michael Tonry. Chicago: University of Chicago Press.

————, and Loretta J. Stalans. 1997. *Public Opinion, Crime, and Criminal Justice*. Boulder, Colo.: Westview Press.

————, Loretta J. Stalans, David Indermaur, and Mike Hough. 2002. *Penal Populism and Public Opinion*. New York: Oxford University Press.

Rose, Dina, and Todd R. Clear. 1998. "Incarceration, Social Capital, and Crime: Implications for Social Disorganization Theory." *Criminology* 36(3): 441–80.

Rothman, David J. 1980. *Conscience and Convenience*. Boston: Little, Brown.

Schulhofer, Stephen J., and Ilene H. Nagel. 1997. "Plea Negotiations under the Federal Sentencing Guidelines." *Northwestern University Law Review* 91: 1284–1316.

Schünemann, Bernd. 1998. "Zum Stellenwert derpositiven Generolprävention in einer dualistischen Straftheorie." In *Positive Generalpravention*, ed. Andrew von Hirsch, Bernd Schünemann, and Nils Jareborg. Heidelberg: C. F. Mueller Verlag.

Simon, Jonathan. 2001. "Fear and Loathing in Late Modernity: Reflections on the Cultural Sources of Mass Imprisonment in the United States." *Punishment and Society* 3(1): 21–34.

———, and Malcolm M. Feeley. 1995. "True Crime: The New Penology and the Public Discourse on Crime." In *Punishment and Social Control*, ed. Thomas G. Blomberg and Stanley Cohen. New York: Aldine de Gruyter.

Spierenburg, Pieter, ed. 1984. *The Emergence of Carceral Institutions: Prisons, Galleys, and Lunatic Asylums, 1550–1900.* Rotterdam: Erasmus Universiteit.

Stanko, Elizabeth A. 2000. "Victims R US: The Life History of 'Fear of Crime' and the Politicization of Violence." In *Crime, Risk and Insecurity: Law and Order in Everyday Life and Political Discourse*, ed. Tim Hope and Richard Sparks. London: Routledge.

Stenson, Kevin. 2000. "Some Day Our Prince Will Come: Zero Tolerance Policing and Liberal Government." In *Crime, Risk and Insecurity: Law and Order in Everyday Life and Political Discourse*, ed. Tim Hope and Richard Sparks. London: Routledge.

———, and Robert R. Sullivan, eds. 2001. *Crime, Risk and Justice: The Politics of Crime Control in Liberal Democracies.* Cullompton, Devon: Willan.

Sutherland, Edwin H. 1950. "The Diffusion of Sexual Psychopath Laws." *American Journal of Sociology* 56: 142–48.

Tak, Peter J. P. 2001. "Sentencing and Punishment in The Netherlands." In *Sentencing and Sanctions in Western Countries*, ed. Michael Tonry and Richard S. Frase. New York: Oxford University Press.

Tonry, Michael. 1994. "Proportionality, Parsimony, and Inter-changeability of Punishments." In *Penal Theory and Practice*, ed. R. A. Duff, S. E. Marshall, R. E. Dobash, and R. P. Dobash. Manchester, U.K.: Manchester University Press.

———. 1995. *Malign Neglect: Race, Crime, and Punishment in America*. New York: Oxford University Press.

———. 1996. *Sentencing Matters*. New York: Oxford University Press.

———. 1997. "Ethnicity, Crime, and Immigration." In *Ethnicity, Crime and Immigration: Comparative and Cross-national Perspectives*, ed. Michael Tonry. Chicago: University of Chicago Press.

———, ed. 2001. *Penal Reform in Overcrowded Times*. New York: Oxford University Press.

———, and Richard S. Frase, eds. 2001. *Sentencing and Sanctions in Western Countries*. New York: Oxford University Press.

———, and David A. Green. 2003. "Criminology and Public Policy in the U.S. and U.K." In *The Criminological Foundations of Penal Policy*, a volume prepared in honour of Professor Roger Hood, ed. Lucia Zedner and Andrew Ashworth. Oxford: Oxford University Press.

———, and Kate Hamilton, eds. 1995. *Intermediate Sanctions in Overcrowded Times*. Boston: Northeastern University Press.

———, and Kathleen Hatlestad, eds. 1997. *Sentencing Reform in Overcrowded Times: A Comparative Perspective*. New York: Oxford University Press.

———, Lloyd E. Ohlin, and David P. Farrington. 1991. *Human Development and Criminal Behavior*. New York: Springer-Verlag.

Törnudd, Patrik. 1993. *Fifteen Years of Declining Prisoner Rates*. Helsinki: National Research Institute of Legal Policy.

———. 1997. "Sentencing and Punishment in Finland." In *Sentencing Reform in Overcrowded Times: A Comparative Perspective*, ed. Michael Tonry and Kathleen Hatlestad. New York: Oxford University Press.

Tremblay, Richard, and Wendy M. Craig. 1995. "Developmental Crime Prevention." In *Building a Safer Society: Strategic Approaches to Crime Prevention*, ed. Michael Tonry and David

P. Farrington. Vol. 19 of *Crime and Justice: A Review of Research*, ed. Michael Tonry. Chicago: University of Chicago Press.

Turner, S., P. W. Greenwood, E. Chen, and J. Fain. 1999. "The Impacts of Truth-in-Sentencing and Three-Strikes Laws: Prison Populations, State Budgets, and Crime Rates." *Stanford Law and Policy Review* 11: 75–91.

Tyler, Tom. 1990. *Why People Obey the Law*. New Haven, Conn.: Yale University Press.

———. 2003. "Procedural Justice, Legitimacy, and the Effective Rule of Law." In *Crime and Justice: A Review of Research*, vol. 30, ed. Michael Tonry. Chicago: University of Chicago Press.

———, and Robert Boeckmann. 1997. "Three Strikes and You're Out, But Why?" *Law and Society Review* 31: 237–65.

Virginia Criminal Sentencing Commission. 1997. *Annual Report*. Richmond: Virginia Criminal Sentencing Commission.

von Hirsch, Andrew. 1993. *Censure and Sanctions*. Oxford: Clarendon.

———, and Andrew Ashworth, eds. 1998. *Principled Sentencing*. 2d ed. Oxford: Hart Publishing.

Wacquant, Loic. 2001. "Deadly Symbiosis: When Ghetto and Prison Meet and Merge." *Punishment & Society* 3: 95–134.

Walker, Nigel. 1991. *Why Punish?* Oxford: Oxford University Press.

———. 1999. *Aggravation, Mitigation, and Mercy in English Criminal Law*. London: Blackstone.

Walker, Samuel. 1977. *A Critical History of Police Reform: The Emergence of Professionalism*. Lexington, Mass.: Lexington Books.

———. 1998. *Popular Justice: A History of American Criminal Justice*. 2d ed. New York: Oxford University Press.

Weigend, Thomas. 1997. "Germany Reduces Use of Prison Sentences." In *Sentencing Reform in Overcrowded Times*, ed. Michael Tonry and Kathleen Hatlestad. New York: Oxford University Press.

———. 2001. "Sentencing and Punishment in Germany." In *Sentencing and Sanctions in Western Countries*, ed. Michael

Tonry and Richard S. Frase. New York: Oxford University Press.

Weiss, Carole H. 1983. "Ideology, Interests, and Information: The Basis of Policy Decisions." In *Ethics, the Social Sciences, and Policy Analysis*, edited by D. Callahan and B. Jennings. London: Plenum Press.

————. 1986. "Research and Policy-Making: A Limited Partnership." In *The Use and Abuse of Social Science*, ed. F. Heller. London: Sage.

Whitman, James Q. 2003. *Harsh Justice: Criminal Punishment and the Widening Divide between American and Europe.* New York: Oxford University Press.

Wilson, James Q. 1993. *The Moral Sense.* New York: Free Press.

————. 1995. "Crime and Public Policy." In *Crime*, ed. James Q. Wilson and Joan Petersilia. San Francisco, Calif.: ICS Press, Institute for Contemporary Studies.

————, and Richard Herrnstein. 1985. *Crime and Human Nature.* New York: Simon and Schuster.

Wright, Ronald F. 2002. "Counting the Cost of Sentencing in North Carolina, 1980–2000." In *Crime and Justice—A Review of Research*, vol. 29, ed. Michael Tonry. Chicago: University of Chicago Press.

Yankelovich, Dan. 1991. *Coming to Public Judgment: Making Democracy Work in a Complex World.* Syracuse, N.Y.: Syracuse University Press.

Young, Warren, and Mark Brown. 1993. "Cross-national Comparisons of Imprisonment." In *Crime and Justice: A Review of Research*, vol. 17, ed. Michael Tonry. Chicago: University of Chicago Press.

Zedlewski, Edwin W. 1987. *Making Confinement Decisions.* Washington, D.C.: U.S. Department of Justice, National Institute of Justice.

Zimring, Franklin E. 1982. *The Changing Legal World of Adolescence.* New York: Free Press.

————. 1989. "Toward a Jurisprudence of Family Violence." In *Family Violence*, ed. Lloyd Ohlin and Michael Tonry. Vol. 11 of *Crime and Justice: A Review of Research*, ed. Michael Tonry and Norval Morris. Chicago: University of Chicago Press.

———, and Gordon Hawkins. 1988. "The New Mathematics of Imprisonment." *Crime and Delinquency* 34: 425–36.

———. 1991. *The Scale of Imprisonment.* Chicago: University of Chicago Press.

———. 1995. *Incapacitation: Penal Confinement and the Restraint of Crime.* New York: Oxford University Press.

———. 1997. *Crime is Not the Problem: Lethal Violence in America.* New York: Oxford University Press.

———, Gordon Hawkins, and Sam Kamin. 2001. *Punishment and Democracy: Three Strikes and You're Out in California.* New York: Oxford University Press.